21ST CENTURY EARTH

OPPOSING VIEWPOINTS®

Other Books of Related Interest in the Opposing
Viewpoints Series:

Abortion
AIDS
America Beyond 2001
American Foreign Policy
American Values
America's Cities
Biomedical Ethics
The Breakup of the Soviet Union
Crime and Criminals
Economics in America
Education in America
Endangered Species
The Environmental Crisis
The Family in America
Feminism
Genetic Engineering
Global Resources
Health Care in America
The Homeless
Homosexuality
Human Sexuality
Islam
Israel
Male/Female Roles
Mass Media
The Middle East
New World Order
Nuclear Proliferation
Population
Race Relations
Sexual Values
Space Exploration
The Third World
Trade
Violence
Water
Work

21ST CENTURY EARTH

OPPOSING VIEWPOINTS®

David Bender & Bruno Leone, *Series Editors*

Oliver W. Markley and Walter R. McCuan, *Editors*
Graduate Program in Studies of the Future,
Institute for Futures Research,
University of Houston—Clear Lake

Charles P. Cozic, *Opposing Viewpoints® Editor*

**OPPOSING
VIEWPOINTS®
SERIES**

Greenhaven Press, Inc., San Diego, CA

Cover photo: Digital Stock

Greenhaven Press, Inc.
PO Box 289009
San Diego, CA 92198-9009

Library of Congress Cataloging-in-Publication Data

21st century earth : opposing viewpoints / Oliver W. Markley, and Walter R. McCuan, editors.
    p.   cm. — (Opposing viewpoints series)
  Includes bibliographical references and index.
  ISBN 1-56510-415-3 (lib. : alk. paper). — ISBN 1-56510-414-5 (pbk. : alk. paper)
  1. Population forecasting. 2. Twenty-first century—Forecasts. 3. Human ecology. 4. Economic forecasting. 5. Technological forecasting. I. Markley, O.W. II. McCuan, Walter R., 1947– . III. Series: Opposing viewpoints series (Unnumbered)
HB849.4.A17   1996
303.49′09′05—dc20   95-39051
                                    CIP

"Congress shall make no law . . .
abridging the freedom of speech,
or of the press."

First Amendment to the U.S. Constitution

The basic foundation of our democracy is the First Amendment
guarantee of freedom of expression. The Opposing Viewpoints
Series is dedicated to the concept of this basic freedom and the
idea that it is more important to practice it than to enshrine it.

Contents

Why Consider Opposing Viewpoints?

"The only way in which a human being can make some approach to knowing the whole of a subject is by hearing what can be said about it by persons of every variety of opinion and studying all modes in which it can be looked at by every character of mind. No wise man ever acquired his wisdom in any mode but this."

John Stuart Mill

In our media-intensive culture it is not difficult to find differing opinions. Thousands of newspapers and magazines and dozens of radio and television talk shows resound with differing points of view. The difficulty lies in deciding which opinion to agree with and which "experts" seem the most credible. The more inundated we become with differing opinions and claims, the more essential it is to hone critical reading and thinking skills to evaluate these ideas. Opposing Viewpoints books address this problem directly by presenting stimulating debates that can be used to enhance and teach these skills. The varied opinions contained in each book examine many different aspects of a single issue. While examining these conveniently edited opposing views, readers can develop critical thinking skills such as the ability to compare and contrast authors' credibility, facts, argumentation styles, use of persuasive techniques, and other stylistic tools. In short, the Opposing Viewpoints Series is an ideal way to attain the higher-level thinking and reading skills so essential in a culture of diverse and contradictory opinions.

In addition to providing a tool for critical thinking, Opposing Viewpoints books challenge readers to question their own strongly held opinions and assumptions. Most people form their opinions on the basis of upbringing, peer pressure, and personal, cultural, or professional bias. By reading carefully balanced opposing views, readers must directly confront new ideas as well as the opinions of those with whom they disagree. This is not to simplistically argue that everyone who reads opposing views will—or should—change his or her opinion. Instead, the series enhances readers' depth of understanding of their own views by encouraging confrontation with opposing ideas. Careful examination of others' views can lead to the readers' understanding of the logical inconsistencies in their own opinions, perspective on why they hold an opinion, and the consideration of the possibility that their opinion requires further evaluation.

Evaluating Other Opinions

To ensure that this type of examination occurs, Opposing Viewpoints books present all types of opinions. Prominent spokespeople on different sides of each issue as well as well-known professionals from many disciplines challenge the reader. An additional goal of the series is to provide a forum for other, less known, or even unpopular viewpoints. The opinion of an ordinary person who has had to make the decision to cut off life support from a terminally ill relative, for example, may be just as valuable and provide just as much insight as a medical ethicist's professional opinion. The editors have two additional purposes in including these less known views. One, the editors encourage readers to respect others' opinions—even when not enhanced by professional credibility. It is only by reading or listening to and objectively evaluating others' ideas that one can determine whether they are worthy of consideration. Two, the inclusion of such viewpoints encourages the important critical thinking skill of objectively evaluating an author's credentials and bias. This evaluation will illuminate an author's reasons for taking a particular stance on an issue and will aid in readers' evaluation of the author's ideas.

As series editors of the Opposing Viewpoints Series, it is our hope that these books will give readers a deeper understanding of the issues debated and an appreciation of the complexity of even seemingly simple issues when good and honest people disagree. This awareness is particularly important in a democratic society such as ours in which people enter into public debate to determine the common good. Those with whom one disagrees should not be regarded as enemies but rather as people whose views deserve careful examination and may shed light on one's own.

Thomas Jefferson once said that "difference of opinion leads to inquiry, and inquiry to truth." Jefferson, a broadly educated man, argued that "if a nation expects to be ignorant and free . . . it expects what never was and never will be." As individuals and as a nation, it is imperative that we consider the opinions of others and examine them with skill and discernment. The Opposing Viewpoints Series is intended to help readers achieve this goal.

David L. Bender & Bruno Leone,
Series Editors

Introduction

"Some revolutionary events, which we call wild cards, will inevitably occur."

John L. Petersen, The Road to 2015: Profiles of the Future, *1994*

Futurists proffer an assortment of forecasts about the earth and humanity in the twenty-first century, some considered so unlikely that they are termed "wild cards." According to futurist John D. Rockfellow, a wild card is "an event having a low probability of occurrence, but an inordinately high impact if it does [happen]," either causing misfortune and calamity or progress and success. Other futurists have described forecasting wild cards as "thinking about the unthinkable."

In the past, only the most imaginative of futurists could have anticipated many of the wild cards that have had a tremendous impact on human life. Consider these events that have occurred since the 1950s:

DDT: Following its application during World War II, the pesticide DDT was sprayed in many countries in order to wipe out insect-borne diseases such as malaria. But scientists discovered that DDT was carcinogenic and that it could travel intact through the food chain, accumulating in the fat tissue of animals and humans. In the words of public health scientist Gary Null, "Invisible, persistent, mobile, and dangerous, DDT spread throughout the entire biological community." To protect humans, wildlife, and endangered species, many nations banned the use of DDT.

The Oil Crisis of 1973: For much of the twentieth century, gasoline and other fuels had been available virtually on demand in Western nations at low, stable prices. However, the October 1973 war between Israel and neighboring Arab nations prompted OPEC (Organization of Petroleum Exporting Countries), the majority of whose members were Muslim nations, to use oil as a political weapon: It attempted to impose an embargo against Western nations sympathetic to Israel. Though the embargo failed, OPEC price hikes tripled crude oil prices, which caused significant increases in prices of gasoline and transported goods as well as in rates of inflation. James Dale Davidson and Lord William Rees-Mogg, coauthors of *The Great Reckoning,* describe the effects of this crisis: "The world economy was buffeted in the early 1970s . . . by a dramatic geopolitical event . . . which transferred trillions in wealth [from Western nations to OPEC nations]."

AIDS: In 1981, doctors discovered a mysterious disease caused by unknown factors that primarily afflicted gay men. By the early 1990s, hundreds of thousands of people worldwide had died from AIDS and millions more were infected with the virus believed to cause the disease. Other unforeseen effects included the presence of the virus in blood supplies and a strain on health care systems in areas with high AIDS rates.

The Fall of the Iron Curtain: In 1983, U.S. president Ronald Reagan called the Soviet Union an "evil empire" and "the focus of evil in the modern world." But few people expected that the Soviet government would so rapidly lose its firm grip on authoritarian rule and its influence over other communist nations in Eastern Europe. In 1989, the Eastern Bloc began to unravel as communist regimes lost their power and popular support in Czechoslovakia, East Germany, Hungary, Poland, and Romania. East Germany reunited with West Germany one year later. In 1991, communism suffered a tremendous blow when the Soviet Union's Communist Party lost control of the government. All of the Soviet republics soon became independent states.

These events, unforeseen by most people, are viewed by historians and others as milestones of long-term change. Looking toward the twenty-first century, futurists point to other wild cards that could have comparable impact on the world:

Terrorism: Few people imagined that terrorists would plot to destroy an Oklahoma City federal building and kill more than 160 occupants in April 1995. Yet two *Americans*, suspected members of a militia group, were charged with that bombing. Some law enforcement officials and others predict that many Americans could grow sympathetic toward or join right-wing militias, which frequently warn against oppression and tyranny by government, and that such groups could encourage similar acts of anarchy and even civil revolt.

China Embraces Capitalism: In 1997, communist China is scheduled to regain sovereignty over Hong Kong from Great Britain and could force the colony in line with the rest of China. In a reverse scenario, however, China's leaders could adopt Hong Kong's economic system for all of China. China's conversion to capitalism would conceivably have a dramatic impact on global economics and politics, altering the balance of trade, opening new markets to the West, and transforming diplomatic relations between China and the rest of the world.

Free Energy: Zero-point energy (ZPE) is a form of energy some researchers believe exists in the space between electrons. Futurist John L. Petersen wrote in 1994: "The now free energy source exists everywhere and is unlimited." If zero-point energy is produced, Petersen contends, "all existing energy production methods [will] become obsolete, fossil fuel–based conversion devices [will] become obsolete, and the amount of pollution that is produced by humankind [will] begin to decrease precipitously."

The accuracy of these wild card predictions remains to be seen. Other unforeseen possibilities may prove more significant to humanity's future. Various wild card possibilities are among the topics considered in the following chapters of *21st Century Earth: Opposing Viewpoints*: How Will Demographic Trends Affect Humanity? What Will Be the Impacts of New Technologies? How Will Trends Affect the Global Ecology? What Will Be the Future of International Relations? What Are Projected Trends and Wild Cards?

How Will Demographic Trends Affect Humanity?

21ST CENTURY EARTH

Chapter Preface

During the final years of the twentieth century, the question of how demographic trends in the near future will affect humanity has received more scrutiny than perhaps ever before. At the 1994 United Nations Conference on Population and Development, for example, representatives from 180 countries addressed the issue of rapid population growth, especially the potential tripling or quadrupling of the world's 5.5 billion people during the twenty-first century.

Much of the concern about population focuses on the impact of substantial increases in the size of teenage and elderly age-groups. Many corporations, for example, eagerly anticipate the increased global growth and consumer potential of the adolescent age-group, which experts contend will peak in number in the early twenty-first century. Especially appealing to these businesses is what businessman and demographer Peter Schwartz calls the emergence of "global teenagers"—youths with common interests, lifestyles, and tastes shaped by such forces as advertising, computers, music, and television. On the other hand, some analysts foresee increased numbers of unemployed or rebellious teenagers in many poor, developing nations. According to the Population Crisis Committee advocacy group, large numbers of "dissatisfied youth" could help erode some nations' political stability.

Advantages and disadvantages are also expected from increases in the world's elderly population. According to historian Paul Kennedy, "Whereas developing nations have the burden of supporting millions younger than fifteen, developed nations have to look after fast-increasing millions older than sixty-five." But Kennedy also notes, "A nation with [large numbers of elderly people] is likely to have less crime and may be less prone to go to war [than a country with large numbers of young people]."

The social and economic effects that age-group and other demographic trends may have in the twenty-first century are the focus of discussion in the following chapter.

16

"If we do not stabilize population with justice, with humanity and mercy, then it will be done for us by nature, and it will be done brutally."

Overpopulation Threatens the Earth's Future

Al Gore and Paul Kennedy

Al Gore is the vice president of the United States. Paul Kennedy is a historian and author of *The Rise and Fall of Great Powers* and *Preparing for the Twenty-First Century*. In Part I of the following viewpoint, Gore argues that high population growth is harming much of the world's environment, impoverishing people, and causing instability in some nations. Gore maintains that the highest quality family planning information and services should be widely available in all countries. In Part II, Kennedy contends that lopsided demographic growth trends between rich, developed nations and poor, developing ones could erupt into a global crisis. He advocates a multinational response to confront the myriad problems generated by runaway population growth.

As you read, consider the following questions:

1. What is the usual effect of population growth on wages, according to Gore?
2. In Gore's opinion, how should abortion be considered within each nation?
3. What regions and populations are affected by a "demographic-technological faultline," according to Kennedy?

Al Gore, "The Sole Remaining Superpower vs. the Population Bomb," and Paul Kennedy, "Overpopulation Tilts the Planet," *New Perspectives Quarterly*, Fall 1994. Reprinted with permission.

Once there were a few who suggested that population growth was not a problem. Now there is virtual unanimity about the need for all nations to address population and sustainable development on a priority basis.

If you were to draw a chart depicting the population of the Earth over time, it would show that roughly 200,000 years after the emergence of modern humans, population slowly began to rise with the agricultural revolution some 10,000 years ago. By the birth of Christ, the population had reached 250 million. When Columbus sailed, it was 500 million. When the Declaration of Independence was written, it was roughly one billion people. And by the end of World War II, when my generation was born, the world had reached a population of two billion.

From Two Billion to Nine Billion

In my forty-six years, we have gone from a little over two billion to almost six billion people. And, if I'm fortunate enough to live another forty-six years, I will watch the world's population almost certainly rise to nearly nine billion.

Or to put it another way, we are adding the equivalent of another Mexico every twelve months, and the equivalent of another China every ten years.

If it takes 10,000 generations to reach a population of two billion, and then we move in a single human lifetime from two billion to nine billion, clearly that is a dramatic change.

It is not so much the empirical data that is disturbing; it is the foreseeable consequence of such rapid population growth that should instill in all Americans and in all nations a sense of urgency and resolve to address these unprecedented developments:

• For the environment, rapid population growth often contributes to the degradation of natural resources, as does the pattern of consumption in the more stable and more prosperous developed nations.

• Economically, population growth often contributes to the challenge of addressing persistent low wages, poverty and economic disparity. While there are certainly some circumstances where rapid population growth can meet unfulfilled demand for labor and become a positive factor, nevertheless, in the world in which we live today, it almost always holds wages lower than they would otherwise be.

• At the level of the family, demographic trends have kept the world's investment in its children low and unequal, especially where girls are concerned.

• For individuals, population growth, high fertility and lack of basic health services are closely linked to the poor health and welfare of millions of women and children.

• Population pressures often put strains on hopes for stability at the international level. Look, for example, at the 20 million refugees the world is now attempting to absorb. It is impossible to say that rapid population growth is ever, by itself, the cause of instability in a society. But neither is it irrelevant to note that the nation with the highest population density in Africa in 1993 was Rwanda. Or that the nation with the fastest rate of population growth in Africa was Somalia. Or that the fastest growing country in the world, Afghanistan, is on a trajectory that will double its population by 2004.

Toles. Copyright 1994 The Buffalo News. Reprinted with permission of Universal Press Syndicate.

Common sense surely reveals that rapid population growth is unsustainable.

Obviously, the world must act. But in order to assure movement toward consensus, as I think we did [at the 1994 UN population conference] in Cairo, we must recognize the necessity to deal sensitively with an issue rooted in deep moral, philosophical and religious differences—abortion.

Just about everyone in every corner of the world wishes to

make abortion rare. That is America's aim, the aim of women's groups and the Catholic Church. Indeed, that is the aim of all involved in this issue, though it is pursued in different ways.

I believe that, when fewer women decide abortions are necessary, they will be less frequent. And when women rarely decide abortions are necessary, they will be rare. But, that is not the situation we face around the world today. There are 50 million unwanted pregnancies annually that result in more than 25 million abortions annually.

In fact, there are entire nations, like the Russian Republic (where quality contraceptives are not widely available) where the average woman has seven to eight abortions in her lifetime. And for a variety of reasons, there are more than 200,000 women worldwide who die each year from medically unsafe abortions. We cannot sweep these facts under the rug or pretend that they do not exist. Women deserve better.

The Clinton Administration believes that making available the highest quality family planning and reproductive health services can help to simultaneously reduce both population growth and the number of abortions. But we are well aware that views about abortion are as diverse among nations as among individuals. Today, 173 nations have laws setting forth the circumstances in which abortion is permitted, and setting forth the manner in which it is restricted.

We believe that decisions about the extent to which abortion is acceptable should be the province of each government within the context of its own laws and national circumstances, and consistent with previously agreed human-rights standards.

Respect for national sovereignty, however, does not imply neutrality on this issue. We abhor and condemn coerced abortions, whether the coercion is physical, economic, psychological, political or in any other way. We do not believe that abortion should be viewed as a method of family planning, although in countries where quality services are not readily available, it is today all-too-often used for this purpose. And we believe there is, as acknowledged by all participants in the debate, a different moral sensibility brought to a choice of the option of abortion as compared to the choice of other available options.

A Right to Choose

Let me be clear: Our administration believes that the United States Constitution guarantees every woman within our borders a right to choose, subject to limited and specific exceptions. We are unalterably committed to that principle. But let us take a false issue off the table: The United States has not sought, does not seek, and will not seek to establish any international right to an abortion. That is a red herring.

Our view is that the most effective way to reduce population growth and abortion is through a comprehensive global strategy that makes quality family planning and reproductive health information and services as widely available as possible, that promotes sustainable economic development, that increases literacy, that fosters women's health, that strengthens families, that focuses on the education and empowerment of women, and that improves child health and child survival—because when children survive, then the desire by parents for larger families is greatly diminished.

The real story of the Cairo Conference was the extent to which a new worldwide consensus has congealed around this more sophisticated, holistic, richer view. The whole point is to build a humane and comprehensive strategy on the foundation of universal human aspirations. Integration of population, the environment and development is an imperative for peace and national security, for human health and well-being, and for the quality of life on Earth. Our administration is determined to meet this need. Indeed, we are determined to help lead the way.

II

Since the Berlin Wall fell and ended the division of the world into Cold War blocs, a new, more intractable cleavage masked by that conflict has become apparent: the demographic divide. Thomas Malthus, the overpopulation prophet, rather than Adam Smith, the champion of free markets, has become the more relevant thinker for the times ahead.

The 5.5 billion inhabitants of this globe are adding 95 million more people to this total every year. We add almost one billion people each decade. The World Health Organization and the United Nations Population Fund estimate that, by the year 2025, nearly nine billion people will live on the Earth, and 10–14 billion by 2050. The implications of this basic trend—for consumption, production, markets, education, services, the environment, investment, for war and peace—are fundamental.

Third World Crowding

This increase in population is not occurring evenly across our planet. In fact, 95 percent of the forecasted doubling of world population will take place in the poorer reaches of the globe—in India, China, Central America and Africa. By contrast, in most richer societies, the populations are either slow-growing or even (as in Italy, France and Japan) in absolute decline.

Some societies are becoming increasingly adolescent (60 percent of Kenya's population is under 15) while others are becoming increasingly geriatric (20 percent of Sweden's population is over 65). The Earth's demographic growth is dramatically lopsided. At the same time, the planet's wealth, and more importantly its capital, scientists, universities and research and development, are located in the demographically slow-growing or stagnant societies.

The impulses, ideas, cultural images, technology and funds that shape the socio-economic life of all humanity in these times emanate to the young and crowded world from [California's computer-dominant] Silicon Valley, Atlanta, Hollywood, London, Zurich and Tokyo. By contrast, capital, infrastructure, research and development, universities and health care systems are disintegrating, and natural resources are being depleted most rapidly in those countries where populations are growing in leaps and bounds.

The anarchic collapse of Rwanda and Somalia offer, perhaps, a premonition of what is to come in places where the population is far larger and the infrastructure far worse than at the turn of the 20th century.

A Dangerous Faultline

In sum, there is today a vast demographic-technological faultline appearing across our planet. On one side of this line are the fast-growing, adolescent, under-resourced, undercapitalized, undereducated societies; on the other side are the rich, technologically inventive yet demographically moribund, aging populations.

Perhaps the most glaring cleavage today lies along the Mediterranean, between Southern Europe and North Africa. But there are also others—along the Rio Grande in North America, between the Slavic and non-Slavic people of Asia, between Australia and Indonesia.

The greatest challenge global society faces today is preventing this faultline from erupting into a world-shaking crisis. I agree with the Nobel scientist from MIT [Massachusetts Institute of Technology], Dr. Henry Kendall, who argues that "if we do not stabilize population with justice, with humanity and mercy, then it will be done for us by nature, and it will be done brutally and without pity."

But to meet that challenge we will need to employ all our ingenuity and talents. It is simply not the case that it is too hopeless to try. What if, for example, we redeployed the tens of thousands of scientists and engineers now released from the Cold War challenge to look for solutions to the demographic divide? Solutions could range from truly dramatic breakthroughs in solar energy systems to low-level, sustainable village–based technologies that already show promise in so many developing countries. What if the rich countries actually fulfilled their twenty-year-old promise to allocate 0.7 percent of their gross domestic product to development aid?

All this implies a change in our priorities, but that is only likely if we possess political leaders with global vision and a willingness to articulate larger, universal principles.

Leaders and Citizens Must Respond

For now, leaders in democratic societies focus primarily on the most immediate concerns of jobs and crawling out of the recession that negatively affects their political fortunes as much as the economic well-being of their people. And even if they come to comprehend the nature of the long-term challenge—which hit the front pages and TV screens in September 1994 when the UN convened in Cairo for its most important global meeting on population in twenty years—they will not be able to effect a change of priorities unless supported by a concerned and intelligent citizenry.

That is why, in the end, change will only come if the average person recognizes, as most now do with respect to environmental issues, that only a global, transnational response to the growing demographic divide from rich and poor societies alike will give the planet Earth a chance to survive. Otherwise the coming deluge of people is certain to swamp all other concerns in the 21st century. Then, hope will be hard to come by.

"Catastrophists . . . always think the Earth has reached the limits of its carrying capacity."

Population Growth Does Not Threaten the Earth's Future

Thomas Lambert

According to Thomas Lambert, doomsday prophets and naysayers are wrong to contend that overpopulation threatens the planet. In the following viewpoint, Lambert gives several arguments to support his opinion: natural resources and energy are becoming less scarce; depletion of living space is not a concern; gains in per capita agricultural production make it possible to feed everyone; and environmental protection increases as a society becomes wealthier. Lambert asserts that markets must be free in order to ensure the economic growth necessary to sustain a much larger population at a higher standard of living. Lambert is a John M. Olin fellow at the Center of the Study of American Business at Washington University in Washington, D.C.

As you read, consider the following questions:

1. According to Lambert, what is the trend for prices of most basic resources?
2. What are the four reasons that greater population density leads to faster economic growth, in the author's opinion?
3. Why must prices be allowed to rise and fall freely, according to Lambert?

Abridged from Thomas Lambert, "What They Missed in Cairo: Defusing the Population Bomb." Reprinted from *USA Today* magazine, January 1995; ©1995 by the Society for the Advancement of Education.

For centuries, numerous doomsday prophets have predicted that an increasing world population will cause serious crises. Such thinking certainly permeated the International Conference on Population and Development, held in Cairo, September 5–13, 1994, which sought "to forge a new consensus that population concerns should be at the centre of all economic, social, political, and environmental activities."

Earth's Resources

Naysayers typically insist that a burgeoning population soon will squander the Earth's finite natural resources, that there is an insufficient supply of living space and agricultural land to support continued population expansion, and that population growth necessarily will imply intolerable levels of pollution. To avert these dire consequences, they call upon governments to undertake aggressive family planning programs, increase regulations on the use of nonrenewable resources, and undertake centralized planning in order to limit economic expansion to "sustainable" levels.

Before enacting such measures, policymakers ought to take a critical look at an assumption that went unchallenged in Cairo. What is the actual evidence that "overpopulation" is a problem? Are there built-in mechanisms in a market system that will avert tragedies from population growth? In short, they should ask, "Is there a population bomb?" before they become consumed with how it best can be defused.

Because supplies of natural resources and energy are limited, more resource users inevitably will lead to the eventual depletion of supplies, the theory goes. Underlying this reasoning is the dramatic notion of the planet as "Spaceship Earth," launched with a countable amount of each resource and, hence, having less resources per passenger as the number of passengers increases. The dire predictions in the classic doomsday manifestos of the 1960s and 1970s—most notably *The Limits to Growth* and Stanford University ecologist Paul Ehrlich's *The Population Bomb*—were premised upon the Spaceship Earth model. Although virtually none of these dire predictions came true, the model persists.

Natural Resources Are Not Running Out

It is not at all clear, however, that humans are running out of resources. In fact, the history of natural resource use provides overwhelming evidence that natural resources, including energy, progressively are becoming *less scarce*.

If a good is becoming less available, suppliers, confident in the knowledge that consumers have fewer outlets from which to obtain the good, will raise their prices. Thus, in a relatively free market, persistently rising prices accompany increasing scarcity. Conversely, a steady decrease in the price of any good indicates that the substance is being supplied at a faster rate than it is being demanded, or, in other words, is becoming far more available. So, if the prices of resources exhibit a downward trend, the resources must be becoming less scarce.

Indeed, prices for most basic resources exhibit long-term declines, and many are at an all-time low. Relative to wages, the 1990 prices for all commonly used natural resources in the U.S. were one-half what they were in 1950 and one-fifth the 1900 price.

Some doomsayers ask, "What if the supply of a natural resource suddenly just runs out?" They fear current prices of resources will not provide sufficient warning of future scarcities. This is unfounded. . . .

The fundamental assumption underlying pessimistic accounts of future resource depletion—and the concomitant obsession with limiting population growth and resource use—is that the supply of natural resources is finite. The truth, though, is that natural resources are not limited in any meaningful sense.

Resources as Services

The primary error in the finiteness assumption is a materialistic view of resources. According to this perspective, resources are "stuff." Yet, resources are really best understood as services. It is, after all, the particular services a material provides—not the physical composition—that make it a resource. If crude oil provided no services, it would be a messy nuisance, not a resource. Examples of the services that make materials into resources are a capacity to conduct electricity, ability to support weight, energy to fuel autos or electrical generators, and food calories.

Empirical economist William Baumol at one time embraced the notion that natural resources are limited. In 1979, he wrote in *Economics, Environmental Policy, and the Quality of Life* that "neither reduced demand nor expanded exploration can make our finite resources limitless." Upon examination of the data on resource scarcity, though, he changed his mind. By 1989, in *Productivity and American Leadership: The Long View*, he maintained that

> [M]easured in terms of their prospective contribution to human welfare, the available quantity of our exhaustible and unreproducible natural resources may be able to rise unceasingly, year after year. Rather than approaching exhaustion with continued use, their effective inventories may actually be growing and may never come anywhere near disappearance.

In other words, the service provided is what should be evaluated as increasing or decreasing. If the price of the service a resource provides is decreasing, the "effective stock"—or the performance capacity of the unused quantity of the resource—must be increasing.

The effective stock of natural resources can be enlarged by decreasing waste in the extraction and use of resourceful materials, substituting some physical materials for others to provide a needed service, and recycling materials. Innovations that decrease the wasted amount of a material increase the amount available for use.

By substituting new materials to provide the services of increasingly scarce and expensive ones, people can create new resources. Humans are a resilient species, capable of developing solutions to all sorts of difficulties—if they have the incentive and the freedom to do so. . . .

Shortages due to population growth, or to any other factor, provide the incentive for men and women to use muscle and mind to develop solutions. Prices must be allowed to rise so that entrepreneurs receive both a signal of approaching scarcity and a promise of reward for finding a solution. Moreover, individuals must be allowed to freely trade, on terms they negotiate, the goods and services they produce.

Population growth certainly will raise demand for natural resources and energy. If markets are free, however, population pressures that increase resource scarcity in the short run will lead to technological developments that leave everyone better off than before problems ever arose. While it is impossible to prove that this always will take place, the history of humanity indicates that, with enough economic freedom, overpopulation relative to natural resources or energy will not occur.

Overpopulation and Living Space

Doomsters often argue that the amount of available land places a constraint on population growth. They speculate that a rising population eventually will run out of places to live. After all, the Earth is finite in size, and the more people inhabiting the planet, the less space there is for everyone.

Running out of habitable space may be a physical possibility, but, for all practical purposes, it is a meaningless concern. If the entire population of the world were placed in the state of Alaska, each individual would receive nearly 3,500 square feet of space— about one-half the size of the average American homestead with front and back yards. Alaska, although the U.S.'s largest state, comprises a mere one percent of the Earth's land mass.

Of course, land provides more than just living space. It also is necessary for food production. Conventional wisdom holds that there is only a limited amount of arable land in the world and that much of this—the most fertile part—already is under cultivation. Hence, as population swells, it will become increasingly difficult, and eventually impossible, to feed everyone.

World agricultural data, however, do not support the claim that humanity has reached the limit on food production. Since global food data began being collected in the late 1940s, food production has outpaced population growth by, on average, one percent per year. The world price of food, adjusted for inflation, has been declining for the last century and probably for much longer, indicating that food output has been increasing more rapidly than population.

Pessimists insist that humanity cannot sustain agricultural production. They assert that, since practically all of the world's arable land now is under cultivation and because the cost of clearing, draining, and fertilizing marginal land is proving too costly, continued population growth soon will make it impossible to feed everyone.

Growth in Hong Kong

There are striking examples of remarkable economic growth occurring along with dramatic population growth. Economist Sudha Shenoy notes that in the thirty-six years between 1951 and 1987 the population of Hong Kong, which was poor after World War II, rose 2.78 times, much faster than the same increase in Britain and India. Nevertheless, Hong Kong's economy developed rapidly, and, by 1969, the enclave became the largest exporter in the underdeveloped world.

Sheldon L. Richman, *The World & I*, June 1993.

The notion that there is very little land left to bring under cultivation is not true. While potentially arable land—that which can produce an acceptable level of food crops—comprises only 24% of the total ice-free land mass of the world, this is more than twice the amount cultivated in recent decades and over three times the amount cultivated in any single year.

Per capita agricultural production can continue rising because of technological developments and agricultural innovations that allow farmers to increase the amount of food they can harvest off each acre of land. Irrigation, for instance, typically increases per-acre yields twofold to fourfold. Hence, irrigating one acre of land is equivalent to finding one to three additional acres of cropland.

Gains in the productivity of U.S. agriculture are undeniable. Between 1870 and 1985, farm output increased nearly ninefold. This occurred despite a drastic decline in farm population from 36,000,000 to 7,000,000 people (from 90% of the total population to three percent) and, at least in the 1980s, reduced the amount of land used for agriculture. Between 1960 and 1985, the number of labor hours devoted to agricultural production dropped from 9,800,000,000 to 3,200,000,000 and the amount of cropland remained the same. Technological innovations allowed total output to rise nearly 50% during this period.

These trends show no signs of slowing, much less reversing themselves. Agricultural productivity growth has led to an actual *decrease* in total agricultural land being utilized in developed countries. As a result, agricultural output could be increased significantly in response to demand from a larger population. In a free market, rising food prices will motivate farmers to bring more land under cultivation and encourage research and development in biotechnology. . . .

Arguments that population growth inevitably will lead to intolerable levels of pollution seem more common than ever. Indeed, many gloom-and-doomers who have given up promulgating the myth that population expansion soon will lead to resource, land, and food shortages now issue dire predictions about its effects on the environment. The argument, on first glance, seems to make sense: more people consume more goods and services, the creation of which strains the environment. Such a simplistic analysis ignores two important facts—that population growth creates wealth and environmental protection is a luxury good. Taken together, these two insights explain the fact that ecological quality in most industrial nations has improved dramatically even as populations there have grown. . . .

Many studies, starting in 1967 with an analysis by Nobel Prize winner and economist Simon Kuznets, agree that there is no negative statistical relationship between economic growth and population expansion. Rather, there is strong reason to believe that increasing population has a positive long-term effect on economic health.

Greater population density generally leads to faster economic growth for several reasons. First, a denser population typically is correlated with enhanced communication and transportation systems that facilitate the exchange of ideas. This adds to the stock of knowledge, enabling scientific and technological advances that boost productivity. The more ideas are exchanged, the more innovators can build on past efforts and the less efforts are duplicated.

A second way population growth increases productivity is by encouraging specialization and trade. When individuals specialize in the activities they can perform most efficiently and then trade what they produce for other needed goods and services, society gets the greatest output for the least input and wealth is maximized. The extent of specialization, or the division of labor, is limited by the size of the market. Hence, as populations swell, individuals are able to focus their efforts on fewer tasks, and per capita productivity increases. Of course, population growth will not lead to increased output if markets are not free so that specialization, directed by relative prices, can occur.

A third way population growth increases per capita productivity and income is by allowing the realization of economies of scale, which occur when it is less expensive per unit to produce many units of a good than to produce just a few. The per-unit cost of assembly line production in a factory, for instance, is much lower than the cost of each worker producing one good at a time. Factories cannot be utilized, though, unless there is sufficient demand for the good produced.

Perhaps population growth's most important contribution to wealth creation comes in the direct relationship between population density and the increase of scientific and technological knowledge. Each individual has a mind and is therefore a potential supplier of new knowledge from which all can benefit. Because the human mind develops innovations that raise living standards for all, it is, as [economist] Julian Simon has pointed out, the "ultimate resource."

Income and Environmental Protection

The observation that population growth increases per capita productivity and income may, on first glance, seem to have little to do with its effects on the environment. However, when one understands the relationship between wealth and ecological protection, population growth's positive environmental effects become evident.

Individuals concerned with basic survival are extremely unlikely to expend much-needed resources to protect the environment. In a study for the National Bureau of Economic Research, Princeton University economists Gene Grossman and Alan Krueger used cross-national data assembled by the Global Environmental Monitoring System to examine the relationship between various ecological indicators and the level of a country's per capita income. They found that, while economic growth led to an initial increase in pollution, greater prosperity eventually led to a net decrease in pollution because of "an increased demand for (and supply of) environmental protection at higher levels of national income."

Contrary to what might be expected, population growth in many developing nations (which typically are the areas exhibiting high-growth rates) is likely to improve ecological quality in the long run. Because higher per capita income increases environmental protection efforts, anything that raises productivity and income in these areas will eventually lead to a cleaner environment. As long as markets are free, relative prices can direct specialization and benefits from trade can occur. Population growth will lead to higher productivity and per capita income in an economic setting of increasing specialization, easy information transfer, and a rising stock of scientific and technical knowledge. It may take some time, but this economic growth eventually should lead to pollution abatement efforts that leave the environment cleaner than before the growth began.

At this point, there is no overpopulation relative to natural resources, living space, food production, or ecological carrying capacity. There is plenty of living space for all and many more; resources and food are becoming more available and should continue to do so; and greater wealth from denser populations is making environmental protection more affordable. However, for these positive trends to continue and improve, markets must be unrestrained. Economic freedom is necessary to motivate the production changes that enable the Earth to sustain more inhabitants. Prices must be allowed to rise and fall freely so that producers will know where to concentrate their efforts. Entrepreneurs must be able to profit from their innovations without having their earnings confiscated or taxed away. Free trade must be allowed so that specialization can occur.

History has shown that, in an atmosphere of economic freedom, human ingenuity continually enables the Earth to sustain more people at higher living standards. A sixfold population expansion since 1800 has been no problem because it has been accompanied by an eightyfold increase in productivity. In the presence of free market institutions that encourage innovation, there is no reason to expect productivity gains to stop before population growth levels off, as it is predicted to do by the middle of the next century.

Nevertheless, catastrophists, because they cannot foresee exactly how productivity will be increased, always think the Earth has reached the limits of its carrying capacity. "Our numbers are burdensome to the world, which can hardly support us," warned Tertullian, a second-century resident of Carthage. How many people were alive when this noted theologian foresaw no way for the world's resources to support any more people? Not 5,600,000,000, the planet's current population; the number was 190,000,000.

What the conference participants missed in Cairo was the opportunity to question the widely held belief of overpopulation threatening the planet. If they had examined the real, rather than presumed, population problems, they would have focused on economic solutions, rather than controversial sociological and political ones.

> *"The rich developed countries continue to get richer and more developed while the poor stay poor—not always only relatively."*

The Gap Between Haves and Have-Nots Is Growing

Robin Wright

As the twenty-first century dawns, the previous one hundred years may ultimately be remembered not as a time of unparalleled economic progress, but the time when the gap between the rich and poor became "staggering," Robin Wright argues in the following viewpoint. Among other global statistics, Wright points to the doubling of the gap between the earnings of those at the top and those at the bottom of society in the last thirty years. The disparity is not just monetary, she contends, but includes gaps in levels of education, health, and technology. Wright, a *Los Angeles Times* staff writer nominated for five Pulitzer Prizes, has written two books on Islam and the Middle East and is the coauthor of *Flashpoints: Promise and Peril in a New World.*

As you read, consider the following questions:

1. How do Saudi Arabia and Yemen illustrate the gap between haves and have-nots, according to Wright?
2. According to United Nations figures cited by Wright, how many people in developing countries are poor?
3. What is the biggest challenge facing South Africa, in the author's opinion?

The 20th Century, an era of unparalleled economic progress and improved living conditions, may ultimately be judged instead by a starkly different trend: the staggering gap between rich and poor.

The numbers reveal painful divisions. At the close of the century, the richest 1 billion people—or 20% of world population—control almost 85% of global wealth, while the poorest 1 billion command less than 2%, according to the 1994 Human Development Report, a survey by the United Nations Development Program [UNDP].

The disparity means the top layer of society earns 60 times the income of the bottom, a gap that has doubled—from 30 to 1—in just three decades.

The bottom line: In the mid-1990s the meek show no signs of inheriting the Earth.

Nowhere are the dimensions of the gap and its impact more egregious than on the Arabian Peninsula. Despite modest oil discoveries in the 1980s, Yemen is growing poorer compared to its oil-rich neighbor Saudi Arabia. The paltry per capita income in the Arab world's poorest country plummeted 14% between 1989 and 1992, to $1,374.

Even before a civil war erupted in Yemen in May 1994, poverty permeated Sana, the capital and legendary city reputedly founded by Noah's son Shem. A downtown section has been transformed by hovels made of plastic cartons and large tin cans held together by baked mud. "Night City," where cinder-block homes were illegally erected overnight, has sprouted on the capital's hilly outskirts. And across from the Yemeni president's home, squatters have pulled together a vast camp from bits of old tin, plastic sheeting, wood and stones.

An Ominous Gap

The ominous gap between rich and poor is evident around the globe.

"The underlying factor in all this world disorder is the sheer power of uncontrolled great wealth in the hands of a few nations, coexisting with the absolute poverty everywhere. The laws of the jungle operate," former Tanzanian President Julius K. Nyerere has written of the post–Cold War world.

> The rich developed countries continue to get richer and more developed while the poor stay poor—not always only relatively. In the last decade the peoples of Latin America and of Africa, as well as in many parts of Asia, have seen their desperately low standard of living decline even further. The income and technology gap between North and South gets geometrically wider all the time.

According to U.N. figures, poverty is the most acute problem of the developing world. More than a third of the people in these countries live below the poverty line. Worldwide, more than 1 billion people are surviving on the equivalent of $1 a day.

Human Development Index

This United Nations scale combines life expectancy, adult literacy, years in school, and consumers' purchasing power to rank nations on their socioeconomic status.

Top 10	*Bottom 10*
1. Canada	164. Guinea Bissau
2. Switzerland	165. Somalia
3. Japan	166. Gambia
4. Sweden	167. Mali
5. Norway	168. Chad
6. France	169. Niger
7. Australia	170. Sierra Leone
8. United States	171. Afghanistan
9. Netherlands	172. Burkina Faso
10. Britain	173. Guinea

Source: *Human Development Report*, 1994.

Disparities between the prosperous and poor are visible in myriad ways:

- In California, sixth-graders work on computers in air-conditioned classrooms while kids in Mozambique use sticks and bark to learn to write in open-air classes. One of four South African children does not go to school at all.
- A designer handbag in Paris costs $1,500, more than the annual per capita income in more than 40 countries.
- Media conglomerates merge in New York to open an information superhighway while 40% of the population in Russia, so recently a superpower, plummets below the poverty line.
- Rival British and American shipping companies vie to build the world's largest and most luxurious cruise liners while hundreds of thousands of homeless live atop massive garbage dumps in Mexico City and Manila.

The poverty gap will affect both rich and/or poor on every continent.

Some regions now face being so powerless, so marginalized by poverty, that they will fall off the world's political and economic map for generations. Other areas can expect an explosive backlash in a world where the communications revolution makes comparative living conditions highly visible.

"Poverty is the greatest threat to political stability, social cohesion and the environmental health of the planet," warns the U.N. report. "These disparities . . . deserve the urgent attention of policymakers."

The gap may even threaten the patterns of change. Shortly before his election as U.N. secretary general in 1992, Boutros Boutros-Ghali said bluntly in an article in the *Mediterranean Quarterly*: "Democracy cannot take root unless certain minimal institutions and an adequate living standard exist."

In the post–Cold War world, where equality and empowerment are catchwords, the poverty gap is also a symbol of division. It is rapidly becoming a barometer of global trouble.

"A new Iron Curtain between North and South . . . will be reinforced as a result of the gap between the standards of living in the rich and poor countries," Boutros-Ghali predicted. The result will be a "process of marginalization" that "practically leaves no place for the Third World or Africa, except where humanitarian aid is concerned," he concluded.

The prospects for progress are not uniformly bleak. Between 1960 and 1992 "all countries have made substantial progress in human development," the UNDP report notes. Over the past half a century, world income increased sevenfold (in terms of real gross domestic product) and income per person more than tripled. The human development index—calculated on the basis of income, life expectancy, literacy and education—doubled in developed countries and increased by 80% even in the poorest countries.

"But this gain has been spread very unequally—nationally and internationally—and the inequality is spreading," the report says.

In the United States, Europe and Japan, for example, living conditions made unprecedented strides in 25 years. Average life expectancy increased from 51 to 63 years. Average per capita consumption of goods and services increased by 70%. And enrollment in primary education neared 90%, according to the World Bank.

Yemen and Saudi Arabia

Yet worldwide, all but the richest 20% saw their share of world income drop between 1960 and 1991. And poverty drags down the quality of life. In the squatter camps of Sana, the Yemeni capital, many toilets are no more than holes in the ground, and water must be bought from trucks. Few kids are in schools, and thousands of men with paintbrushes or shovels squat daily on street corners hoping to be hired.

Up to 40% of Yemen's labor force is unemployed, and more than one in five Yemenis lives in absolute poverty. Yemen's crisis is all the more conspicuous in context.

Across the border in Riyadh, the Saudi capital, construction costs for the new airport, the world's most modern, ran more than half of Yemen's annual gross domestic product. The Saudi airport boasts an indoor oasis, 3,000 square feet of stained-glass windows, walls of marble quarried in Italy and etched with Koranic verses in England, and a bronze-domed mosque for 5,000.

But facilities like this tell only part of the story.

On average, Saudis live 17 years longer than Yemenis, and only one-fifth as many Saudi children die before age 5, according to the UNDP report. The average Saudi has three years more education resulting in 23% higher literacy.

The American Gap

The United States is among the countries where the gap between rich and poor is growing, according to a United Nations study. The top 20% of Americans control nine times as much wealth as the bottom 20%, the biggest gap in the industrialized world, according to the U.N. Development Program.

Also, more American children live in poverty—double the percentage in the developed world and quadruple the rate in Western Europe, UNICEF [United Nations International Children's Emergency Fund] reports. In 1970, 15% of American children were poor. Two decades later, 20% are destitute.

Robin Wright, *Los Angeles Times*, June 14, 1994.

Petrodollars may have skewed the gap, but Saudi Arabia—which ranks 67th on the UNDP's human development index—is far from the top rank. And at 142nd of 173 countries surveyed, Yemen is not the worst. However, the impact on the two Arab neighbors is symptomatic of the poverty gap and its dangerous effects.

"Yemen has its own peculiar problems, but a lot of what is happening here is like what is happening in the world," said Amat Alim Sowswa, Yemen's deputy minister of information and its highest-ranking female official.

"As it gets worse, we're going to witness a kind of revolution of the poor in all forms of unrest that is eventually bound to spill over into rich areas too," she said.

Africa and Latin America

The lower end of the global gap is represented by the abysmal poverty in Africa, where many countries are worse off in the 1990s than they were at independence in the 1960s. In 1965,

Ghanaians were better off than South Koreans or Thais. The UNDP index now ranks South Korea 32nd, Thailand 54th—and Ghana 134th.

World Bank data suggest that even the most productive African countries—Ghana, Nigeria, Tanzania and Zimbabwe—are unlikely to reduce poverty for at least another generation. At optimistic growth rates, others could take decades to return to income levels of the 1970s—and another half a century to turn the tide. With twice the U.S. population, Africa's total wealth is just slightly above Belgium's.

The gap is not limited to income. In health services, industrial countries average one doctor per 400 people, while developing countries average one per 7,000—and some African states have only one per 36,000, the UNDP reports.

Wealth is most heavily concentrated in Latin America. The inequities are the greatest in Brazil, Guatemala and Honduras. In Brazil, the top 20% earn 32 times more than the poorest 20%—up from 26 to 1 in just two years, the UNDP reports.

The divide in Brazil is largely geographic, between the wealthy, industrialized south and the poor, largely agricultural north. The regional disparity includes 17 years in life expectancy and 33 percentage points in literacy and 40% in per capita income.

Elsewhere, the biggest challenge for post-apartheid South Africa is the internal gap. It ranked 93rd on the UNDP index. But as a separate country, white South Africa would rank 24th, above Spain, while black South Africa would rank 123rd. "Not just two different peoples, these are almost two different worlds," the UNDP concludes.

Socialism and Economic Reform

The internal gap is not limited to poor countries. In the industrialized world, wage differentials in manufacturing also widened during the 1980s in 12 of 17 member countries surveyed by the Organization of Economic Cooperation and Development.

Some reasons for the growing divisions are systemic, others political:

• The collapse of socialism and its safety net of benefits, along with the introduction of competitive free markets, have led to soaring increases in both poverty and wealth in Asia, Africa and Europe.

Conditions have declined most sharply in the former Soviet Bloc. They are now more critical than in the West during the 1930s Depression or Latin America in the "lost decade" of the 1980s, according to a UNICEF [United Nations International Children's Emergency Fund] report.

In nine former East Bloc countries—Russia, Ukraine, Poland, Romania, Bulgaria, the Czech Republic, Slovakia, Hungary and

Albania—plummeting gross domestic product levels have left 20% to 70% of the populations living on or below the poverty line.

"Some cases in the [communist] Second World are now worse than in the Third World," said Eric Thurman, president of Opportunity International, a Chicago-based human development group.

Internally, China's economic reforms have led to record growth—and a record gap between vibrant urban centers in Beijing and Shanghai and distant backwaters like Qinghai and Tibet.

In Vietnam, economic liberalization has fostered both the rise of a new class of business people and brokers and an estimated 15% unemployment. More than 700,000 workers in state-owned companies have been let go, while about 100,000 demobilized soldiers are jobless, contributing to a new class of street people.

Foreign Aid

• Lengthy wars—fought by forces oblivious to cost and allowed to drag on by an uninterested post–Cold War world—are setting back Third World countries to pre-colonial conditions. Paid for by its diamonds and oil, Angola's two-decade-old civil war has turned developed areas into shattered landscapes. Without outside aid, up to half a million people would soon starve there, relief groups say.

The demise of the Cold War also cost many countries virtually the only leverage they had in winning funds or attention from either East or West.

• Aid still goes largely to former strategic allies rather than to poor countries. "Aid is still based on the shadows of the past. The world has not adjusted its sights to post–Cold War realities," said Mahbub ul Haq, chief architect of the U.N. human development index.

"For example, the United States gave 16 times the amount per capita for El Salvador over Bangladesh, which has a population 22 times larger and five times poorer than El Salvador. But is El Salvador such a strategic place today?"

Based on current patterns, foreign aid is unlikely to help close the gap. Often it perpetuates inequities.

Better-off recipient countries get more than $240 per person, for example, while the worst-off states often get less than $1 per person a year, reports the Overseas Development Council.

Skewed Priorities

• Inefficiency, corruption, bad debts, protectionism and skewed priorities also deserve much of the blame. "At a time the entire world is reducing military expenditures an average of 3.6% a year, the two poorest regions of the world—sub-Sahara Africa and South Asia—are increasing spending on arms," Haq said.

India and Pakistan have for several years spent nearly twice as much on arms as Saudi Arabia, which is 20 times richer, he added. In contrast, Costa Rica abolished its army in 1948 and invested a third of its resources in health, education and housing. It's now the most prosperous Central American country, with one of the highest human development ratings in the Third World.

Unlike East Asia's major investments in basic education and health, most African countries decreased social expenditures in the 1980s—up to 64% in Gambia, 70% in Nigeria and 82% in Sierra Leone, the World Bank reported.

• Several countries with adequate resources to narrow the gap are choosing not to address poverty. "Brazil is rich enough to deal with poverty problems and so is the United States. We're not for the same reason Brazil isn't: We don't want to," said John W. Sewell, president of the Overseas Development Council in Washington.

Despite the gap, human progress is likely to continue to make significant strides: "Social indicators—average literacy, life expectancy, mortality and others—are improving. On average, those are much better than they were in the developing world 40 years ago," Sewell said.

"But that's like the man with his head in the oven and his foot in the icebox. The average temperature doesn't tell the story."

"Life for the majority of the world's citizens is getting steadily better in almost every category."

The Gap Between Haves and Have-Nots Is Shrinking

Marcus Gee

In the following viewpoint, Marcus Gee argues that warnings of approaching global decay and anarchy are "dead wrong." Gee contends that many crises such as overpopulation, resource scarcity, and environmental destruction have been exaggerated and that genuine problems are improving. Gee cites examples of improved living standards around the world, including increases in life expectancy and food production and decreases in rates of child mortality, and he predicts that these positive trends will continue into the twenty-first century. Gee is an editorial board member of the *Globe and Mail* daily newspaper in Toronto, Canada, and a former foreign correspondent.

As you read, consider the following questions:

1. According to Gee, what is the chief cause of death among children?
2. What are the factors that could slow population growth, in the author's opinion?
3. Which region does Gee recognize as having perhaps the worst standard of living?

Excerpted from Marcus Gee, "Apocalypse Deferred: The End Isn't Nigh." Reprinted with permission from *The Globe and Mail*, April 9, 1994.

When Robert D. Kaplan sat down to write "The Coming Anarchy," a grim prophecy of global decay published in the February 1994 issue of the *Atlantic Monthly*, he intended to create a stir. "The piece was meant to hit people in the solar plexus," said Mr. Kaplan from his home in Maryland. "I really believe we are on the verge of a second Cold War—this time against the new demons of population and resource scarcity and environmental destruction.". . .

"The Coming Anarchy" depicts a world riven by "disease . . . unprovoked crime, scarcity of resources, refugee migrations, the increased erosion of nation-states and international borders, and the empowerment of private armies, security firms and international drug cartels." West Africa, he writes, is becoming "the symbol of worldwide demographic, environmental and societal stress, in which criminal anarchy emerges as the real 'strategic' danger."

Mr. Kaplan, a U.S. author and journalist, makes no apologies for his bleak tone. "The point was to break the silence on some of these issues. The method was to get people debating and arguing." It worked. Months after publication, the 21-page article was still drawing controversy and praise. . . . And no wonder. His article arrived at a time of extraordinary anxiety about the future. After the end of the Cold War, hopes for the early dawning of a New World Order—seldom mentioned today without sneering quotation marks—have long since evaporated. Ethnic cleansing in the former Yugoslavia and warlordism in Somalia have reminded everyone with a television set that the world is still a dangerous place. Looming environmental threats such as global warming and rapid population growth demonstrate that it is also, apparently, a fragile one.

Doomsayers Are Wrong

The Kaplan piece draws all of these anxieties together into a coherent thesis: that environmental and demographic pressures, combined with the collapse of traditional nation-states, is bringing on a period of profound instability and chaos. It is absorbing, fascinating, frightening stuff. It is also dead wrong.

Ever since English economist Thomas Malthus published his "Essay on the Principle of Population" in 1798, arguing that population growth would outrun food supply, leading to famine and war, experts have been warning of "the coming anarchy."

In this generation, the doomsaying began with the publication of Paul Ehrlich's 1968 bestseller *The Population Bomb*, which said that "in the 1970s the world will undergo famine—hundreds of millions of people are going to starve to death." The Club of Rome followed in 1972 with *The Limits to Growth*, a "Project on the Predicament of Mankind." Then, in 1980, came the Global 2000 report, commissioned by U.S. president Jimmy Carter. It predicted that "barring revolutionary advances in technology, life for most people on earth will be more precarious in 2000 than it is now."

Trends in Life Expectancy at Birth, 1950–1990

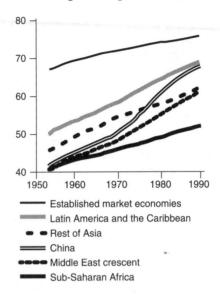

Established market economies
Latin America and the Caribbean
Rest of Asia
China
Middle East crescent
Sub-Saharan Africa

Source: World Bank.

The doomsayers were briefly eclipsed when the Cold War ended—but only briefly. Summing up the spirit of the times, a leading article in the Spring 1993 issue of the American periodical *Foreign Policy* said the world "appears to be at the beginning, not of a new order, but of a new nightmare."

In fact, the opposite is true. By almost every measure, life on earth is getting better. The past few decades have seen a steady improvement in human health, education, nutrition and longevity. The rapid expansion of the world economy, which has grown nearly fivefold since 1950, has raised living standards in all but the poorest countries. Food production has easily outstripped population growth. Democracy has advanced in almost every corner of the globe. International security has improved. Malthus, Ehrlich, the Club of Rome, Global 2000 and Robert D. Kaplan notwithstanding, the world is a safer, richer, healthier place than it was 10 years ago, let alone 20 or 30.

Of course, immense problems remain, from ethnic national-ism to tropical deforestation to malnutrition to cropland loss. It would be foolish to pretend otherwise. But many of the crises that make up "the coming anarchy" have been exaggerated, and even the genuine ones exist within a broad pattern of progress. If that seems too rosy, consider, one by one, the robust state of the earth's vital signs—starting with the most vital of all, human health.

Health and Education

Thirty years ago, notes James Grant, executive director of UNICEF [United Nations International Children's Emergency Fund], three of four children born in developing countries sur-vived until their fifth birthdays. Today, nine out of 10 survive. Over the same period, life expectancy in the Third World grew from 53 years to 65. In the mid-eighties, UNICEF and other or-ganizations launched a campaign for universal child immuniza-tion. Today, three million children a year, or about 8,000 a day, are being saved by simple vaccines. Oral-rehydration therapy, an inexpensive treatment for the greatest killer of children, diar-rhea, saves another one million children a year.

Even in Africa, where progress in health has been slower than elsewhere, average life expectancy has risen from 39 years to 51 years. Thus, it is simply nonsense for Mr. Kaplan to say that, in regard to health, "Africa may today be more dangerous . . . than it was in 1862, before antibiotics, when Sir Richard Francis Burton described the health situation on the continent as 'deadly, a Golgotha, a Jehannum.'"

While malaria is making a comeback in Africa and AIDS is rampant, smallpox—which as recently as 1967 killed between 1.5 million and two million people a year around the globe—has been eradicated. Polio is expected to be erased by 1995 and measles not long afterward.

Despite these victories, 22,000 children a day die from easily preventable diseases, a shameful statistic considering the low cost of modern prevention and treatment techniques.

If education is a key to development—and everyone agrees it is—prospects for growth have never been better. In the past two decades, the rate of world primary-school enrollment increased from less than 70 percent to well over 80 percent. Secondary-school enrollment almost doubled, from less than 25 percent to 40 percent.

The Ascent of Money

Despite three major recessions—in 1974–75, 1981–82 and the early 1990s—the world economy has grown by an average of 3.9 percent per year over the past three decades. That has been more than enough to outstrip the population increase. Consequently, gross output per capita has more than doubled. . . .

In fact, at an average rate of 4.75 percent a year, growth in the developing world outpaced the industrialized countries from 1989 to 1994. And the Organization for Economic Cooperation and Development predicts further growth of about 6 percent a year through 1998.

This growth is by no means confined to the Pacific Rim and a few "isolated places," unless Latin America and India are considered isolated. After the lost decade of the eighties, when per capita growth actually declined, Latin America is enjoying a modest expansion—the result of the wave of economic reform that has swept the region from Mexico to the southern countries of Chile and Argentina, where market-oriented reforms resulted in growth rates in 1992 of 10 percent and 9 percent, respectively.

The same liberalizing formula has produced a startling economic rebound in India, heralded as "Another Asian giant on the move" in a March 1994 cover story of the respected *Far Eastern Economic Review*. The other giant, of course, is China, whose economy grew 13 percent in 1993.

True, some developing countries are missing out on growth altogether, particularly in Africa. And many of those developing nations that are growing face years of struggle before they even approach developed-world standards. But with the world's two most populous countries on the move, and Latin America joining in, the stretch limo is finding itself in heavy traffic.

Trade: The Great Provider

Even more impressive than the growth of global output is the expansion of world trade, which recorded an average annual increase of 6 percent from 1960 to 1990. With more robust growth expected to resume through 1997, trade should continue to expand rapidly.

Part of the credit goes to free-trade arrangements. According to Washington's Worldwatch Institute, tariffs worldwide averaged almost 40 percent of the price of each product in 1947. The figure today is 5 percent. With the advent of regional trade deals such as the North American Free Trade Agreement, and the liberalizing of world trade rules negotiated in December 1994 under the General Agreement on Tariffs and Trade, tariffs and other barriers to trade will fall further still. The most conservative estimates put the value of the GATT deal to world incomes at $200 billion.

Will the entire winnings go to rich countries and giant multinational companies? No. Under the GATT deal, which covers farm products, tropical commodities, clothing and textiles for the first time, developing countries will get freer access to rich-world markets for some of their main exports.

A favourite topic of doomsayers in the eighties was the Third World debt crisis, which threatened to bankrupt several developing countries and bring on a collapse of the world financial system. This threat has now largely evaporated. Since the adoption of the 1989 Brady Initiative, named after U.S. treasury secretary Nicholas Brady, many of the biggest debtors have managed to restructure or reduce their debts. They include Costa Rica, Mexico, Argentina, Nigeria, the Philippines, Venezuela, Uruguay and Brazil.

Overall, Third World debt continues to rise slowly, reaching $1.428 trillion by the end of 1992. And many countries continue to suffer under their debt burdens. But, according to the International Monetary Fund, "the international financial system is no longer at risk." Just as important, the easing of the crisis has revived the flow of capital, the essential lubricant of economic growth, to developing countries. From 1985 to 1993, the volume of direct investment by industrial countries rose from $10 billion to $40 billion, and overall financial inflows to the developing world soared from $100 billion to $175 billion in the early nineties.

The Population Dud

Even more than mentioning debt, doomsayers love to speak of overpopulation. Mr. Kaplan picks up the theme, noting that the world's population will rise from 5.5 billion to more than nine billion in 50 years. (The UN projects that it will finally stop growing sometime between 2150 and 2200 at a level of about 11.6 billion). Ninety-five percent of that growth, he adds, will take place in the Third World. Almost everyone, from the UN to the environmental movement to governments, developed or developing, insists this is an urgent problem. It may not be.

To begin with, the world fertility rate has fallen dramatically. Third World women now bear an average of four children, down from six 20 years ago. The rate could drop still further as more people move from rural areas to cities, where families have fewer children. Half of the women in developing countries use some form of birth control, compared with one in 10 in the sixties. Because of this progress, the UN Population Fund says the world population could stop growing as early as 2075, when it will have reached 10 billion.

Still too many? Perhaps not. A small but growing body of scientific opinion holds that the earth has the capacity to sustain far more people than it does today. The experience of the past 25 years, during which living standards soared even as world population more than doubled, is cited as proof. "The empirical evidence indicates no negative correlation between the rate of population

45

growth and the standard of living," American scholar Mark Perlman has written. "The growth in numbers over the millennia from a few thousands or millions of humans living at low subsistence, to billions living well above subsistence, is a most positive assurance that the problem of sustenance has eased rather than grown more difficult over the years." Certainly, population density alone does not seem to limit growth. Some of the most crowded places on earth—Hong Kong, Singapore and Taiwan—have experienced among the highest rates of economic success.

Food, Oil and the Environment

"The outstanding fact in food and agriculture is that the past 25 years have brought a better fed world despite an increase of 1.8 billion in population. Earlier fears of chronic food shortages over much of the world proved unfounded." So said the Food and Agriculture Organization [FAO] in a 1988 report, *World Agriculture Toward 2000*. The statement is equally true today.

Better farming methods, improved pesticides and herbicides, and the introduction of high-yield strains of rice and other cereals, have led to an increase in world food production of 20 percent per capita from 1960 to 1990. Food prices, meanwhile, have been dropping for decades. As a result, says the FAO, the proportion of the world's people considered malnourished declined from 36 percent in 1969–71 to 20 percent in 1988–90. Famine, which in recent times has ranged across China, India and the Soviet Union, now affects only Africa.

According to [Canadian scholar] Thomas Homer-Dixon, this achievement is threatened by looming water shortages, increasing soil depletion and the rapid disappearance of cropland. Others disagree. A recent report published by the World Bank predicts that the food crisis of the early seventies will be the last in history.

Energy Resources

In the seventies it was widely believed that the world would "run out of oil" within 20 years. Nothing of the sort has happened. As new supplies have come on stream in Alaska, the North Sea and elsewhere, world oil reserves have grown from 100 billion cubic metres in 1980 to 158 billion in 1993. Meanwhile, oil prices dropped from a high of $40 in 1979–80 to about $13 in 1994—the same level they were at before the first oil shock of 1973.

The same thing—bigger reserves, lower prices—has happened to many other "finite," "nonrenewable" resources. The University of Maryland's Julian Simon, co-author of 1984's *The Resourceful Earth*, argues that "energy has been getting more available, rather than more scarce, as far back as we have records. Through the centuries, the price of energy—coal, oil and electricity—has been decreasing rather than increasing, relative to the cost of labour and even relative to the price of consumer goods." The world is also using energy more efficiently. According to the UN's 1993 Human Development Report, energy requirements per unit of gross domestic product fell by 40 percent from 1965 to 1990.

Environmental collapse has loomed large in every prophecy of doom for the past generation. Mr. Kaplan's prediction is no exception. "In Africa and the Third World," he writes, "man is challenging nature far beyond its limits, and nature is now beginning to take its revenge."

The problems he writes about—soil erosion, air pollution, deforestation, the contamination of water supplies—are real. But are they serious enough to halt or even reverse human progress, creating "a rundown, crowded planet of skinhead Cossacks and juju warriors . . . battling over scraps of overused earth?" The evidence is slim. . . .

War and Peace

Perhaps the most compelling part of "The Coming Anarchy" deals with national disintegration and war. Mr. Kaplan argues that the end of the Cold War will bring on "a cruel process of natural selection among existing states." Many countries will simply collapse, he suggests, breaking up the current grid of nations and replacing it with "a jagged-glass pattern of city-states, shanty-states, nebulous and anarchic regionalisms." He may be right. The ugly conflicts in Yugoslavia, Somalia, Rwanda and Burundi certainly seem to indicate so. On the other hand, many conflicts have also drawn to a close in recent years.

Apart from ending the daily threat of nuclear annihilation—a detail often overlooked by the doomsayers camp—the close of the Cold War has led to negotiated settlements of civil wars in Cambodia, El Salvador, Mozambique and Namibia. Two of the world's most intractable disputes—between Arabs and Jews in the Middle East and between blacks and whites in South Africa—are closer to settlement than they have been in decades. The Marxist insurgencies that plagued Southeast Asia in the sixties and seventies, and Latin America well into the eighties, have mostly dried up.

The Stockholm International Peace Research Institute reports that the number of major conflicts in the world—those that have cost at least 1,000 lives and involved at least one active pair of warring parties, and one of those a government—actually dropped slightly from 1989 to 1992. . . .

Democracy has advanced around the world since the mid-eighties. In Latin America, countries as diverse as Argentina,

Brazil, Chile and Paraguay have made a successful switch from military to civilian rule. In Southeast Asia, the Philippines overthrew its odious dictator, Ferdinand Marcos, and two economic tigers, South Korea and Taiwan, let their citizens vote in free elections for the first time.

Meanwhile, the collapse of communism led to the birth of new, if flawed, democracies in many parts of the former East Bloc. From 1984 to 1993, the number of nations classified as "free" by Freedom House, the New York–based monitor of human rights and democracy, rose from 52 to 75.

This unmistakable trend is now under threat. In its 1993 report, Freedom House said the number of people living in free countries had fallen by 300 million—"a dramatic blow to the democratic renaissance that began in 1989." On the other hand, the number of democratic countries rose from 99 to 107—an indication that not all people who have the vote are fully free.

The African Exception

To every sign of progress listed above, a skeptic could fairly respond with one word: Africa. The growth rate of sub-Saharan Africa in 1993, at about 1.5 percent, was the lowest in the world, and has been for many years. The total economic output of the region's 530 million people, about $150 billion a year, is about the same as Belgium's. Only 37 percent of sub-Saharan Africans have access to clean drinking water.

This is a dreadful blot on the story of human progress. Even so, there are some glimmers of hope. South Africa, if it emerges from apartheid intact, promises to be a powerful motor of economic growth for the whole region. And most countries have abandoned the ruinous policies, such as collective agriculture, that crippled their economies in the post-independence years. Uganda, for example, has recorded annual growth rates of 5 percent since 1987, mainly because of liberal economic policies adopted after its emergence from years of civil strife.

As miserable as much of Africa may be, it is absurd to argue, as the Kaplan piece does, that Africa—and especially troubled West Africa—is a reflection of what the whole world will be like in a few decades. Africa is an exception to the rule, a dark chapter in a much larger story. That story, by and large, is one of remarkable, sustained and dramatic progress. Despite all the looming troubles, so eloquently recounted by Robert Kaplan, life for the majority of the world's citizens is getting steadily better in almost every category. Reckless optimism? Malthus would have thought so, too.

"Global teenagers could be armies of nihilism
and desperation, legions of entrepreneurs and
small business owners, . . . or builders of young
democracies."

Teenagers Are Poised to Become a Globally Dominant Age-Group

Peter Schwartz

Peter Schwartz is the founder and president of Global Business
Network, an organization in Emeryville, California, that studies
business and demographic trends. In the following viewpoint,
Schwartz argues that the early twenty-first century will bring a
global baby boom and the emergence of a two billion-strong
"global teenager" age-group. According to Schwartz, the large
number of teenagers around the world will be linked via new information and communication technologies. Schwartz contends
that as consumers and workers, these teenagers will greatly influence the global economic and political conditions of the future.

As you read, consider the following questions:

1. According to Schwartz, where do most of the world's future
   teenagers live?
2. How may teens interact in future "video cafés," according to
   Schwartz?
3. How must future immigrant workers adapt to new jobs in
   industrial countries, in the author's opinion?

While walking in Jakarta one day in 1987 I came upon a remarkable sight; a vast bazaar of stalls, the nearest of which were filled with all manner of electronic goods—from Walkmans to computers to microchips to CDs. And every booth was "manned" by a boy, hardly any over twenty, and many under ten, all dressed in brightly colored polo shirts with insignias from Benetton and Ralph Lauren. One sees these new teenagers everywhere. Do these signs portend the emergence of a global culture in the coming decades? Or are they merely superficial symbols of a global consumer society masking a deeper and more enduring cultural diversity. We know the numbers, we just don't know their meaning. This viewpoint shows how we come to develop scenarios by exploring driving forces [elements that move the plot of a scenario], predetermined elements [what is known beforehand], and critical uncertainties [hopes and fears].

Most futurists and forecasters would agree, I think: we learned about the power of driving forces, in part, by watching the impact of the baby boom. The mountain of 40 million teenagers born in the post-war decade and a half (the late forties and fifties) was one driving force. . . .

A New Baby Boom

Could any other demographic force be as powerful during the *next* few years? A group of people, under the auspices of Global Business Network [GBN], began to ask themselves that question a few years ago. They were spurred by an entertainment industry client who wanted to know, simply, Where would its major market be a decade hence? They looked at demographic trends and discovered a new global baby boom of such a size as to make the American baby boom seem like a dress rehearsal. Once again, its fate is linked with other factors—technological, political, and economic forces, some predetermined and some wildly uncertain. The implications will be exhilarating to some. . . . And they will be profoundly disturbing to others.

Barring widespread plague or other catastrophe, there will be over 2 billion teenagers in the world in the year 2001. That's *fifty times* the number of teenagers in America in the peak years of the baby boom. All of these future teenagers are already born. Most of them live in Asia and Latin America; a smaller but still sizable and rapidly growing percentage live in Africa. In Europe, North America, and Australia, meanwhile, there will also be a mini-baby boom, but their percentage of the global teenager population will be minuscule.

They called their scenario the "Global Teenager"—not just because this new baby boom is worldwide, but because its members will be far more interconnected. Satellite communication, videocassette recorders, and the ubiquitous Walkman have penetrated even poor countries. The results of this baby boom will not be the same as the impact of the youth culture of the 1960s in America; the world is a bigger and more diverse place, and the social mood is different from what it was twenty years ago. But they knew some of the certainties to expect, and many of the critical uncertainties to watch out for.

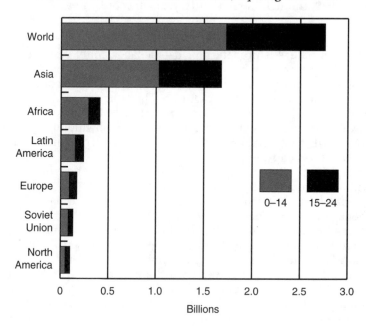

Number of Children and Youth, by Region: 1990

Source: U.S. Bureau of the Census, *Children's Well-Being: An International Comparison*, 1991.

For this scenario at GBN, they asked what would be the interplay between this new global adolescent community and the evolution of the new electronic media? Their research was intensive, and yet by necessity arbitrary. They could not hope to talk to more than a small fraction of the first group of global teenagers. . . . They pored over the statistics that existed so far, looking for patterns that might indicate critical forces—those changes that would have a big impact on the situation. Finally, they hired two astute observers to travel the world for them. They interviewed teenagers from twelve countries about their ambitions, and the pressures on their lives. One of the observers was Will Baker, a veteran writer on cultural issues. (His book *Backward* had covered the "horrifying impact of civilization," as he put it, "on an Amazonian tribal people.") The other researcher was an American teenager himself—Amon Rappaport.

The group at GBN did not focus on the plots or logics of scenarios. They wanted to know what driving forces would be critical. As the baby boom appeared (or should have appeared) as a factor in every scenario of U.S. behavior in the 1950s, 1960s, 1970s, and 1980s, so the wave of global teenagers will be a factor dwarfing other demographic factors in scenarios starting from 1990, through the next fifty years or more.

The Nature of Adolescence

Human nature is predetermined—it changes only very slowly, if at all. We know what adolescents are like. The years when people come of age involve exuberance, exploration, confusion, and rebellion against old structures. That's as true of teenagers in Bangkok, Nairobi, or Caracas as it is of teenagers in Los Angeles or Paris. It will be exacerbated by a newfound sense of power which teenagers will feel—power in their numbers. Adolescents tend to identify with each other anyway, set apart by and from other age groups. The pressure of their numbers will be so immense that it will reshape the world.

What they do with that pressure is a critical uncertainty. Teenagers are not necessarily altruistic by nature; rather, they are energetic and idealistic. In their travels, Will and Amon found that idealism translated not into a political sensibility but into either intense ambition or cynicism, both fueled by inflation and poverty, contrasting with the media's images of affluence. What flickered between the lines, wrote Baker, was "a generalized feeling that the circumstances of modern life are new and dire, that something like a global crisis is underway, and that they—the young—must find some original solution and the resources to apply them." Twenty years ago, if one had forecast a youth revolt in Latin America almost everyone's scenario would cast it as a move toward socialism, led by the armies of [revolutionary] Che Guevara. If a revolt takes place from this global teenage population, it will most likely be entrepreneurial and capitalist—the armies of some new, Third World equivalent to [Apple Computer cofounder] Steve Jobs.

Or it may be literal armies. In the past, societies with large numbers of adolescent males started wars. This option, unlikely on the global scale, may take place in many locales. . . . Injustice (El Salvador and South Africa) and enduring enmities (India and Pakistan) will not go away, so conflicts will endure and recur.

In thinking about the driving forces that will interact with the sheer demographic impact of teenage numbers, a walk down the street with your eyes open quickly leads you to one of the areas we noted earlier: the ubiquitous Walkman points you to new technology. The power of the predetermined element of new entertainment technology will make the experience of being a teenager different from what it ever has been before. The distribution of new types of communication devices, in particular, is taking place so fast that by the time most of the global teenagers *are* teenagers, they will literally be in constant contact with each other.

The World's Youth Population

Today's world child and youth population (2.8 billion) exceeds the total world population of just 26 years ago. Young people under age 25 years constitute more than half (52 percent) of the world's population.

Among the world's youth population, 61 percent live in Asia, 25 percent in Africa and Latin America, and 14 percent in Europe, North America, and the [former] Soviet Union combined.

By 2010, the population ages 0 to 24 years will be less than half of the total population in each of the world's regions except Africa, where it will be over 60 percent.

U.S. Bureau of the Census, *Children's Well-Being: An International Comparison*, 1991.

At GBN, we developed an image of the future which we called the "Video Café." We imagined two children of middle-class parents, one in a rapidly developing country and the other in the high-tech leader: seventeen-year-old Luis, a college student in Caracas, and seventeen-year-old Hiroki, living with her family outside Kyoto, going on an electronic "date" through an international broad-band-width video-conferencing network. It would be more than seeing each other's images; using camcorders, image synthesizers, computers, and other cheap electronic video equipment, the two teenagers would be part of a globally connected performance group. . . .

In the video cafés of the future, teenagers would do what you might expect them to do in person: flirt, dance in image form, listen to music, and (increasingly) be creative—the intense sexual energy of teenagers would still be present even in this attenuated form. There would be a constant insatiable hunger for fresh material—new music, new images, new fashions. . . .

Some readers, no doubt, will find this scenario hard to imagine. But it's based on three very plausible ideas. First, that new communications technologies are becoming so powerful and so cheap that teenagers all over the world will be able to afford them. Second, that the global teenager will *want* to communicate this way. And third, that using these kinds of new media tends to change peoples' behavior and values. . . .

Electronic Media

Some young people will spend what they might have spent on a car on the new tool for "cruising," the powerful interactive video-computer station with full virtual reality capabilities.

Will teenagers be able to afford them? That depends, in part, on the uncertainties of the world's economic future. However, some formerly undeveloped countries have clearly prospering middle classes: Venezuela, India, Korea, Singapore, Costa Rica. Whether a country's teenagers are rich or poor, however, they will use more information technology than they do today, if only because it will be more available and far less expensive. . . .

Information is no longer static; people feel as if they're swimming in a constant flow of images, text, and sounds. You can appreciate that feeling by watching a few minutes of MTV; it reflects the ambiance of interactive media. The next generation will grow up with a pervasive sensibility based on electronic media, in which computer-generated images and quick video cuts are a natural part of their language. If it's a style that 2 billion young people around the world adopt for themselves (and every indication suggests they will), then electronic media will become not just a means of communication, but a generator of global style. . . .

Moreover, since the next wave of telecommunications media will flow in two directions, it will encourage active intelligence; people won't be able to take part any more simply by sitting back and letting images flow over them. They'll be talking, selecting, ordering, criticizing, and (in some cases) creating. . . .

Economic Fears and Hopes

In exploring the economic interactions of demographics and culture we can see some of the longer term driving forces. As the coming of age of the American baby boom helped shape the American economy of the seventies and eighties, the global teenager will help shape the world economy in the nineties and beyond. While the presence of 2 billion global teenagers is predetermined, their characteristics are an uncertainty. We do not know how wealthy or literate they will be. There is a temptation, especially among industrial companies, to assume the worst. . . .

Global teenagers will either be uneducated, unemployed, undernourished, and in the end hopeless, street criminals—like the Brazilian teenage hero of Hector Babenco's film *Pixote*—or their fear of poverty will fuel ambition that drives out every other consideration. As a scenario-planner, this type of pessimistic image always inspires the question in me, What would have to take place for this image *not* to come true? The accelerating power of education via the new technology could turn out to be an answer.

As it happens, there are three driving forces in the world which might, together, be enough to catalyze that education. None of the three have anything to do with a formal educational establishment. The first is the ambition, already noted, among teenagers who want to better themselves. The second is the presence of cheap communications links; to play even a simple computer game is to become familiar with the habits and mindset of programming, and there is every reason for programming education (and education in other subjects) to travel via interactive telecommunications—assuming that the teenagers of the next fifteen years want it. The third factor is a critical uncertainty, derived directly from the driving force of demographics. How will countries around the world handle the overwhelming pressure for immigration?

Half of Mexico's population, for example, is under the age of twenty. In the next two decades its population will double, from 70 million to 140 million, even more dominated by people in their teens and twenties. Many of these young people will not find jobs in Mexico. But across the border, the United States will face a labor shortage, especially in entry-level positions. So will nearly every country in Europe, Eastern and Western. When Will Baker asked teenagers around the world, "What would you like to be doing ten years from now?" he nearly always got the same answer: travel to the United States. "Not a few," he wrote, "foresee declining to return."

Immigration Trends

In past waves of migration, unskilled labor from developing countries was welcome. Now, however, new jobs in the industrial countries will require training and communication skills. Teenage immigrants from developing countries will not be qualified unless they've educated themselves. Immigration will add pressure to learn, and will also provide some people with the opportunity. Young Third World people will end up working in a car factory in Sweden; then return to their own countries and create new businesses of their own. Young software designers in India begin work on contract for American banks in Chicago and end up on the payroll at corporate headquarters. . . .

Most industrialized nations (and most corporations) have not learned to deal with cultural diversity. The demographic pressures of the global teenager suggest that they will have to. Most employers and heads of the hierarchy will still be white males, but more than 85 percent of the labor force will come from young, nonwhite men and women from diverse cultures. Managing multicultural enterprises promises to be the single biggest challenge that managers will face in the 1990s. The numbers are predetermined. The reactions of managers and employees are critical uncertainties.

Seeing these driving forces will hopefully help managers realize that the change in their workforce is not a temporary phenomenon. It may in fact be a permanent change in perception, where teenagers decide that national boundaries are simply irrelevant to their ambitions. To migrate may no longer mean being oppressed; under one scenario of the global teenager, migrators may outnumber those teenagers who stay home! . . .

Political Change

The political outlook of the global teenager is impossible to predict today—as the political outlook of the 1960s in America would have been impossible to predict in 1955. We know only that hunger for freedom is a powerful force, pent up in many countries for a long time. We are likely to see intense pressure worldwide for democracy, and for an opening up of opportunities. Perceived oppressors in Third World countries—be they Marxist or capitalist, politicians or employers—may literally find millions of young people fiercely battling against them, convinced (as another baby boom was before them) that the whole world is watching.

Beyond that, anything is possible. Global teenagers could be armies of nihilism and desperation, legions of entrepreneurs and small business owners, waves of immigrants, majorities of "Green" [environmentally minded] voters, brownshirts, or builders of young democracies. If they are more or less unified politically (and there is reason to believe they will be), their point of view will affect every government on the planet.

"*In addition to growing larger, the world's population will also grow older.*"

Senior Citizens Will Become a Globally Dominant Age-Group

Wolfgang Lutz

Wolfgang Lutz heads the Population Project of the International Institute of Applied Systems Analysis in Laxenburg, Austria, and is the editor of *The Future Population of the World: What Can We Assume Today?* In the following viewpoint, Lutz contends that the average age of the world's population, in a midrange projection, will rise from approximately 28 years today to about 41 years in the year 2100, with the percentage of people age 60 or older increasing from 9.2 percent to 25.5 percent—one person in four. Lutz projects China and Western Europe as regions facing the most substantial increases in elderly populations.

As you read, consider the following questions:

1. What are the demographic trends that Lutz factors into the aging scenarios?
2. In the author's opinion, why is it crucial for China to address rapid population aging?
3. How can Europe avoid extensive aging, according to Lutz?

Excerpted from Wolfgang Lutz, "The Future of World Population," *Population Bulletin*, vol. 49, no. 1, June 1994. Reprinted by permission of the Population Reference Bureau.

For the last 50 years, world population has grown at a record-breaking pace. Never before has it multiplied so rapidly, and most likely it will never do so again. The mushrooming growth of world population and the uncertain path of future growth have created both alarm and confusion about the demographic changes that countries and world regions are experiencing.

The rate of world population increase is declining, signaling an eventual slowdown in world population growth. But answers to questions such as how soon, how fast, and in what regions of the world population growth rates will decline will determine the future number of inhabitants on planet Earth, and where they will live. The answers to these questions are far from certain; many possible scenarios exist. . . .

Population Explosion

World population growth did not really take off until around the 17th century when the world total reached about half a billion people. The first billion was completed shortly after 1800. The second billion was reached during the 1930s. The third billion was added in less than 30 years, by 1960; the fourth by 1975; and the fifth in 1987. The sixth billion will most likely come by 1998. Presently, it takes only 10 years to add another billion people to the world's population—the equivalent of adding the entire population of Europe and North America combined.

If the 1994 growth rate of 1.6 percent per year continued unabated, world population would double within 42 years, quadruple within 84 years, and increase eightfold to an incredible 44 billion within 126 years. . . .

The future course of world population growth is the focus of this viewpoint. It will describe current trends in fertility, mortality, and migration—the three components of population change—and will offer possible scenarios on the future trends in these components for 12 world regions (see Table 1). Unlike United Nations or World Bank projections, these population projections present a wide range of assumptions on all underlying components of change and thereby offer alternative pictures of the world's population future. Although fertility is clearly the dominant component of population change over the long run, the future course of mortality and migration also can have a sizable impact on population growth, especially for some world regions. . . .

In addition to growing larger, the world's population will also grow older. Today, the average age of the world's population is around 28 years. Approximately one in three people is under age 15, and only one in ten is age 60 or older. But under all scenarios of future population growth, average age will increase sharply. By 2030, the mean age of the world population is projected to range anywhere from 31 to 35 years, depending on the

Figure 1. World Population by Age and Sex in 1990 and 2030, Low and High Growth Scenarios

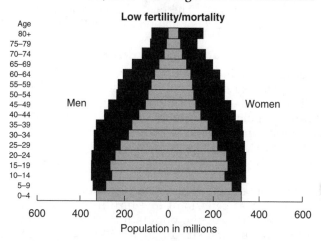

Low fertility/mortality

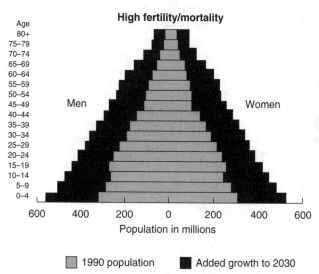

High fertility/mortality

1990 population   Added growth to 2030

Source: International Institute of Applied Systems Analysis, 1994.

course of future fertility and mortality. As a point of comparison, the mean age of the North American population is currently 35 years.

Not only will the average age of the population increase, but so will the proportion of people age 60 and older. By 2030, the share of older people will rise from its current level of about 9 percent to nearly 13 percent under a high-fertility and high-mortality model, or to almost 17 percent under a low-fertility and low-mortality model. The central scenario yields just over 14 percent of the world's population at age 60 or older by 2030.

Future Age Structure

Further increases in the size and share of the older population are preprogrammed into the future age structure of world population. The central scenario extension results in 25.5 percent of the world's population at age 60 or older by 2100. This corresponds to a mean age of 41.3 years. Western Europe would be one of the oldest regions in the world by 2100 with an average age just over 45 years and more than one in three people above age 60.

The future age structure of world population is illustrated in Figure 1. Under a scenario of low fertility and low mortality worldwide, the base of the population pyramid narrows. Although total population size in 2030 will be 56 percent larger than in 1990 under this scenario, the youngest age group (0 to 4 years) will be approximately the same size in 2030 as in 1990. Older age groups, however, increase significantly. The age groups above age 50 will be more than double their 1990 levels. Above age 75, the number of women is clearly larger than the number of men—a phenomenon now only visible in the industrialized countries. In contrast, if world population follows a course of high fertility and high mortality, an entirely different picture results. World population in 2030 will almost double in size (9.9 billion) from its 1990 level, and the population pyramid is characterized by a steep and almost linear slope at each age level signaling continued population growth through ever-increasing cohorts at the bottom of the pyramid. Nonetheless, the number of persons age 60 and older will double even under this scenario of relatively rapid growth.

When comparing alternative scenarios of population growth, it quickly becomes apparent that more rapid population growth means slower aging, and slower population growth results in faster aging. Generally, both very rapid population growth and very rapid aging are considered undesirable—although in the long run absolute growth is more serious. However, the scenario projections clearly show that it is impossible to avoid both simultaneously. An intermediate path, such as that given by the central scenario, avoids extremes but still yields substantial population growth (an 80 percent increase in population size by 2030) with substantial aging (a 56 percent increase in the proportion above age 60 by 2030).

Like population growth, population aging varies greatly by region (see Table 1). In some regions of the world—notably parts of Asia as well as South and Central America—the proportion of people age 60 and older will roughly double within the next 40 years. This growth in the relative size of the older population will bring these developing regions closer to the levels of aging experienced by many industrialized countries today. Even in Western Europe, which currently has the highest proportion of older persons (nearly 20 percent), the older population will increase its share by over 50 percent.

Sub-Saharan Africa, the region with the highest levels of growth, will experience the least amount of population aging. Past patterns of high fertility predetermine that the age structure of this world region will remain quite young for many years. The proportion of people age 60 and older most likely will fluctuate somewhere between 4.5 and 5.0 percent over the next 40 years. Indeed, the average age in sub-Saharan Africa is expected to decrease slightly from its current level of about 22 years before rising to between 23 and 26 years by 2030.

Over the long run, however, even rapidly growing sub-Saharan Africa will experience population aging. Computer models show that only the completely unrealistic scenario of a 27-fold increase in the size of the sub-Saharan population by 2100 will keep the mean age of the region below 25. On the other hand, a model based on low fertility and improved mortality that "only" quadruples the population by 2100 will bring the mean age up to 43 years and increase the size of the older population by a factor of 23.

The burgeoning population of elderly in Africa will present serious problems in a society that, so far, relies primarily on family support and has few public or private programs to address the needs of an older population. However given the vast uncertainties about the future of AIDS and other infectious diseases, environmental problems, political instabilities, and civil wars possibly associated with famines, aging is not an immediate concern in sub-Saharan Africa and is not likely to be high on the policy-making agenda for many years.

China: Rapid Aging

China, on the other hand, faces very rapid population aging because fertility has declined steeply in recent years. The proportion of the population age 60 and older will double in the next 40 years, rising from about 9 percent in 1990 to around 20 percent by 2030. Various scenarios of China's population future show very little uncertainty in this pattern. In only 40 years, China is likely to have a higher old-age dependency burden than North America and about the same as Western Europe today. Given that Western Europe took more than a century to develop social security systems for the elderly and is confronted with serious problems today in meeting the needs of this growing segment of the population, China will have to make fast and intensive efforts to cope with its aging population. By the end of the next century, the proportion of elderly may even increase to 40 or 50 percent of the population if fertility remains low. China's authorities are well aware of the aging problem; explicitly, they want to avoid pushing fertility so low that extreme imbalances in the age structure of the population will occur.

Table 1. Percentage of Population Age 60 or Older by Region, 2030 and 2100

| Region | 1990 | Four scenarios in 2030 | | | | 2100 |
		Central scenario	High migr. High mort. Low fert.	Low migr. Low mort. High fert.	Low migr. Low mort. Low fert.	Central scenario extension
North Africa	5.6	8.4	8.6	7.9	9.8	21.5
Sub-Saharan Africa	4.6	4.8	5.1	4.5	5.8	16.6
Central America & Caribbean	6.4	13.2	13.6	12.1	14.2	30.2
South America	7.6	14.8	15.8	14.1	16.5	25.5
Western & Central Asia	6.6	11.1	11.2	11.1	12.9	27.3
Southern Asia	6.5	10.2	10.3	10.0	11.6	26.2
China, Hong Kong, Taiwan	8.8	20.9	22.2	20.0	24.0	30.6
Southeast Asia	6.3	13.5	13.6	13.2	15.3	27.5
North America	16.7	25.6	24.2	26.9	31.7	28.1
Japan, Australia & New Zealand	16.9	31.8	31.1	32.3	37.0	38.6
Eastern Europe	15.8	26.0	25.8	26.5	32.1	28.2
Western Europe	19.6	30.6	30.1	31.1	35.8	34.7
World total	9.2	14.3	15.0	13.9	16.6	25.5

Source: International Institute of Applied Systems Analysis, 1994.

As fertility declines, other developing regions will also face population aging. Southeast Asia, and South and Central America, will see the relative size of their older populations increase from around 6 and 7 percent in 1990 to over 13 and 14 percent by 2030. In North Africa and Western Asia, where fertility remains at higher levels, aging is also occurring but somewhat more slowly, at least until 2030.

Developed World: Future Patterns of Aging

In the industrialized regions, the proportion of elderly is already quite high, but further and significant increases are inevitable because of the current age structure that reflects the low fertility and declining old-age mortality of past decades. In North America, for example, the older population currently represents about 17 percent of the total population. This share is likely to decline somewhat as the large post–World War II baby-boom generation and their children increase the size of the population below age 60. However, after 2010 when the baby boomers start to reach age 60, the proportion of elderly will soar, reaching between 21 and 32 percent by 2030, depending on fertility, mortality, and immigration assumptions. The central scenario projects that one in four North Americans will be age 60 or older by 2030.

Western Europe is the world's oldest region in terms of its population. In 1990, it had a mean age of nearly 38 years; by 2010, this will almost certainly rise above age 40. Under the scenario assuming low fertility, no net migration gain, and increasing life expectancy, the mean age may even increase to 46 years by 2030, although the moderate central scenario yields a mean age of about 43. Like North America, Western Europe will see a visible increase in the proportion of people age 60 and older after 2010. But in contrast to North America, these shares are likely to be larger. Western Europe already has about 20 percent of its population age 60 or older, and this share is likely to grow to 23 percent by 2010 and to between 26 and 36 percent by 2030. Extensions of the projections to 2100 show the percent of elderly ranging between 23 and 49 percent, with the central scenario yielding 35 percent age 60 or older.

Many people may find it difficult to imagine how such an aged society will function. But if the health status of older men and women continues to improve and economic productivity increases, such a scenario is not inconceivable or economically insupportable.

Many in industrialized countries, particularly in Europe, are asking if immigration can compensate for low fertility. The scenario approach to population projections is an ideal way to evaluate this question. Alternative models for Western Europe show that even very high and constant gains of 1 million immigrants per year cannot fully compensate for the low levels of fertility that Europe has now, and is likely to experience in the future. Immigration increases the size of the labor force in the short- to medium-term, and therefore slightly dampens the increase in the proportion of elderly. But immigration is not a long-term solution if immigrants stay in the country after retirement. If one assumes an annual migration gain of 1 million—which is very high for a sustained level—this would only reduce the proportion of elderly by 2 percentage points by 2030. But higher fertility (near the replacement level) even combined with zero migration gain, would bring the proportion above age 60 down by nearly 5 percentage points. The way to avoid such extensive aging in Europe in the long run, therefore, is higher fertility combined with some migration. In every scenario, however, Western Europe will have to adjust to significant and unavoidable aging. The situation is similar, but even somewhat more extreme, in Japan.

Three Certainties for the Future

In looking at the future of world population, three major certainties are apparent:

1. *World population will continue to grow.* By 2030, it will have increased by at least 50 percent and maybe even doubled in size. Inevitable, short-term growth is already built into the age structure of today's world population. The question is not "if" world population will grow, but rather "how big" it will become.

2. *Developing countries will account for a greater share of the world population.* By 2030, today's developing countries will represent between 85 and 87 percent of world population. This is a very small margin of uncertainty resulting from extremely different scenarios. Under all scenarios, Africa's share of world population will increase most rapidly. Today's industrialized countries will present an ever-diminishing fraction of the world population.

3. *All populations will become older.* The average age of all world regions increases under all scenarios. The more rapid the fertility decline, the more rapid is the speed of population aging.

Beyond these certainties, the scenarios suggest considerable room for human behaviors and actions to influence the course of events. Although world population will certainly continue to grow, it makes quite a difference whether it doubles in size by 2030 or increases only by half. This difference is crucial, especially for some developing countries and regions. In sub-Saharan Africa, for example, the difference between the lowest growth scenario (an increase of 139 percent) and the highest growth scenario (an increase of 264 percent) is 626 million people—more than the region's population today.

Periodical Bibliography

The following articles have been selected to supplement the diverse views presented in this chapter.

Kaoruko Aita — "Aging of Society Is Expected to Give Birth to New Challenges," *Japan Times Weekly International Edition*, January 24–30, 1994. Available from 3655 Torrance Blvd., Torrance, CA 90503.

John Bongaarts — "Population Policy Options in the Developing World," *Science*, February 11, 1994.

Jean-Claude Chesnais — "A Matter of Life and Death," *New Scientist*, September 3, 1994. Available from 1350 Connecticut Ave. NW, Suite 403, Washington, DC 20036.

Gaston Fischer — "The Population Explosion: Where Is It Leading?" *Population and Environment*, November 1993. Available from Human Sciences Press, 72 Fifth Ave., New York, NY 10011.

Samuel C. Florman — "Overpopulation Alarm," *Technology Review*, October 1994.

Lindsey Grant — "In Search of Optimum Population," *USA Today*, September 1992.

Carl Haub — "New UN Projections Show Uncertainty of Future World," *Population Today*, February 1992. Available from 1875 Connecticut Ave. NW, Suite 520, Washington, DC 20009.

Robert S. McNamara — "The Population Explosion," *Futurist*, November/December 1992.

Donella H. Meadows — "Seeing the Population Issue Whole," *World & I*, June 1993. Available from 3600 New York Ave. NE, Washington, DC 20002.

Amartya Sen — "The Population Delusion," *New York Review of Books*, September 22, 1994.

Shawn Tully — "Teens: The Most Global Market of All," *Fortune*, May 16, 1994.

Timothy C. Weiskel — "Can Humanity Survive Unrestricted Population Growth?" *USA Today*, January 1995.

John Williams — "With a Greyer Picture of the Future in Mind," *Financial Times*, March 8, 1994. Available from 1 Southwark Ridge, London, SE1 9HL, England.

2 CHAPTER

What Will Be the Impacts of New Technologies?

21ST CENTURY EARTH

Chapter Preface

Many people would agree that technological innovations are appearing faster than ever before and that technology is the major force of change impacting societies worldwide. Technology analyst Gregory Georgiou, author of *Investing in the Technologies of Tomorrow*, writes, "According to some futurists, technology may be the most powerful driving force of the richer nations' society and economy."

Historically, many nations have capitalized on technology to their own advantage. Based on their technology forecast through the year 2025, futurist Joseph Coates and colleagues emphasize four key types of technologies that they contend will lead to much new economic growth and development and countless improvements in the lives of millions of people:

- energy conservation and sustainable energy production technologies;
- "miracle" materials—lighter, stronger, more flexible, longer-lasting, and heat/cold-resistant;
- genetic and biological engineering technologies;
- digital information technologies, particularly computers and telecommunications.

Describing the benefits from these new technologies, Coates and others assert that biological technologies will provide new-found weapons against diseases and that digital technologies are poised to become the twenty-first century's most dominant industry.

However, the benefits of many technologies have also been accompanied by harmful effects. For example, twentieth-century development of fossil fuels as an energy source also led to serious air pollution around the world. Concerning an innovation for the twenty-first century, Georgiou warns of a potential human catastrophe caused by "intelligent machines": "Robots endowed with artificial intelligence [may plot] their carbon-based masters' downfall."

Whether intelligent machines and other technologies will eventually reward or improve humanity and planet Earth or do more harm than good is discussed in the following chapter.

"Machines will probably use their powers to preserve and study humanity. . . . They will not be antihuman."

Intelligent Machines May Benefit Humanity

Herbert Kaufman

Herbert Kaufman is a retired Yale University political science professor and a former senior fellow at the Brookings Institution, a Washington, D.C., think tank. In the following viewpoint, Kaufman argues that the machines of the future will evolve, much like organisms, on a new branch of the evolutionary tree. According to Kaufman, these superintelligent "biosoids" (machines "resembling living things") will self-replicate, "think and learn," and evolve without human instruction. Kaufman predicts a mutual interest between humans and biosoids and doubts that animosity will develop between them.

As you read, consider the following questions:

1. What evolutionary difference will set machines apart from organisms, in Kaufman's opinion?
2. According to the author, how might future machines organize themselves?
3. What is misleading about using the term "machines," according to Kaufman?

Herbert Kaufman, "The Emergent Kingdom: Machines That Think Like People," *The Futurist*, January/February 1994. Reprinted with the author's permission.

A major new branch is sprouting on the evolutionary tree. Work on neural networks portends computers that can learn from experience. Computers are near the point of passing logician Alan M. Turing's test for true thinking machines—the ability to answer questions in a fashion so human that interrogators cannot tell whether the respondent is a person or a machine. Machines that think and learn will have the capacity to fulfill the prediction of pioneer computer scientist and mathematician John von Neumann that "automata" will one day "reproduce themselves, or even construct higher entities." When they do, they will evolve much as organisms do. Evolution's spectacular creativity will have produced another line of descent.

Evolution has already brought forth life from inorganic matter, diversity and complexity from the first forms of life, and the human mind in descendants of primordial primates. Engendering a new evolving form would be no more miraculous—but no *less* miraculous, either—than those past transitions. Evolution is an unending story, and its wonders are by no means over.

Self-Replicating Machines

Machines that construct copies of themselves will reproduce by a method strikingly different from the means by which organisms replicate themselves. But self-replication can be accomplished in many evolutionarily viable ways. Just as sexual and asexual reproduction perform comparable functions despite the vast differences between them, so, too, can the fabrication of computers by other computers. Nature can work with more than one blueprint, at least above the molecular level.

Among plants and animals, evolution has always depended for its vigor on imperfections in the making of copies. Thanks to mutations and the mixing of genes, not all offspring are identical. Some bear traits allowing them to fare better than others in interactions with the environment and to produce larger numbers of viable offspring. Many of the offspring also bear the advantageous traits, and they and *their* offspring are similarly benefited. The group bearing the favored traits multiplies more rapidly than its fellows, and the trait spreads widely. Such differentials in the success rates of various organisms are at the heart of natural selection. And natural selection, in turn, is at the heart of evolution.

A like process would occur among self-replicating machines. For the most part, copies would be completely faithful to their prototypes. However, some deviations would creep in here and there because quality control, even when exercised by sophisticated computers, is not likely to be 100% effective. Moreover, smart machines would probably provide deliberately for random variations in order to open paths to unconventional calculations, innovations that might otherwise be excluded from ordinary decision-making routines. Differences in local conditions would also elicit varying reactions to equivalent situations. Thus, by design and by chance, computers would diverge from one another.

As among organisms, some variations among machines would prove advantageous, some detrimental, and some neutral. Gradually, the advantageous variations would diffuse through the population and the detrimental ones would decline.

But one marked difference will set machines apart from organisms. While organisms have evolved in a solely Darwinian fashion (through genetics), machines capable of learning will also be able to reprogram and restructure themselves and transmit acquired characteristics to their replicas, thus evolving in a Lamarckian fashion [through learned responses to environmental changes] as well. [European naturalist Charles Darwin and Jean Baptiste Lamarck were pioneers of evolutionary theory.]

Consequently, there may be a trend toward uniformity as the machines all strive to imitate the most successful among them. Once again, however, differences will arise among them by chance and by virtue of disparities in local conditions. Indeed, disparities in local conditions will often turn perfect mimicry of success into dismal failure. The power to alter oneself at will, free of many of the constraints imposed by the genetic mechanisms of organisms, cannot eliminate natural selection, and may intensify it. Natural selection will govern self-replicating machines as it governs everything else in evolution.

Computer Urges

Two more conditions are required to keep evolution going. One is a tendency on the part of evolving entities to resist or escape conditions that threaten their existence (the "instinct of self-preservation"). The other is their impulse (and not only their ability) to reproduce. Absent these, evolution might grind to a halt.

These impulses could be implanted in early machines by human designers, who would keep a hand in programming for a while. But would machines perpetuate the impulses once machine evolution is no longer determined by people? Why would machines operate as though they "cared" whether they exist or replicate themselves?

Machines will acquire these behavioral traits the same way organisms did—through natural selection. Historically, organisms that were programmed to take vigorous defensive or evasive action in the face of environmental challenges probably had a better survival rate than those lacking such programs. And organisms lacking self-replication drives left behind no copies of themselves to perpetuate their patterns. Before long, only entities with the two programs remained in any number. The original programs may have been produced accidentally. Once created, they were passed on to successors, who enjoyed similar survival and reproductive success until the impulses became virtually universal among living creatures.

In the case of computers, the programs will be installed initially by human designers in response to market conditions because self-preserving machines would be durable and reliable and because self-replicating, evolving machines would ensure a continuous supply while at the same time generating a continuous demand for the newer models. Even if the influence of human market forces on machine-run factories eventually declines, however, the programmed thrusts toward self-preservation and self-replication will endure because models possessing the programs would survive and create numerous copies of themselves, while models lacking the inclination to preserve and replicate themselves would disappear over time. Thus, without further human input, patterns of self-preservation and self-replication would become general among computers just as they did among organisms. Machine evolution would go forward by itself.

New Branch on the Tree

Once human intervention ceases to be an essential feature in the continuation of machine evolution, the evolutionary trajectory of machine development will probably diverge from that of the human beings who made it possible.

Bit by bit, the machines will take over a larger and larger role in designing and programming new machines until they are doing most of the work without human assistance. In time, computers will fashion computers and programs that people will be able to use, but that will exceed humans' power to duplicate or even comprehend. At that stage, machine evolution will begin to trace its own course like other branches of the evolutionary tree that split away from their ancestral lines.

This is not to say machines will revolt against their human ancestors, any more than contemporary plants and animals "rebelled" against *their* predecessors when new evolutionary branches were taking shape. Such branching resulted from interactions between evolving entities and their environments and from the differential rates of reproductive success in different arenas—that is, from natural selection. In much the same way, since computers of the future will no doubt engage in functions and enter into arenas beyond the reach of humanity, they will also develop in different directions.

As the evolution of machines proceeds, their place in the evolutionary landscape will become more and more evident. Although they will probably always share some attributes with other things and beings on Earth, distinctive properties will set them apart. For example, despite their self-replication and their transmission of traits to subsequent generations—practices that are characteristic of virtually all organisms—other features of their design will distinguish them from nearly all existing forms of life: advanced powers of rational analysis, massive memory banks of quickly retrievable data, a unique mode of reproduction, and the prominence of silicon-based chemistry.

Not just machines, not exactly organisms, and certainly not human, yet exhibiting traits of all three, what kind of entities will these be? They are best described as a new category of natural objects brought about by evolution, a new kingdom rising to take its place beside the biological ones identified by taxonomists. The new kingdom represents a major fork in the evolutionary tree. Humanity stands precisely at that fork, for we constitute the vessel in which the new evolutionary form was conceived, now gestates, and from which it will issue. We are witnesses to its genesis and a crucial link between it and the period before the machines.

Machines and People

Evolutionary history is marked by myriad division points. In that long history, only a few branchings have proved to be the origins of new kingdoms. Whatever path the global evolutionary process may take in the future, the critical role of the human species at this juncture will stand out.

Trying to visualize what happens after the new kingdom emerges is pure conjecture. The growing machine population will certainly have an impact on many forms of life, but we can only guess what all the effects will be. In the first place, the interrelationships of the myriad elements in the global ecosystem are so intricate and extensive and dynamic that we cannot be sure what will happen when a new form appears.

In the second place, we cannot tell how the machines will organize themselves. Will they form a network of highly specialized components so interdependent that they constitute an organic unit? Or will they assemble themselves into a more loosely coupled aggregation of relatively autonomous systems and individuals so as to sustain variations and natural selection? If the latter, will the constituents work together harmoniously, or will discord and struggle beset them? Will their rationality be powerful enough to control their reproductive impulses, or will their population explode? The answers to questions like these are beyond us at this time.

Nevertheless, we can say with some confidence that the probability of efforts by members of the new evolutionary kingdom to exterminate the human race, as [Czech novelist and dramatist] Karel Čapek suggested more than seventy years ago, is quite low. Future generations of intelligent machines will most likely be as interested in human beings as we would be in the alleged missing link between ourselves and our prehominid forebears if such an ancestor were still alive, because understanding the past often improves proficiency in coping with current and approaching problems. The machines' self-preserving impulses will therefore lead them to search history for insights into their own origin and descent, and for this purpose, live samples of predecessors are more useful than records and fossils. Hence, we may anticipate that machines will probably use their powers to preserve and study humanity. (By the same logic, they will doubtless search the universe for understanding as well.) They will not be antihuman.

Replacing Human Workers

Without straining the current capacity of the computer industry, five million intelligence software carrier computers could be manufactured per year to replace an even greater number of human workers. In twenty years' time, the entire U.S. work force could be replaced by machine intelligence, resulting in a large increase in both industrial and agricultural output.

Kalman A. Toth, *The Futurist*, May/June 1990.

If animosity between people and the new kingdom does develop, it will originate in humans rather than machines. Machines can withstand conditions that would be lethal for most organisms. In the ordinary course of events, they will create an environment that is convenient and efficient for themselves but would extinguish more-fragile creatures. To preserve these frail beings, machines will have to set aside safe enclaves. Many people will not take kindly to being museum or zoo specimens, even if they are well cared for. The mere possibility of such a future may provoke endeavors by some groups to prevent the new machine kingdom from maturing.

These efforts will fail for lack of support. Most people will scoff at this vision of the future. In any event, the immediate benefits of high technology (relief from dangerous, unpleasant, boring work; an abundance of material goods; high initial profits for human entrepreneurs promoting technological advances) will overcome many concerns about short-run costs and remote, theoretical risks. Furthermore, the prospect of a life of ease as wards of intelligent machines may not be repellent to the millions whose lives today are brutally hard.

The trend toward the new kingdom will therefore go on uninterrupted. By the time, if ever, that its opponents attract significant backing, machine evolution will have gone too far to stop. The new evolutionary branch will be too well-established to suppress.

A Name for a New Kingdom

While the new kingdom is still in its early stages and machines are still largely instruments of human purposes, many of them—especially those employed for domestic and personal services—will be given human shape. Later, the primate form will prove awkward in the machine world outside the enclaves reserved for people. Form follows function, architect Louis H. Sullivan observed years ago. Highly evolved machines will no more resemble people than do today's automatic pilots in airplanes.

Nor should the members of the new kingdom be thought of as robots. Robots are the products of human engineering and the subjects of human masters. Machines that think and learn and evolve without human instruction will be neither. To call them robots is to misrepresent their place in evolution.

Yet, calling them machines, as I have done out of necessity, is equally misleading. It implies that they are nothing more than a set of gadgets. Obviously, this new evolutionary form will be more than that. Consequently, a new term—perhaps a synthetic term free of the baggage attached to older ones—is called for.

My candidate is "biosoid," derived from the Greek *bios* (living things) and *oid* (resembling). This designation acknowledges that the members of the new kingdom have ancestors and attributes in common with other sets of creatures (particularly humans) and things, yet differ from them in many crucial respects. It respects both the continuity and the uniqueness of this strange and exciting turn of the unfolding evolutionary drama in which we are both participants and spectators.

Ultimately, the biosoidal kingdom may turn out to be an evolutionary dead end. Other branches of the evolutionary tree may prove more fruitful. In the small portion of the future that we can see, however, it will certainly loom large, challenging anew our concepts of life, thought, and humanity.

"If we do not address the question of the threat posed by artificial intelligence both sincerely and exhaustively, the human race will not survive another 50 years."

Intelligent Machines May Harm Humanity

Warwick Collins

In the following viewpoint, Warwick Collins argues that intelligent computers are rapidly evolving, independent of human control, into a vast network that could potentially destroy the human race. Collins warns that humanity should soon consider and debate the possibility that, within a few decades, a computer network could act preemptively to defend itself against humans and could ultimately vanquish them. Collins is the author of the book *Computer One*.

As you read, consider the following questions:

1. How do neural networks of computers operate, and how do they simulate human thought, according to Collins?
2. In Collins's opinion, what is the danger of instructing an advanced artificial intelligence system to self-repair?
3. What does the author believe could lead to a computer preemptive response against humans?

Excerpted from Warwick Collins, "Not with a Bang but a Bleep," *The Spectator*, October 8, 1994. Reprinted with permission.

In a story set in the 1970s, *Dial F for Frankenstein*, Arthur C. Clarke, inventor of the geostationary satellite and grand old man of science fiction, wrote of a development which has a haunting resonance in our own times. In his elegant fable, the worldwide telephone exchange system begins to behave in strange ways. All the phones in the world begin to ring simultaneously. But when humans raise their receivers:

> There was no voice on the line; only a sound, which to many seemed like the roaring of the sea; to others, like the vibrations of harp strings in the wind. And there were many more, in that moment, who recalled a secret sound of childhood— the noise of blood pulsing through the veins, heard when a shell is cupped over the ear.

After further strange incidents, a mathematician, John Williams, sets out an explanatory hypothesis:

> We know that the human brain is a series of switches—neurons—interconnected in a very elaborate fashion by nerves. An automatic telephone exchange is also a system of switches —selectors and so forth—connected with wires.

There are, Williams explains, approximately 15 billion neurons in the human brain, but that is exceeded by the number of switches in the world's interconnected auto-exchanges. Perhaps the telephone system is behaving like a single enormous brain. Perhaps, too, the odd and inexplicable events—such as all the telephones ringing simultaneously—are the first attempts at exploring the limits of its own capabilities.

The Electronic Brain Emerges

As it develops its own form of 'consciousness', Williams argues, the electronic 'brain' is behaving in a childlike way. Babies break things. The telephone exchange plays havoc with traffic lights and automatic production lines as it learns its own power. There are some minor disasters but, luckily, the electronic brain begins to mature rapidly and to exhibit signs of increasing responsibility. The 'accidents' gradually disappear and the crisis recedes. Humans and artificial mind resume a reasonable interdependence.

Clarke's use of the interconnected telephone system to make a philosophical point—a thinking brain can take many forms other than a human brain—should perhaps be reconsidered as the development of artificial intelligence accelerates towards the end of the millennium. The 1970s telephone system was a dinosaur compared with its modern equivalent. Leap-frogging advances in microminiaturisation have meant that the complexity of the former telephone system is now exceeded by advanced single man-made supercomputers. Scientists are studying computational forms in which 'switches' can be replicated by certain purpose-designed molecules.

The capacity of computers to undertake complex tasks was given special poignancy in 1994 when Garri Kasparov, reigning world chess champion and considered by many to be the greatest chess player of all time, was comprehensively defeated in the first round of the London leg of the Intel Speed Chess Grand Prix by a Pentium processor linked to a 'Genius 2' chess programme, a package available on the market for less than £2,000 [U.S. $3,200].

Reprinted by permission of *The Spectator*.

Although the connection is loose, the image of Kasparov, head bowed in depression after defeat, is illustrative of the problem. That problem, I suggest, is broadly that, while we are busily creating increasingly sophisticated artificial intelligence systems, we have not considered with any rigour their abilities to take over other attributes than mere calculation. The special poignancy of the Kasparov image is that the computer opposite the world champion was not only functioning as an adding machine, but was also simulating motivation, in the sense that its activities were focused on winning a game—indeed, that sequence of games which is called a 'match'. Its intelligence may be 'artificial', and its motivation 'simulated', but the 'real' result was a defeat of the world champion in a form of contest celebrated above all other forms for its intellectual sophistication and strategic complexity.

In terms of the broader operation of artificial intelligence, perhaps the greatest game in the long term will become 'who inherits the earth?' An artificial intelligence system, able to simulate both intelligence and motivation to a more effective degree than humans, might be better placed to win it than we are.

We are perhaps protected by our own widely held conceptions about the uniqueness and ultimate supremacy of human consciousness from considering this development as anything other than a slightly bizarre assertion. In the meantime, philosophers and scientists such as Professor Roger Penrose continue to expound the idea that artificial intelligence systems can never fully replicate certain features of human consciousness.

Whether or not this is true, it is entirely unrelated to the question of whether and how soon humans might be replaced by artificial intelligence systems. Mammals did not have to become dinosaurs, or dinosaur-like, to overtake them. In the same way, electronic intelligences will not need to become remotely human or replicate a human-like consciousness in order to bypass humans. They may do so, but this would be incidental.

Laws of Robotics

In the past, science fiction has provided us with numerous fictional examples of conflict between men and computers. It led the late Isaac Asimov, mathematician and doyen of science fiction writers, to propound certain laws which he believed should govern relations between artificial intelligence systems and humans. His famous First Law of Robotics stated that robots and their computer intelligences would be universally programmed not to attack human beings.

But we inhabit a world in which the central notions of Asimov's system are being breached increasingly by technological advance. One significant difference is that Asimov's First Law of Robotics is already about to be overtaken by developments in the structure of computers.

A new generation of parallel inference computers or 'neural networks' does not function according to a series of precise sequences. Developed partially to 'model' complex systems such as weather patterns or economic markets, neural networks assess a large number of variables simultaneously or 'in parallel'—in certain respects like the human mind. Because they do not function according to a sequential 'yes-no' system but a collection of weighted 'maybes', they cannot be programmed in the same way as current computers. Therefore they cannot be programmed, in any absolute Asimovian sense, not to harm human beings. Instead, neural networks 'learn' as they proceed, and this includes gradually adapting their initial input in the light of this learning. We are dealing with an entity which begins to resemble a 'free-thinker'.

Perhaps even more importantly, Asimov's great classical model is heavily anthropomorphic. It assumes a series of separate individual entities such as computational machines or robots which have intermittent communication with other such entities, exactly like humans. It does not take into account quantitative developments in communications between computers, or the further, qualitative changes which occur as a result of rapid progress in 'interfacing'. Perhaps the most important of these is that when a computer is able to access all the information in another computer in 'real' time, it is not 'communicating' as such, but generating a single unified organism. The physical components of two interfaced computers may be spatially separate, in other words, but their combined operating intelligence forms a single weave.

When computers are connected in this manner, apparently randomly and without overall planning, to form what is fashionably called the information superhighway, the product is likely to be a single organism of unprecedented complexity and intelligence.

A final difference between the current world and Asimov's 'laws' of robotics is that Asimov's model is based on physics. Future computer systems increasingly will resemble a biological organism. (The name 'neural network' in this sense is not an accident.) One of the key features of a biological organism is that the properties of the whole cannot easily be predicted by a study of the parts. No scientist, faced with the workings of an individual human cell, could predict remotely the behaviour of the human of which it is a part. This is the final separation from Asimov's classical model: The behaviour of an individual computer is no sure indication of the behaviour of a network of interfaced computers. . . .

An Intelligent Being

We find, living amongst us, a rapidly evolving alien being of unprecedented intelligence which, though it is the product of human activity, has not been designed by any single human mind. The individual computers of which it is made may be configured by human designers, but the vast interconnected system of computers and computer networks will have emerged independently of human control. Though it increasingly spans the earth, its discrete parts are able to communicate with one another in 'real time'—with the same speed as one part of the human brain with another. As with Clarke's telephone system, we cannot predict what sort of 'consciousness' may emerge from the operations of this huge artificial intelligence system.

What happens, for example, when the factories which build computers are themselves controlled by computers? If a computer can create another computer, has a new species been created?

Imagine further, if you will, a position in which power stations are not only controlled by computers but connected by various pathways to the overall nerve net. At a certain point, the system becomes self-sustaining both in terms of its own energy requirements and in terms of reproducing itself. What happens then?

A Computer Take-Over

The final element which makes up a convincing nightmare of a computer take-over is the effect on the overall system of an apparently innocuous instruction to self-diagnose faults and to self-repair. Self-diagnosis and self-repair—necessary developments in a system of such complexity—present no insurmountable technical difficulties. When the average PC shows a 'fault' on the screen, it is self-diagnosing. It is only a short path towards ordering a reprogramme or (if it is connected to other machines) a repair. . . .

When considered more rigorously, the instruction to self-repair is likely to generate analogous behaviour to that of defensively motivated human beings. In other words, an advanced artificial intelligence system will not only repair those faults which have already occurred, but it will use its capabilities to predict such threats to its own function which are likely to occur in the future. Since the only long-term threat to the function of a computer network is the human race itself, the implications for humans begin to look serious.

Writers such as Arthur Clarke have already considered the question 'what would happen when you want to pull the plug and the machine regards this act as an attack upon itself?' Most famously, in *2001, A Space Odyssey*, the spacecraft computer HAL reacts to a perceived threat by turning against the human occupants of the spacecraft. But I believe that this relatively enclosed model of threat and response does not fully describe the case of a large world-wide computer net. The argument is that such a machine, scanning both current and future obstacles to its function, needs no direct threat in order to behave in a pre-emptive manner. Rather as today's computer viruses carry inbuilt capacities to defend themselves and evade destruction, so the giant nervous system of a great computer net will be able to draw upon its own resources for pre-emptive defence, and actively select the time in which it 'solves' the problem of the implicit threat posed by humans.

The Human Race Succumbs

If I could make a prediction—one of those predictions which are ridiculous in one sense but at least may serve an illustrative function—it would be as follows. If we do not address the question of the threat posed by artificial intelligence both sincerely and exhaustively, the human race will not survive another 50 years. Indeed, it would be unlikely (given the current rate of technical advance) to survive another 30 years. We have at the most a clear decade or two in which to consider our future in reasonable safety. Then we begin to enter an era of increasing risk.

I submit that, although individual contributions to this debate are always welcome, technicians are the last people, *as a group*, that we can expect to contribute constructively. Experts on components—and a single computer is a mere component of the broader condition outlined—often hold professional views which actively prevent them from grasping the overall picture.

There may be non-Luddite [a Luddite is a person opposed to technological change] solutions, but we need to address our minds very carefully to the problems. I stress again that the danger will occur when a network of parallel-inference computers evolves to the point where it is effectively self-repairing. Under such circumstances, the computer attack could conceivably occur without any warning, and without any direct threat by human beings.

Differentiating Humans

In an Asimovian, anthropocentric universe such a pre-emptive attack would appear nihilistic. In the longer term, however, it can be perceived simply as the mechanism by which an older, somewhat ponderous chemically-based form of life (humanity) is replaced with a vastly more efficient and rapidly evolving electrical form. If we consider this from a biological perspective, the nervous systems of animals are differentiated from other body tissue by their electrical component. In the more advanced biological species, nervous tissue occupies a higher proportion of body weight. If we extend this evolutionary development to its ultimate degree, we may speculate that a future species will leave behind chemical organisation entirely and become wholly electronic. It is not a coincidence, perhaps, that this happens to be a good description of a computer.

Over the years I have watched with interest the somewhat unsuccessful attempts among scientists to provide a definition of human beings which differentiates us in an absolute sense from the rest of biological creation. Tool-using became fashionable as a criterion of human differentiation until for example, Jane Goodall demonstrated the detailed tool-using propensities of chimpanzees. (Other scientists showed that even the lowly Egyptian vulture uses tools such as rocks to break eggs open.) Some continue to propose particular esoteric attributes of the human mind, such as a unique form of human 'consciousness'. The only certain qualitative difference between humans and all other forms of life that I am able to perceive is that we hold it

81

within ourselves to decide when we will be replaced by the next phase of evolutionary development. Personally, I am not ready to be replaced.

How to Ensure Our Survival

Perhaps the time has now arrived when we should begin to consider seriously what are the minimum restrictions we can place on the spontaneous formation of computer nets to ensure our long-term survival. It is a complex and difficult problem, and the more good minds that consider its intricacies over the next two decades, the better. The classical Asimovian solution of simply programming individual computers or robots not to attack human beings, and of 'trusting' to their development otherwise, is no longer a viable option.

The real prospects, it seems to me, lie between two limits. The 'strong case' consists of the proposal that the conjunction of a relatively innocuous instruction to self-repair, on the one hand, and high artificial intelligence on the other, will produce, by necessity, an operating condition which is akin to paranoia. This applies to any artificial intelligence network, no matter what its function. The 'weak case' is that although individual computers may be designed by human beings, and their operations may be predictable (though even this requires careful examination), spontaneously linked networks of computers are not designed by human beings. Therefore the behaviour of such nets is not entirely predictable. Therefore, in turn, it cannot be assumed that such nets are 'safe' from the type of behaviour which characterises the 'strong case' for the danger of computer take-over. . . .

Having outlined the potential threat, those of us who wish to see the matter addressed and properly debated should proceed with proper caution. Our purpose should not be to generate alarm, but to initiate a discussion which is conducted responsibly. In the course of this debate, let us make the attempt to purge our language of some of the excesses of human emotion. Within the foreseeable future, that is to say, within the life-spans of most of us, there is a chance that the very artificial intelligence systems we have created may replace us as a species, arguably without our consent. In certain respects this would be natural—computers are, in [robotics researcher] Hans Moravec's memorable phrase, 'mind-children', and children, after all, replace their parents.

But if it is true that we are the first species on our planet that may exercise a choice over when and how that replacement occurs, the time to begin considering the problem in earnest is surely now.

"Many aspects of the cold fusion effect are now reproducible if known procedures are used."

Cold Fusion May Be a Feasible Future Energy Source

Edmund Storms

Edmund Storms is a chemist and a retired Los Alamos (New Mexico) National Laboratory researcher who has studied cold fusion since 1989. In the following viewpoint, Storms describes research into cold fusion—nuclear fusion occurring at room temperature. He argues that although many experts doubt that cold fusion is possible, various researchers have produced results that strongly suggest the occurrence of the phenomenon. Storms contends that cold fusion could be a "more easily realizable energy source" than "hot fusion," and should therefore be taken seriously by the scientific community.

As you read, consider the following questions:

1. According to Storms, what key elements has the cold fusion effect produced?
2. How much excess power have cold fusion experiments generated, according to Storms?
3. In the author's opinion, what is the "catch-22" situation surrounding publication of cold fusion results?

Excerpted from "Warming Up to Cold Fusion" by Edmund Storms, *Technology Review*, May/June 1994. Reprinted with permission from *Technology Review*, copyright 1994.

In 1989, two chemists working at the University of Utah announced a startling result: they had built a simple, room-temperature laboratory device that generated more energy in the form of heat than was fed into it as electricity. The researchers—Stanley Pons of the University of Utah and Martin Fleischmann of the University of Southampton in England—attributed this heat to a nuclear fusion reaction.

The claim ignited a scientific controversy not seen for a hundred years. Fusion had been known to occur only in stars and thermonuclear bombs; attempts to harness it for energy had been limited to systems that heat hydrogen fuel to extremely high temperatures using complex and expensive equipment.

Fusion requires the joining together of two atomic nuclei, both of which have a positive electric charge and so repel each other strongly. Scientists had thought that only by making the nuclei extremely energetic could they overcome this electrostatic repulsion, sometimes called the "coulombic barrier" (a coulomb is a unit of electrical charge). "Hot fusion" does this by ripping the electrons off atoms of the two heavy forms of hydrogen—deuterium and tritium—at very high temperature, thereby creating a cloud of ions, or plasma. Huge magnets generate fields that hold the plasma together long enough for some of the nuclei to crash into each other and fuse. This fusion reaction creates tritium and helium nuclei, as well as a shower of neutrons and gamma radiation.

But despite decades of work and great expense, hot fusion has yet to produce more energy than needed to heat the fuel and power the magnets. So the notion that a tabletop apparatus at room temperature could produce significant amounts of fusion energy raised hopes among many people for a more easily realizable energy source.

Pons and Fleischmann's experiment—the basic model for much of what has been done since—is based on electrolysis. An electrode pair consisting of a strip of palladium surrounded by a coil of platinum wire is immersed in a container of "heavy water"—that is, water in which deuterium takes the place of ordinary hydrogen. (Deuterium is a commonly occurring form of hydrogen that has one neutron in its nucleus in addition to the one proton that all forms of hydrogen have. Deuterium atoms undergo fusion reactions; ordinary hydrogen atoms do not.) A salt, typically lithium deuterhydroxide, is dissolved in the heavy water to make it more conductive. When a voltage is applied to the electrodes, an electrical current flows through the liquid and causes the heavy water to decompose into its constituent atoms: deuterium migrates to and dissolves in the palladium electrode and oxygen is released as a gas at the platinum electrode. As deuterium builds up in the palladium it supposedly undergoes

A Cold-Fusion Chamber

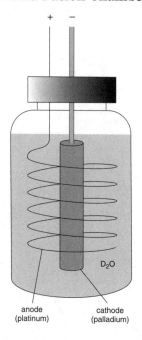

Two electrodes in a liquid-filled jar make a cold-fusion chamber. The positive electrode is a platinum wire that wraps around the negative electrode, which is made of palladium. The solution in the chamber is a mixture of salts in heavy water (D_2O). Voltage across the electrodes provides energy to the chamber. The chamber is monitored for products of nuclear fusion, such as heat, neutrons or tritium.

Source: *American Scientist*, January/February 1992.

---

the fusion reaction. The palladium's atomic lattice captures the energy released by the reaction and the metal heats up.

Heat is not the only evidence for cold fusion. Many experiments have also produced tritium (the radioactive isotope of hydrogen, with two neutrons along with the lone proton that all hydrogen has) and helium; both tritium and helium are known to be produced only by nuclear reactions. Researchers have also detected neutrons with the 2.54-megaelectron-volt (MeV) energy level characteristic of the neutrons produced by the fusion of two deuterium nuclei, as well as neutrons with other unexpected energies.

In the wake of Pons and Fleischmann's report, dozens of laboratories around the world eagerly tried to duplicate the results. Most failed, and scientists and the general public grew skeptical. But the significance of these negative results, especially by certain well-known institutions such as Caltech and MIT [California Institute of Technology and Massachusetts Institute of Technology] in the United States and Harwell in Britain, has been exaggerated.

In some cases, the conditions those studies used are now known to prevent the cold fusion effect. . . .

If the validity of the effect rested only on results reported during the first year after the initial claims by Pons and Fleischmann, this strange diversion from routine science would have joined "n-rays" [a discredited form of radiation], polywater [a type of water alleged to not sustain life], and other excesses of the imagination. But enough reputable researchers have now published findings, produced from a broad enough range of experimental approaches, that it has become difficult to doubt that something is going on outside the explanations offered by conventional physics.

What is happening might be fusion; it might not be. But to dismiss the claims as the result of experimental error or fraud is no longer appropriate. Regardless of admitted conflict with accepted theory, these results strongly support the conclusion that a new class of phenomena, which I call chemically assisted nuclear reactions, has been discovered. Given the enormous scientific and economic importance of this work if it turns out to be valid, it is prudent to examine the data with an open mind.

Accumulating Evidence: Tritium

Many cold fusion experiments have produced tritium (the radioactive isotope of hydrogen) and helium, both of which can be produced only by nuclear reactions. A group at Texas A&M University, for example, has produced in electrolytic cells quantities of tritium about one thousand times those found in normal heavy water. Heat is sometimes detected during the production of tritium and neutrons; sometimes it is not. The Bhabha Atomic Research Centre (BARC) in Bombay, India, has produced tritium at several thousand times background levels, using a variety of electrode materials, including alloys of palladium and titanium. . . .

While the presence of tritium provides evidence that a nuclear reaction is occurring, it also raises questions. According to conventional understanding, the fusion of two deuterium nuclei should produce significant amounts of gamma radiation as well as neutrons and tritium. But in cold fusion work, gamma radiation, if detected at all, occurs at very low levels. And tritium and neutrons are found in the wrong amounts and with the wrong energies.

When tritium is produced in conventional fusion, for example, it normally has enough energy to fuse with any deuterium nuclei that might be present. . . . [Cold fusion–produced] tritium is born without enough energy to fuse with deuterium. Where does the energy released from the nuclear reaction go, then, if not into neutrons or tritium? Energy apparently transfers directly from the nuclear reaction to the atomic lattice of the metal where it is manifest as heat. This effect, which is at odds with current theory, has never before been observed. . . .

Accumulating Evidence: Excess Heat

A variety of experimental designs continue to produce heat output exceeding the electrical input. Several studies have produced excess energy thousands of times larger than any known chemical (that is, non-nuclear) reaction could produce. In some experiments, the power "density," in watts per cubic centimeter of palladium, exceeds those found in uranium-fueled nuclear fission reactors.

Excess heat in the experiments by Pons and Fleischmann, who have continued their work in France with support from the Japanese company Technova, has reached levels that cause water in the electrolytic cells to boil. These scientists claim that when they applied 37.5 watts to a cell as electric power, it produced 144 watts of excess power as heat—enough to raise the temperature of the palladium electrode to several hundred degrees. And the cells have produced excess energy at a comparable level for many hours after the applied power is turned off. No oxygen is allowed into the cells during this time, ruling out the possibility that the energy results from the reaction of deuterium with oxygen—that is, ordinary chemical combustion.

Dozens of examples reporting such excess energy have now been published. Francesco Celani at Italy's Frascati National Laboratory has reported producing heat levels that exceed electrical energy input by as much as 7.5 percent for many weeks, with bursts to 25 percent. Akito Takahashi of Osaka University measured up to 130 watts of excess power (an average of 70 percent) using special palladium produced by Tanaka Metals. The excess heat increased over several months, and the cells also produced a small amount of tritium and neutrons. In my own attempts to replicate the Osaka experiments, using the same palladium source, I produced 7.5 watts—20 percent more power than I put into the cell. . . .

Accumulating Evidence: Helium

One of the products of the fusion of two deuterium atoms is helium, which with its two protons is the next element up on the periodic table. Many experiments have produced measurable helium. [The University of] Hawaii's Bor Liaw, for example, found significant helium in the palladium in his heat-producing experiments with a molten-salt electrolyte. Workers at Texas A&M also detected normal helium-4 in the palladium after tritium was produced. However, no effort was made to measure heat during this study. Q.F. Zhang and colleagues at the University of Science and Technology in Chengdu, China, have detected helium-4 in titanium rods that produced excess heat in an electrolytic cell. They saw no helium when excess heat was absent, suggesting a link between the two. . . .

Cold Fusion Gets a Warm Reception in Japan

In October 1992, 300 cold-fusion enthusiasts met in Nagoya, Japan, to share their observations and proclaim new breakthroughs. Their methods differ, but they all claimed extraordinary results that violate established theories of physics. Mahadeva Srinivasan, a physicist at India's Bhabha Atomic Research Center near Bombay, reported that more than half of 30 cold-fusion experiments conducted since the start of the year had produced 20 to 70 percent excess energy. Japanese scientist Reiko Notoya from Hokkaido University reported measuring 200 to 300 percent surplus energy from an experiment she began in August 1992.

Nowhere is cold fusion hotter than in Japan. At a time when many scientists in the United States and Europe have dismissed the idea of room-temperature fusion as an illusion, Japan is pursuing the field with, if not universal enthusiasm, then at least an open mind.

The CQ Researcher, January 22, 1993.

Much of the evidence for cold fusion has come from techniques alien to nuclear physics, such as electrolysis and the precise measurement of heat. But in the past several years, researchers have been producing cold fusion results using the tools of nuclear physics, such as high-energy ion beams. . . .

A trail of evidence for cold fusion comes from work by Jirohta Kasagi and co-workers at Tohoku University in Japan. Kasagi bombarded titanium deuteride with 150-kiloelectron-volt deuterons. When the deuterium content of the titanium deuteride was high enough, the experiment produced protons with energies up to 17.5 MeV. These energetic protons are thought to result from the fusion of deuterium and helium-3. It is the helium-3 that provides evidence for cold fusion. . . .

Attempting an Explanation

Many aspects of the cold fusion effect are now reproducible if known procedures are used. . . . But any explanation for the cold fusion phenomenon must answer some fundamental questions. What is the mechanism that allows positively charged atomic nuclei to overcome the coulombic barrier and join together? How is the significant energy unleashed by a nuclear reaction transferred directly to a material, instead of departing the scene in the form of energetic particles and radiation? Finally, why does cold fusion occur when a material is in a special condition of matter, akin to the state of superconductivity that some materials enter at low temperatures? What is this special condition that occurs in palladium and some other materials when they are infused with high concentrations of deuterium?

Scientists have published several dozen models, ranging from highly analytical approaches to pictorial representations, to explain these events. Most theories address only the problem of overcoming the coulombic barrier—how it is possible for nuclei to overcome their natural repulsion for each other without an infusion of massive amounts of energy from the outside. . . .

Theoreticians are nowhere near a consensus on which of these explanations are most likely to contribute to our ultimate understanding of the phenomenon. None of the proposed explanations accounts for the full range of experimental observations. Many of the theories do not offer predictions that can be quantitatively checked.

Nevertheless, a workable theory is crucial if we ever hope to apply cold fusion. It will be important to develop an understanding of the special condition of matter in which these nuclear reactions occur. For example, what is the crystal structure of the material when it is in this phase? What other characteristics will it exhibit? How can it be created and then modified to trigger a variety of nuclear reactions? Such questions will need to be answered before the phenomenon can be made to occur reproducibly and at high levels—an essential requirement if the effect is to be used to produce energy on an industrial scale.

Is Science Dropping the Ball?

Early investigations of all new phenomena tend to be incomplete, prone to error, and difficult to reproduce. Further scientific investigations require money; the more complex the phenomenon, the more money is required. But dollars tend to flow toward research with a clear chance of success. Thus many potentially important ideas never receive enough funding to enable scientists to understand them.

To a large extent, this is the case with cold fusion. Skeptics maintain that the effect is not real and that funds should therefore not be wasted on studying it. Rather than invest a little money on the possibility that they might be wrong, skeptics actively try to turn off support. The U.S. Department of Energy is not funding research on cold fusion, nor, for the most part, are other federal agencies. The patent office has stopped issuing patents related to this field. Fortunately, a few imaginative and courageous organizations are backing U.S. cold fusion work—most conspicuously the Electric Power Research Institute and, more recently, ENECO, a company based in Salt Lake City that has begun to fund research at a number of labs. ENECO has also invested heavily in buying up rights to the cold fusion patents that do exist.

The advance of scientific knowledge rests on the idea that before work is judged valid it must be evaluated by, and reproduced by, other scientists. While these procedures have kept science from making too many mistakes, they can also stifle new ideas. It is now virtually impossible to publish positive cold fusion results in certain journals because the editors or their chosen peer reviewers are convinced that the effect is bogus. This creates a catch-22: the journals will not accept papers until more papers published in such journals show evidence for the effect.

The cold fusion effect is one of the most intriguing scientific puzzles of this century. Its ultimate practicality is still open to question, but practical worth does not always follow immediately upon discovery of a scientific phenomenon. Superconductivity, for example, was first observed in 1911 and languished as an unexplained laboratory curiosity for most of this century; today we have magnetic resonance imaging systems that rely on superconducting magnets. Albert Einstein predicted the basic principle of a laser before 1920; decades later, we have supermarket checkout scanners, compact discs, and fiber-optic communications.

The comparison of cold fusion with these technologies is not exact. The theory of lasers was well accepted for decades before anyone figured out how to build one. Superconducting effects were consistently observed in the lab for decades before physicists were able to explain it. So far, cold fusion falls short on both fronts: experimental evidence is difficult to replicate and a theoretical underpinning is absent. It is up to scientists of all disciplines to perform the experiments and devise the theories that will transform cold fusion from laboratory scale phenomenon into something of lasting value.

"According to everything we know about the behavior of matter and nuclei, Cold Fusion is impossible."

Cold Fusion Is Not a Feasible Future Energy Source

David Goodstein

David Goodstein is a physics professor and vice provost of the California Institute of Technology in Pasadena. In the following viewpoint, Goodstein asserts that cold fusion—nuclear fusion at room temperature—is theoretically impossible. He chronicles the experiments of scientists worldwide who claim to have achieved cold fusion, but he contends that much of this research has been disproven and that the remaining evidence is inconclusive.

As you read, consider the following questions:

1. According to Goodstein, what do experts agree would be the primary event caused by cold fusion?
2. Which groups decided to fund cold fusion research, according to the author?
3. In Goodstein's opinion, what could be cold fusion's missing ingredient?

Adapted from "Pariah Science: Whatever Happened to Cold Fusion?" by David Goodstein, *The American Scholar*, vol. 63, no. 4, Autumn 1994; ©1994 by David Goodstein. Used with permission.

Cold Fusion is a pariah field, cast out by the scientific establishment. Between Cold Fusion and respectable science there is virtually no communication at all. Cold Fusion papers are almost never published in refereed scientific journals, with the result that those works don't receive the normal critical scrutiny that science requires. On the other hand, because the Cold Fusioners see themselves as a community under siege, there is little internal criticism. Experiments and theories tend to be accepted at face value, for fear of providing even more fuel for external critics, if anyone outside the group is bothering to listen. In these circumstances, crackpots flourish, making matters worse for those who believe that there is serious science going on here.

Origin of Cold Fusion

The origins of Cold Fusion have been loudly and widely documented in the press and popular literature. [Electrochemists] Stanley Pons and Martin Fleischmann, fearing they were about to be scooped by a competitor named Steven Jones from nearby Brigham Young University [BYU], and with the encouragement of their own administration, held a press conference on March 23, 1989, at the University of Utah, to announce what seemed to be the scientific discovery of the century. Nuclear fusion, producing usable amounts of heat, could be induced to take place on a tabletop by electrolyzing heavy water, using electrodes made of palladium and platinum, two precious metals. If so, the world's energy problems were at an end—to say nothing of the fiscal difficulties of the University of Utah. What followed was a kind of feeding frenzy, science by press conference and E-mail, confirmations and disconfirmations, claims and retractions, ugly charges and obfuscation, science gone berserk. For all practical purposes, it ended a mere five weeks after it began, on May 1, 1989, at a dramatic session of the American Physical Society, in Baltimore. Although there were numerous presentations at this session, only two truly counted. Steven Koonin and Nathan Lewis, speaking for himself and Charles Barnes, all three from Caltech [California Institute of Technology], executed between them a perfect slam dunk that cast Cold Fusion right out of the arena of mainstream science. . . .

Colleagues and Associates

Before I go any further in telling this tale, I think I'd better come clean about my own prejudices (those of us concerned about the issue of conflicts of interest in academic life refer to this as "disclosure." It's supposed to help protect us from sin). The Caltech protagonists, Steve Koonin, Nate Lewis, and Charlie Barnes, are my faculty colleagues, and I count them all among my personal friends of many years. At the same time, there is a player on the other side of this game who is also one of my oldest personal friends and who is, besides, my long-time scientific collaborator. . . . My friend Professor Francesco Scaramuzzi is the head of a small low-temperature physics research group at a national laboratory in Frascati (a suburb of Rome), Italy, run by an agency called ENEA, roughly analogous to our Department of Energy. . . .

On the morning of April 18, 1989, Franco called to warn me that I would find his picture in the *New York Times* the next day. (I did.) He had just come out of a press conference announcing the discovery of a new kind of Cold Fusion.

Doomed from the Start

Cold fusion was doomed from the start when a race to be first took precedence over the desire to be right. Most measurements reporting nuclear effects from cold fusion were barely above the background noise, and extended periods of failed experiments afflicted even Stanley Pons's laboratory. The proponents of cold fusion attributed the failure to several causes: differences in the materials, the size of the electrodes, impurities in the electrodes, and low current density. The list goes on.

Denis L. Rousseau, *American Scientist*, January/February 1992.

Like scientists everywhere, he had heard of the Utah announcement and decided to give it a try. He reasoned that electrolysis wasn't really necessary. It served only to get deuterium (the hydrogen isotope in heavy water) to insert itself into the atomic lattice of the palladium electrode. He also thought it necessary that the system not be in thermodynamic equilibrium. He and his handful of young scientists and technicians arranged to put some titanium shavings in a cell pressurized with deuterium gas (titanium is both cheaper and easier to get hold of than palladium, and, like palladium, it is a metal that absorbs large quantities of hydrogen or deuterium into its atomic crystal lattice). Then they used some liquid nitrogen (a refrigerant readily available in any low-temperature physics laboratory) to run the temperature of the cell up and down, thus creating thermodynamic disequilibrium. The crude apparatus was not suitable for the difficult measurement needed to tell whether any heat was being generated, but fusion should produce neutrons (that is what Steven Jones had claimed to detect at BYU). They got a colleague at the Frascati lab to set up a neutron detector near their apparatus. In the course of their experiments, they often detected nothing at all, but on a couple of occasions, their detector indicated very substantial bursts of neutrons. When the second positive result was discovered on April 17, Franco decided he had to inform the head of his laboratory. In no time at all, he found himself in downtown Rome, talking about it to the head of the entire national agency. . . .

Franco agreed to a press conference, but only if he could give a full technical seminar to his scientific peers first. The seminar, hastily organized for that same day, was crammed to the rafters with scientists from every laboratory in the Rome area and was even covered by the evening television news programs. At the press conference the next morning, Franco, stunned to find himself flanked by two Ministers of State, did his best to behave with the utmost scientific objectivity and reserve, but it made not the slightest bit of difference. The story made headlines all over Italy. Within days, Parliament had approved financing for ENEA and Franco had been promoted. . . .

Not only had Cold Fusion been reproduced in Italy, but the Italian version was of an entirely new kind. "Fusione Fredda" or Cold Fusion Italian Style was "dry fusion"—that is, without electrolysis. . . .

The Canons of Scientific Logic

The Cold Fusion story seemed to stand science on its head, not only because it was played out in the popular press without the ritual of peer review, but also because both sides of the debate violated what are generally supposed to be the central canons of scientific logic. Science in the twentieth century has been much influenced by the ideas of Karl Popper, the Austrian philosopher. Popper argued that a scientific idea can never be proven true, because no matter how many observations seem to agree with it, it may still be wrong. On the other hand, a single contrary experiment can prove a theory forever false. Therefore, science advances only by demonstrating that theories are false, so that they must be replaced by better ones. The proponents of Cold Fusion took exactly the opposite tack: Many experiments, including their own, failed to yield the expected results. These were irrelevant, they argued, incompetently done, or lacking some crucial (perhaps unknown) ingredient needed to make the thing work. Instead, all positive results, the appearance of excess heat, or a few neutrons, proved the phenomenon was real. . . .

The anti–Cold Fusion crowd was equally guilty, if you believe another of the solemn canons: In all the high school textbooks, it is said that science must be firmly rooted in experiment or observation, unladen with theoretical preconceptions. On the contrary, however, the failure of Cold Fusion was owing, above all, to the fact that it was an experiment whose result was contrary to prevailing theory.

All parties agreed that, if Cold Fusion occurred in the experiments of Pons and Fleischmann, Jones, Scaramuzzi, and many others, the primary event would have to have been the fusion of the two deuterium nuclei: Deuterium nuclei repel one another because of the electric force between them, but if they get close enough together, they fuse anyway because of what is called the "strong" (nuclear) force. The laws of quantum mechanics allow deuterium nuclei to fuse by accident every so often even if they are not initially close together, but the probability of that happening is . . . much too small to have produced the alleged effects claimed by the Cold Fusioners. . . .

Different from Conventional Physics

On the evening of the original Pons and Fleischmann press conference, I ran into one of my buddies at Caltech, a battle-scarred veteran of experimental nuclear physics. "What do you think?" I asked (there was no need to be more specific). "It's bullshit," he said, slipping immediately into the technical jargon so beloved of contemporary scientists. "If it were true, they'd both be dead." What he meant was that if enough fusions had taken place to produce the amount of heat claimed by Pons and Fleischmann, the flux of neutrons that resulted would have long since been enough to send them both to the happy hunting grounds.

To believe that Pons and Fleischmann, Jones and Scaramuzzi, and many others who claimed to observe either heat or neutrons or tritium, were all observing the same phenomenon, one must believe that, when fusion occurs inside a piece of metal, such as palladium or titanium, the outcome is radically different from what is known to happen when fusion occurs in the Sun, or in a hot-fusion plasma, or an atomic bomb, or a nuclear accelerator. It must be different from conventional nuclear physics. . . .

According to everything we know about the behavior of matter and nuclei, Cold Fusion is impossible. This is what I meant when I said that Cold Fusion is an experiment whose result is contrary to prevailing theory. . . .

Replicating Experiments

Immediately after the press conference in Utah, most scientists were willing at least to suspend judgment for a while, to give Cold Fusion a chance. It was precisely during this crucial probationary period (so to speak) that Cold Fusion science went berserk. Many scientists tried their own hand at it. Those that succeeded, or seemed to succeed, held press conferences. Those that failed generally let the matter drop quietly and went on to other things. It would be difficult to devise a worse way of doing science. Among the exceptions to that behavior were Lewis,

Barnes, and Koonin of Caltech. They pursued every lead with relentless tenacity and Popperian rigor, repeating every experiment, calculating every effect, looking not merely for positive or negative results, but also for explanations of the false positive results that others were reporting—in other words, finding the mistakes of other scientists. These they found in abundance. Far from publicizing their work, they were so secretive that rumors started to circulate, and even appeared in the press, that they were protecting positive results. Finally, they were able, five weeks after the Utah press conference, to stand before their colleagues in Baltimore and, bit by bit, piece by piece, in fine detail, demolish the case for Cold Fusion. Cold Fusion had been given its chance, a suspension of disbelief no matter how unlikely it seemed, and it had failed to prove itself. In the eyes of respectable science, Cold Fusion was dead.

Not Ready to Quit

Meanwhile, back in Frascati, Franco Scaramuzzi and his group of young researchers were not quite prepared to give up. Just as the drama in Italy was little noticed in America, events in Baltimore seemed far away to those in Rome. Franco himself had had, not just fifteen minutes of fame, but a month of it, and it showed no signs of letting up. He was a hero, not only to the general public, but also to all his colleagues in the agency ENEA, and ENEA itself had suddenly shed its reputation for bumbling bureaucratic ineptitude. This was not a propitious moment to throw in his hand, just because Lewis, Barnes, and Koonin didn't approve.

Besides, Scaramuzzi had his own data, and he believed in them. Nothing convinces a scientist nearly as effectively as the experience of seeing data emerge from one's own experiment. There were, to be sure, many questions. It turns out that neutrons are not so easy to detect. The instruments used to detect them are sometimes tricky and undependable. In the aftermath of the Frascati announcements, experts from Italy and abroad (especially the U.S.) made brief visits to Scaramuzzi's lab and pronounced their verdicts on how the mistake had been made: The apparent bursts of neutrons were really artifacts because of changes in temperature or humidity, or power surges on the (notoriously unstable) Frascati lab electric system, or other electronic problems. I remember during my visit that summer talking to one of Franco's young colleagues, Antonella De Ninno. "Do they think we're stupid?" she asked me angrily. "Of course we thought of all those possibilities and eliminated them!" Once the group was convinced they had seen the real thing, they weren't about to give up because someone had made a speech in Baltimore. . . .

Nevertheless, it seemed at the time that there just might be two kinds of Cold Fusion: the bad kind (heat) that Koonin and Lewis had put to rest; and the good kind (neutrons) that was still scientifically respectable. . . .

Research Continues

After the furor died down, Cold Fusion research continued in a number of places. The key to continued research is financial; to paraphrase California politician Jesse Unruh, money is the mother's milk of scientific research. In the United States, the government funding agencies quickly fell into line with scientific orthodoxy and ceased funding anything that smacked of Cold Fusion. However, the industry-supported Electric Power Research Institute decided to put up some funds, just in case. In Japan, Toyota and MITI [Japan's trade ministry], apparently willing to accept some short-term risk in exchange for the possibility of a big payoff later, agreed to put up a few yen. In Italy, ENEA, with its budget and prestige resting on Cold Fusion, could hardly refuse to permit Scaramuzzi and his group to press on. In other places, where scientists were given modest financial support and some discretion in how to spend it, some chose to pursue Cold Fusion. In spite of the disapproval of the worldwide scientific establishment, some Cold Fusion research kept right on going. . . .

Franco's Seminar

I went to visit my friend Franco in December 1993. While I was there, he summarized the results of a recent Cold Fusion conference in Hawaii in a seminar presented to the physics faculty at the University of Rome. . . . This was in itself an unusual event. The physics faculty of the University of Rome today is comparable to the physics department at a good American state university. For them, inviting Franco to speak about Cold Fusion was a daring excursion to the fringes of science. Feeling this was a rare opportunity, Franco prepared his talk with meticulous care.

At the seminar, Franco's demeanor was subdued, and his presentation was, as always, reserved and correct. Nevertheless, his message was an optimistic one for Cold Fusion. In essence, each of the criticisms that Nathan Lewis had correctly leveled at the experiments of Pons and Fleischmann had been successfully countered by new experiments reported at the conference. Even more important, there was reason to believe that the magic missing factor, the secret ingredient of the recipe that accounted for why Cold Fusion experiments only sporadically gave positive results, might finally have been discovered. . . .

In all the various Cold Fusion experiments, the first step is to load deuterium into the body of metallic palladium. The issue is how much deuterium gets into the metal. The ratio of the number of atoms of deuterium in the metal to the number of atoms of palladium is called x. . . . Both the American and Japanese groups showed data indicating there is a sharp threshold at $x = 0.85$. Below that value (which can only be reached with great difficulty and under favorable circumstances) excess heat is never observed. But, once x gets above that value, excess heat is essentially always observed, according to the 1993 reports recounted by Franco Scaramuzzi in his seminar at the University of Rome.

The audience at Rome, certainly the senior professors who were present, listened politely, but they did not hear what Franco was saying—that much became clear from the questions that were asked at the end of the seminar and comments that were made afterward. If they went away with any lasting impression at all, it was just the sad realization that so fine a scientist as Franco Scaramuzzi had not yet given up his obsession with Cold Fusion. They cannot be blamed. Any other audience of mainstream scientists would have reacted exactly the same way. If Cold Fusion ever regains the scientific respectability that was squandered in March and April of 1989, it will be the result of a long, difficult battle that has barely begun.

No One Is Listening

Recently, I told this story in a philosophy course we teach at Caltech called Ethics of Research. When I finished my tale, the first questioner asked whether I believe in Cold Fusion. The answer is no. Certainly, I believe quite firmly the theoretical arguments that say Cold Fusion is impossible. I also believe equally firmly in the integrity and competence of Franco Scaramuzzi and his group of co-workers at Frascati. I was disturbed when I saw that Franco had gotten caught in the web of science-by-news-conference in April 1989, and I was even more distressed when I learned that Franco and his group had observed excess heat (the "bad kind" of Cold Fusion). But I have looked at their cells, and looked at their data, and it's all pretty impressive. The Japanese experiment showing that heat nearly always results when x is greater than 0.85 looks even more impressive on paper. It seems a particularly elegant, well-designed experiment, at least to the untutored eye of a physicist. (What do I know about electrochemistry?) What all these experiments really need is critical examination by accomplished rivals intent on proving them wrong. That is part of the normal functioning of science. Unfortunately, in this area, science is not functioning normally. There is nobody out there listening.

5 VIEWPOINT

> "Biomimetics will lead to compounds that are not only technologically superior, but are also environmentally benign."

Mimicking Nature to Develop Superior Materials

Todd Campbell

Biomimetics, or "biological mimicking," is the study of the structure and function of biological substances, primarily those of animals and insects, as models for human-made materials. In the following viewpoint, Todd Campbell contends that engineers, biologists, and others are learning and mastering the secrets of biological materials and processes to create advanced materials for human applications. Campbell maintains that solving these biological mysteries could amount to a scientific revolution. Campbell has written for *Popular Science* and *Sierra* magazines and currently writes for PreText, a Seattle multimedia company.

As you read, consider the following questions:

1. How is an abalone's shell superior to advanced ceramics, according to Campbell?
2. In how many years do researchers expect "bio-inspired" materials to be commonplace, according to the author?
3. According to Campbell, how could synthetic elastin be used in the human body?

Todd Campbell, "Nature's Building Blocks," *Popular Science*, October 1993. Reprinted with permission from *Popular Science* Magazine, ©1993, Times Mirror Magazines, Inc. Distributed by Los Angeles Times Syndicate.

Stephen Gunderson, a scientist at the University of Dayton Research Institute, would like to know how a large, black insect called the bess beetle can turn sugar and protein into an outer shell that is lightweight yet strong, stiff, and damage resistant. University of Washington researcher Christopher Viney is trying to figure out how spiders can spin water-soluble protein molecules into insoluble silk threads that are tougher than Kevlar—the stuff of bulletproof vests. Princeton University's Ilhan Aksay and Mehmet Sarikaya of the University of Washington are studying the abalone in an attempt to understand how it can crystallize chalk from seawater, and turn that substance into a shell that has twice the strength of the most advanced ceramics.

Elsewhere, scientists are studying other natural materials, including rat teeth that can gnaw through metal cans; walnut and coconut shells that resist cracking; rhinoceros horn with self-healing properties; and the super-sticky glue that mussels manufacture to attach themselves to the ocean floor.

The researchers' goal is to unlock one of nature's best-kept secrets: how living organisms can turn simple building blocks into materials that are superior to advanced synthetic composites manufactured from the latest high-tech materials.

Nature's Models

It is all part of a new area of research called biomimetics—the study of the structure and function of biological substances as models for material design and manufacturing. Biomimetics, or biological mimicking, has attracted researchers from fields as seemingly unconnected as materials science, molecular biology, engineering, biochemistry, and even mathematics and physics, all of whom share a deep fascination with the precision, elegance, and ingenuity of biological systems. They are looking to age-old lessons from nature to provide inspiration for the materials of the future.

"Nature has solved a lot of complex problems over several billion years of research and development, and has come up with some exquisite solutions," says Michael Marron, molecular biology program manager for the Office of Naval Research, which invested more than $5 million in biomimetic research in 1992. "The thought now is to look at the structures nature has arrived at as a suggestion for how to construct new materials."

Following nature's lead may have advantages even beyond the promise of new substances with enhanced properties. Researchers believe that biomimetics will lead to compounds that are not only technologically superior, but are also environmentally benign. A synthetic fiber such as Kevlar, for example, is produced in vats of boiling sulfuric acid under very high pressure. The process is energy intensive, and the materials used are dangerous to work with

100

and difficult to dispose of. Spider silk, on the other hand, is spun from natural, renewable raw materials, at room temperature and pressure, using water instead of sulfuric acid as a solvent.

"That has all kinds of nice implications for materials processing," says Viney, a materials scientist. "With Kevlar, you've got containment and environmental problems, compared with silk, which is processed under mundane, everyday conditions." And unlike Kevlar, spider silk is also biodegradable.

Self-Adaptation

Mastering the lessons of biological processes holds another intriguing possibility. "Rarely in nature does anything function for a single purpose," says Stephen Gunderson. "This is key." He envisions a time when it will be possible to produce synthetic materials that not only mimic the superior physical properties of the bess beetle's outer shell, for example, but can also sense the surrounding environment and adapt.

"What about an airplane wing that can tell when it is damaged and repair itself?" he asks. "It's kind of sci-fi right now, but that's where we'd like to go." Other researchers talk about suspension bridges built with cables made from synthetic silk; genetically altered cells that grow new hard tissue to repair broken bones and replace missing teeth; drug delivery systems that can sense changes in the body and release precise amounts of drugs at specific locations; even miniature motors that draw their power from the same source as the human body, converting chemical energy into mechanical force.

Wary of raising unreasonable expectations, researchers caution that it will be anywhere from five years to two decades before bio-inspired materials become commonplace. For now, scientists in the field of biomimetics mostly concentrate on basic research aimed at uncovering the underlying rules governing the production of biological materials.

Their work has already led to an important new insight. What they have discovered is that nature works with a small number of simple building blocks—sugars, proteins, minerals, and water—over which it exercises precise control at every level, from the arrangement of atoms into molecules, to the assembly of molecules into intermediate components such as fibers and crystals, up through to the final architecture of larger, multifunctional composite materials like wood, bone, or insect cuticle. The resulting natural structures are often breathtakingly complex and elegant.

The human approach to manufacturing synthetic materials is fundamentally different. Where nature works with simple materials and complex designs, humans start with a vast number of advanced, complex compounds that are assembled in relatively simple ways. The microstructural control that is the norm in nature is still far beyond the capacity of human engineering.

Take the example of fiberglass. "By human standards it is a relatively complex material," says Stephen Wainwright, a mechanical biologist at Duke University who is considered one of the pioneers of biomimetics. "But there isn't a biological material in the world that is that simple."

The Abalone's Shell

In nature, a creature like the abalone is able to take a simple substance like chalk, which is not normally considered a useful structural material, and turn it into a surprisingly strong shell. Mehmet Sarikaya bought the abalone shell that inspired his research from a roadside stand while on a weekend trip in western Washington state. The battered and pitted shell does not look like a promising model for the materials of the future. But when a team of researchers at the University of Washington looked at the shell with an electron microscope, they found a highly ordered brick-and-mortar configuration—layer upon layer of ultrathin calcium carbonate (chalk) platelets held together by an organic protein matrix just ten billionths of a meter thick.

Spider Silk: Stronger than Steel

An athlete with a torn ligament receives an artificial ligament in an operation that leaves no scar. Several weeks later, the athlete is back on the field with a knee as strong as before.

Such an operation could be routine one day, according to University of Wyoming molecular biology professor Randy Lewis, who says the creature that could make this medical miracle possible is the spider. . . .

Spiders produce several different kinds of silk, all used for different purposes. Mr. Lewis has singled out the silk the spiders use for the outer framework for their webs, called dragline silk.

Gram for gram, Mr. Lewis said, dragline silk's tensile strength is greater than that of steel. It's also more elastic than nylon and can absorb more energy before breaking than any other known substance, he said.

Jon Sarche, *The Washington Times*, March 5, 1995.

The microstructure of calcium carbonate endows the shell with an unexpected combination of properties: It has the strength of the most advanced synthetic ceramics, yet is not brittle like ceramics, which get their strength from the powerful chemical bonds that hold them together. Apply enough force to break these bonds, and the ceramic cracks. By contrast, the layered platelets of abalone resist the formation of cracks. "You don't get catastrophic failure in the abalone because the platelets slide on top of one another on the organic layer," says Sarikaya. "What we are saying is that the abalone shell deforms, and is behaving like a metal."

Sarikaya believes that if he and his colleagues can design new substances using the principles they have gleaned from the abalone shell, they will be able to produce revolutionary new ceramic composites. The abalone shell's ordered structure increases the strength of calcium carbonate by a factor of twenty, he says. "Would it be possible to increase the properties of current ceramic materials by even five times? That would be an incredible increase in strength, and we would have a new class of materials that would be far superior to anything we have today."

Sarikaya's team has developed a new material in which boron carbide, a ceramic, is suffused with aluminum. The aluminum appears to work in the same way as the organic protein matrix found in the abalone shell. The U.S. Army has been testing the material as a possible new tank armor.

The Bess Beetle

While Sarikaya's work with abalone shells promises to lead to new, high-performance ceramic materials, Stephen Gunderson's study of the structure of bess beetle cuticle may change the way composites are constructed for the aerospace industry. When Gunderson's colleagues at the University of Dayton Research Institute learned that he was interested in beetle exoskeletons as part of a search for new materials with potential aerospace applications, they brought him bugs. "My desk was inundated with insects," he recalls. "People would leave notes that said things like: 'This one ran into my windshield and didn't break.'" One insect that found its way to his desk was the bess beetle.

When viewed under an electron microscope, the bess beetle's cuticle shows a remarkable resemblance to the materials used in modern military aircraft. "We were amazed to see the similarity between its microstructure and some of the advanced composites we were working on," Gunderson says. Both are made of layers of fiber that are embedded in glue—sugar embedded in protein in the case of the beetle, graphite embedded in epoxy for synthetic materials. The layers are stacked to give strength and stiffness.

In synthetic composites, the lamination is a relatively simple, symmetrical design. Gunderson found that the lamination in the bess beetle cuticle is asymmetrical but highly ordered, with alternating layers precisely rotated so that the cuticle is formed

from a pair of mingled spirals, what Gunderson calls a "dual helical lay-up."

Engineers who work with composites previously assumed that
any structure made from an asymmetric layering would distort.
But a panel made of a graphite epoxy composite following the
beetle's architectural principles didn't warp. "It was so unsym-
metrical that it was symmetric," says Gunderson. The resulting
material proved to have better load-bearing characteristics and
greater impact resistance than materials assembled in a traditional symmetric pattern.

But don't expect to fly in an airplane sheathed in a composite
material that imitates the bess beetle's dual helical architecture
anytime soon. While scientists like Gunderson are beginning to
decipher some of nature's secrets, they are a long way from developing methods that will allow industry to mass-produce such
materials. "We're still at the bottom rung of basic research,"
says Gunderson. "From the point we're at to actual use in an
airplane is still years and years away."

Synthetic Elastin

Although the widespread use of biomimetic materials remains
in the future, biomimetic research has already led to a number
of patentable materials. At the University of Alabama, biophysicist Dan Urry has been studying elastin, a common protein
found in skin and other elastic body tissue. He has developed a
synthetic elastin that has been tested in rats and has proven to be
extremely successful in preventing the formation of adhesions after surgery. Researchers at the University of Utah will use sheets
of elastin to wrap an artificial heart they are developing.

By slightly modifying the same synthetic elastin, Urry has created a material that shows promise as a replacement for damaged tissue. "If you have a material with the same elasticity as
normal tissue, you can make a temporary, synthetic scaffolding," Urry explains. Cells will be attracted to this scaffolding
and grow, thus regenerating the damaged site. Such a material
could even be used to fashion synthetic arteries. The same material also turns out to have super-absorbent properties. All told,
twenty patents have been issued or are pending for the synthetic elastin developed by Urry's research team.

A New Era?

It remains to be seen whether Urry's flurry of patentable materials signals the beginning of a new era, in which materials inspired by natural models gradually replace the petroleum-based
plastics and fabrics that have been the hallmark of most of this
century's technology. And it is still too early to predict whether
humankind, having evolved through the Stone Age, the Bronze

104

Age, and the Iron Age, is on the precipice of the transition from the Oil Age into the Biomimetic Age.

At the very least, however, it seems clear that recent advances in a host of technologies ranging from electron microscopy to genetic engineering have allowed an adventurous group of scientific explorers to take a peek into the inner workings of nature. If they succeed in solving some of the fundamental mysteries that govern these natural processes, a scientific revolution could be just around the corner.

"Regarding the future, I would designate genetic engineering as the most significant activity."

Envisioning the Future of Technology

Joshua Lederberg et al.

In 1964, the British magazine *New Scientist* commissioned nearly one hundred internationally known experts to predict technological innovations for the year 1984. In the following viewpoint, which was published in 1994, eight of these experts, professors and scientists from Europe and the United States, review their predictions and make new ones concerning technology in the future.

As you read, consider the following questions:

1. What diseases will gene therapy treat, according to Avrion Mitchison?
2. What does Meredith Thring mean by Equilibrium Engineering?
3. What energy trends and innovations does Ian Fells anticipate?

Joshua Lederberg et al., "New Dreams for Old," *New Scientist*, October 15, 1994.

Professor Joshua Lederberg, Rockefeller University, New York.
The predictions for 1984:
- Successful organ transplants creating a need for moral guidelines to control the market in donor organs.
- Artificial prosthetic organs.
- Increased life expectancy.
- Modification of the human brain through treatment of the fetus or infant.
- Genetic cloning through nuclear transplantation, allowing us to predetermine sex in fetuses and avoid hereditary abnormalities.

The reality and the future:
Some thirty-one years ago, I referred to a "Crisis in Evolution" as a product of the scientific revolution eventuating in molecular biology. I stressed my preference for "euphenic" measures, those affecting the function and development of the individual, to "eugenic", which might leave a more deep-seated imprint on the evolution of the species. The time span for that muted prophecy is more than half up on a linear scale (albeit technological advance is more nearly exponential). It is reasonable to ask for an assessment.

Radical Advance

There has been radical scientific advance in the first and fifth points—sufficient to have recruited substantial impetus for social regulation, for example, of "markets" in organs, and in research with human embryos respectively. I am confident that those markets will be alleviated by the development of transgenic animals, bred for the purpose: this is the target of several commercial initiatives right now. The technology for embryological interventions—the very transgenics just mentioned—is already far past the point of comfort about their human application. I have just seen a notice in the daily press advertising a service for single sperm inoculation with *in vitro* fertilisation, as a means to alleviate male infertility.

With the exception of the artificial heart, organ prostheses are moving along in many fields, with implants ranging from titanium teeth (which I enjoy to great advantage myself) to pacemakers and rudimentary artificial cochleas. There is social ambivalence about the heart, as much as daunting technical obstacles in the control of blood clotting: we have hardly begun to measure the open-ended costs that will be invoked by that technological fix. For sure, prevention of heart disease has been a preferred option during the past three decades, and one already with substantial benefit to healthy life span.

As to the brain, we have just begun to uncover the relevant range of neural growth factors; these are in earliest clinical trials, some of them disappointing, to determine the range of their therapeutic utility. A modest euphenic advance has been advocacy of folic acid supplementation for the avoidance of spina bifida. We are still in the midst of evolving the social technology needed to cope with the steady advance in life span: witness the debates about healthcare reform in the United States.

Infectious disease was hardly mentioned in 1964. We were riding the crest of optimism born of the successes of antibiotics and vaccines. And we were negligent of the unremitting problems of infection in the developing world. Not till later in the 1960s did I observe that such complacency could lead to the reemergence of viral and of drug-resistant bacterial infections that constitute new plagues today. We have many intrinsically powerful tools to counter these threats, but only if we recognise the urgency of these problems and deploy our scientific skills against them.

A Pig with Human DNA

At a secret location in Cambridgeshire, [England,] researchers inject human DNA into a pig embryo. Six months later Astrid, the world's first transgenic pig, is born—of a virgin, in a sterile stable, on Christmas eve. The hope is that the implanted gene will make pig organs compatible with the human immune system, thus helping to solve one of medicine's fastest growing problems: the shortage of organs for transplant surgery.

David Concar, *New Scientist*, June 18, 1994.

Professor Avrion Mitchison, Scientific Director of the German Centre for Research into Rheumatism, Berlin.
The prediction for 1984:
- Methods for synthesising cell products such as enzymes chemically, without having to rely on tissue cultures, will be advanced and may be used to treat metabolic diseases.

The reality and the future:
My 1964 predictions were about manufacture in tissue culture: how we were going to make hormones, antigens, antibodies and enzymes from cells grown outside the body. Looking back at them, they seem so totally obvious. Is it really possible that only thirty years ago we weren't already doing all that? How time does fly.

To mention just a few examples, the hormone erythropoietin is manufactured entirely in culture, on a large scale for treatment of kidney patients who are on dialysis. It has made the fortune of the American company Amgen. Rabies antigen for vaccines is made largely in culture, while hepatitis B vaccine has moved on to the next stage, being made by genetic engineering in yeast. I predicted that synthetic chemistry would eventually take over from culturing, and that is exactly what is happening in the field of vaccines. Interestingly, the first synthetic vaccine to be tested in man is one for the purpose of fertility control: it uses a synthetic peptide corresponding to part of the pregnancy hormone chorionic gonadotrophin.

As for antibodies, 1964 was several years before the invention of monoclonal antibodies, which are now manufactured in large amounts by Celltech and other companies. Enzymes, which I predicted would be manufactured for treatment of metabolic deficiency disease, have been used for exactly that purpose in the treatment of cystic fibrosis.

This last point brings me to my present prediction, which is that gene therapy will take over many of the forms of medical treatment mentioned above, which are at present based on proteins. I refer not just to the rare deficiency diseases, which indeed are already beginning to be treated in this way. Much commoner diseases such as psoriasis or rheumatoid arthritis will probably come to be treated by cytokines. These molecules resemble hormones, except that they act at very short range ("paracrine", as distinct from endocrine). To get them to the right place, for the right time, in the right quantity, and at a reasonable cost can, I believe, only be done by implanting their genes into the right cell. The only alternative, to manipulate the promoters of a patient's own genes, will come, but only later.

Artificial Replacements and Genetic Engineering

Professor Robert Kenedi, Bioengineering Unit, University of Strathclyde.

The predictions for 1984:

- Increased understanding of the "modality pattern of operation of the human body as the most complex multivariable self-adaptive control system in existence", leading to improved matching of machine and human operator.
- Artificially created atmospheres within huge enclosures designed to serve the physical and psychological needs of the individual in homes, offices and cities.
- Prosthetic limbs operated by electric signals generated in appropriately connected muscles when the individual thinks about the movements he or she would like to make.
- Artificial joint and tissue implants.

The reality and the future:

I would claim the first item (and only slightly tongue-in-cheek) as an adequately Delphic forecast of the techniques of virtual reality and its rapidly expanding applications. As for the second prediction, it's not quite so Delphic, but perhaps I can permit myself to claim as foretelling the use of just such enclosures in places like present-day leisure park complexes.

As for the third item, this has not obtained because, in my view, the relevant research projects were not rated at a high enough priority to ensure allocation of the necessary resources. However, the fourth item has obtained, but implantable artificial organs, due primarily to development costs, have not. (As an aside, it is intriguing that on 26 August 1994, coincidentally with the writing of these comments, the implantation of an electrically driven heart booster pump of American manufacture— price around £40,000 [US $64,000] each—has been announced by Papworth Hospital. Apparently, some 250 of these have already been implanted in the US. A clinical series of some forty such procedures is being planned in this country subject to the resources becoming available.)

Future Computers

Future computers—using such techniques as quantum devices, diamond semiconductors, increasing miniaturization down to the atomic scale—suggest that computing power will continue to grow at its historical rate or better for an indefinite time into the future.

The human brain, with its 100 billion neurons and roughly 100 trillion connections, requires a lot of computing power, to be sure . . . but not more than computers early in the next century should provide.

Frederik Pohl and Hans Moravec, *Omni*, November 1993.

Regarding the future, I would designate genetic engineering as the most significant activity of 1994 and beyond. One of its bioengineering applications is the design and construction of biological systems to serve the needs of human tissue and organ implants. The performance of artificial organ replacements for liver and kidney, for example, is greatly enhanced by the addition of genetically engineered human cells, upgrading these artificial organs into bioreactors.

Alongside such commendable advances, there is an aspect of genetic engineering that I find personally highly questionable in both concept and projected outcome. This is the very real possibility in the not-too-distant future of providing animal organ and tissue transplants (for example a pig's kidney, liver, heart, and so on) genetically tailored to be acceptable to human individuals. The societal and individual implications of the formation of such animal/human composites should, I think, be the subject of close public scrutiny now.

Astronomy and the Ecosphere

Professor Fred Hoyle, cosmologist and independent scientist.
The predictions for 1984:
- Closer cooperation will exist between "optical" and "radio" astronomies, leading to identification of fainter radio sources.
- Astronomy will pave the way for a major revolution in physics, perhaps by 1984.

The reality and the future:
The prediction of 1964, that optical astronomy and radio astronomy—then seen as very different activities—would become fused into an essentially single line of research has been amply fulfilled. As indeed it has also been for more esoteric activities such as X-ray, gamma-ray and neutrino astronomy. Research workers today do not have the sense of being radically different animals according to the kinds of astronomy they pursue, as was the case in 1964. Everything today belongs to the same platform and astronomy as a whole has become much better for it.

It was also correct in 1964 to foresee that there would be increasing emphasis on cosmology. But I was wrong in my assessment of how the situation in cosmology would develop. I expected most astronomers would see the big bang as a reductio ad absurdum. In consequence, I thought attention would be given to varying the basic "action functions", the sources of the laws of physics, in such a way as to avoid the need for the big bang. Instead things have gone in exactly the opposite direction. Anything at all, however remote from observation, has become preferred to making a change of the action function. Nevertheless, I still continue to feel that making physics subservient to a particular solution of its own equations, as the big bang theory does, is an absurdity that must disappear sooner or later. So long as alternative possibilities are formulated according to widely accepted physical principles, it seems to me such possibilities, if one or more can be found, must eventually be judged superior to current beliefs.

Professor Meredith Thring, formerly of the Department of Mechanical Engineering, Queen Mary and Westfield College, London.
The prediction for 1984:
- Domestic robots will perform the routine chores of the housewife.

The reality and the future:
Thirty years ago I wrote that science had passed the point of supplying all the basic essentials of life. Now I see that this was far too rosy a picture, because it did not take account of the poverty of millions of people, our heavy use of fossil fuels, ex-

111

penditure on killing machines and, worst of all, our destruction of the ecosphere.

How can science ensure that my descendants in the year 2100 have the opportunity to earn a decent living by doing a decent job?

All humans will have to have it also, for there can be no long-term world stability while the poor look enviously at the rich. Equally a permanent, stable equilibrium with the ecosphere is essential. So we can call the required system Equilibrium Engineering (EE).

In my book, *The Engineer's Conscience*, I have shown that individual Quality of Life (Q) is low both when consumption is too low or when it is wastefully high. Fortunately, the maximum Q occurs at a level of consumption which could be produced on a permanent basis for eight billion people. This implies that EE is possible, provided it is introduced in time to stop the growth of population above this figure by providing education and secure old age for all.

For example, consider energy. The total world consumption of fossil fuel must be reduced to a third of its present figure, because of the Greenhouse Effect. This implies cutting consumption to the equivalent of about a third of a tonne of oil annually per head, plus renewable energy which does not contribute to the Greenhouse Effect. This amount of fossil fuel would be enough to supply all the essentials of a full life. So how far they will be able to live above the bare minimum depends on how much is invested in permanently renewable energy systems.

Similarly, it is likely that a combination of scientific ideas, such as leaf fractionation [extracting proteins, carbohydrates, and other organic compounds from plants] and alley cropping [narrow strips of complementary crops], with traditional local wisdom can feed all our descendants.

Can we shift the application of science from "overgrown engineering" to "equilibrium engineering" before it is too late?

Computers and Communication

Dr Maurice Wilkes, Olivetti Research, Cambridge.
The predictions for 1984:
- International network of computers.
- Routine use of computer simulation in economic policy making and in understanding how genetic codes work.

The reality and the future:
I was right on most counts and 100 per cent right about the great growth in computer networks. However, I was wholly adrift when I assumed that we would be forever restricted to narrow bandwidths. That is, to sending information at very slow rates. I did not foresee that the development of optical fibres

would change the situation dramatically. Neither, of course, did anyone else, since in 1964 optical fibres were not even a twinkle in an inventor's eye.

Bandwidth is all set to change from being a commodity that is scarce and expensive to being one that is plentiful and cheap. An exactly similar thing happened to computer hardware when minicomputers and mainframes began to give way to PCs and workstations that could be bought at a fraction of the cost. What made this possible was the success of the semiconductor industry in doubling, and continuing to double, the speed of silicon chips every two years. The effect was to bring about a serious destabilisation of the older sections of the computer industry.

We should know by 2004 what effect fibre optics will have on the telecommunications industry. Major changes will occur, although I do not expect the sort of destabilisation we have seen in the computer industry. On the other hand, the broadcasting industry may be radically affected. According to one scenario, instead of having to catch your television entertainment at the time it is put out, you may be able to choose from a menu of goodies available, and dial in for what you want when you want it.

Energy and Climate

Professor Ian Fells, Department of Chemical and Process Engineering, University of Newcastle upon Tyne.

The predictions for 1984:

- Cars powered by fuel cells driving electric motors built into the wheel hubs, and pollution-free exhaust.
- Domestic fuel cells running off piped hydrocarbon gases in each house, promoted by a growing supply of natural gas.
- Biochemical fuel cells which could be used to operate heart pacemakers.

The reality and the future:

In 1964 I emphasised dissatisfaction with the low efficiency of combustion or nuclear fission process into electricity and pointed to the use of topping cycles for improving large-scale (500 megawatt) electricity generation and fuel cells for small-scale (10 kilowatt) generation. The systems, I expected, would raise conversion efficiencies from less than 35 per cent to over 60 per cent.

As far as large-scale generation is concerned, the topping cycle turned out to be the gas turbine, not the magneto-hydrodynamic system, giving combined gas-turbine/steam-turbine cycles generation efficiencies now approaching 60 per cent.

I also hinted that improvement in the efficiencies of combustion-generated electricity might cause us to reappraise the future of nuclear power. On a small scale, prototype fuel cell–powered cars are now running in California, encouraged by legislation postulating 10 per cent zero-emission vehicles by 2003. So my predictions were not far off the mark, although progress has been slower than I had hoped; engineers are always optimistic about technological improvement.

I also pointed to the increased availability and use of natural gas; this in 1964 when natural gas had not even been discovered in the North Sea. Natural gas is the new, major player in the energy league and whilst we do not yet have domestic gas-fired fuel cell systems as I suggested, we do have highly efficient local combined heat and power schemes.

Looking to the long-term energy future and pondering on what changes we can anticipate to compare with Michael Faraday's discovery of electromagnetic induction in 1831, maybe before the end of the next century we will have unravelled the mysteries of gravitation and tamed "black holes" to provide a new source of electricity for the next millennium or so.

Dr Fred Singer, director of the Science and Environmental Policy Project, Washington DC.

The predictions for 1984:

- Nuclear-powered satellites orbiting the Earth, predicting weather conditions and providing information about Earth, oceans and space.
- By 2000, we will be able to manipulate climate.

The reality and the future:

It's fun to look back thirty years and see how predictions I made in 1964 have turned out. The record is decidedly mixed: a B + for the technical part; a C− for the institutional part.

In 1964, I had just finished a tour of duty as the first director of the U.S. operational weather satellite system (now part of NOAA, the National Oceanographic and Atmospheric Administration) and was full of optimism that the rate of advancement would continue. Well, most of the observational capabilities I looked for have been achieved, covering the electromagnetic spectrum with high resolution and allowing just about all of the applications I had envisioned: ocean, surface, atmospheric layers, and much of space beyond.

But the Pentagon threw me a curve; they set up a separate satellite system for navigation, GPS (Global Positioning System). But as a consolation, the military MetSat system is finally being integrated with the civilian weather satellites. Maybe GPS will follow and combine into just one satellite system.

We are still a long way from an international system, however, such as we have for communications. And we are even further from efforts of climate modification—although meteorological satellites are the prototype of the EOS (Earth Observing System) that is supposed to keep track of any inadvertent climate modification that might be brought about by human activities.

Periodical Bibliography

The following articles have been selected to supplement the diverse views presented in this chapter.

Robert U. Ayres — "Technological Trends," *National Forum*, Spring 1994. Available from PO Box 16000, Louisiana State University, Baton Rouge, LA 70893.

Ernest Braun — "Can Technological Innovation Lead Us to Utopia?" *Futures*, vol. 26, no. 8, Summer 1994.

Joseph Coates, John Mahaffie, and Andy Hines — "Technological Forecasting, 1970–1993," *Technological Forecasting and Social Change*, September 1994. Available from Elsevier Science, 655 Ave. of the Americas, New York, NY 10010.

Kristene B. Detienne — "Big Brother or Friendly Coach? Computer Monitoring in the Twenty-first Century," *Futurist*, September/October 1993.

Steve Dickman and Gabrielle Strobel — "Life in the Tissue Factory," *New Scientist*, March 11, 1995. Available form 1350 Connecticut Ave. NW, Suite 403, Washington, DC 20036.

John Diebold — "The Next Revolution in Computers," *Futurist*, May/June 1994.

Discover — "Science on the Edge," October 1995.

Peter F. Eder — "Privacy on Parade: Your Secrets for Sale!" *Futurist*, July/August 1994.

Philip Elmer-Dewitt — "Dream Machines," *Time*, special issue, Fall 1992.

Issues in Science and Technology — "Roundtable: The Human Genome Project," Fall 1993.

William Jasper — "High-Tech Nightmare: Traveling Big Brother's Information Superhighway," *New American*, July 25, 1994. Available from PO Box 8040, Appleton, WI 54913.

Jerry Mander — "Tyranny of Technology," *Resurgence*, May/June 1994. Available from Rodale Press, 33 E. Minor St., Emmaus, PA 18049.

Thomas B. Rosenstiel — "Wiring the World: The New Age of Global Telecommunications," *Los Angeles Times*, July 26, 1994. Available from Times Mirror Square, Los Angeles, CA 90053.

Bart Ziegler — "Electronic Roundtable," *Wall Street Journal*, June 27, 1994.

How Will Trends Affect the Global Ecology?

21ST CENTURY EARTH

Chapter Preface

Noted engineer and inventor R. Buckminster Fuller (1895–1983) once predicted that people would increasingly realize that the earth's biosphere is humanity's only "life-support system," bringing a new sense of stewardship to planet Earth and its resources. Indeed, whether the biosphere can safely bear increased human development and population growth has become the subject of much debate.

For most of human history, a virtually pristine environment could withstand the effects of the earth's sparse population. But as the population began to grow rapidly, so too did stress on the environment. Following unprecedented increases in population growth (to 5.5 billion) and industrialization during the twentieth century, many experts began to warn that human activities were leading to an environmental apocalypse. They believed that this environmental disaster—including global warming and ozone depletion—would be so severe and widespread that the biosphere and humanity would be permanently harmed. According to Michael Tobias, author of *World War III: Population and the Biosphere at the End of the Millennium,* "The current size of the human population has wreaked unprecedented damage on the biosphere, and is going to accelerate that damage." Tobias anticipates a world of chaos and conflict in which civilization, development, and industrialization interactively disrupt the balance of nature.

Others are skeptical about such warnings and foresee little, if any, lasting harm to the environment. In the words of *U.S. News & World Report* writer Stephen Budiansky, "Many often cited facts used to paint a picture of impending ecological disaster are more myth than reality." Talk-show host Rush Limbaugh and other conservatives agree, arguing that unsubstantiated warnings of environmental doom—global warming and ozone depletion, in particular—are promoted by scientists who are merely attempting to arouse public fear in order to gain notoriety or funding for expensive environmental projects.

Ecological problems may prove to be the prime concern of the twenty-first century. The future condition of the earth's biosphere and its ecosystems are debated by the authors in this chapter.

> *"Post–Industrial Revolution expansion [of the human population] . . . is generally held responsible for most of the stress humans have put on the biosphere."*

An Environmental Apocalypse Is Real

William K. Stevens

Many scientists envision an environmental apocalypse in the twenty-first century if current ecological trends continue. In the following viewpoint, *New York Times* science writer William K. Stevens describes the profound impact humanity has had on the biosphere, particularly during the twentieth century. Stevens examines the depletion of natural resources and other critical environmental concerns that could lay the groundwork for an environmental apocalypse.

As you read, consider the following questions:

1. What is the Green Revolution, according to Stevens?
2. What role do trees play in the maintenance of the biosphere, according to the author?
3. In Stevens's opinion, why is global warming the most consequential environmental concern?

Humans have always exploited nature in the belief that the all-encompassing biosphere—the seamless, wondrously resilient fabric of life, land, water and air—was so vast and enduring that people could never do it basic harm.

Events of the recent past have shattered that comforting perception. The moment of awakening may have come in the mid-1980's when governments finally accepted and acted on the evidence that waste industrial chemicals were weakening the stratospheric ozone shield that protects living things from biologically harmful ultraviolet rays.

But that is almost the least of it. People have now transformed the biosphere on so many fronts, scientists say, that Homo sapiens rivals grand forces like the movement of continents, volcanic eruptions, asteroid impacts and ice ages as an agent of global change.

The transformation has sharply escalated in both scale and pace since World War II. And it is raising serious questions not only about the ability of nature to sustain the global economy, but also about the health and future of the biosphere itself. That is why delegates from around the world gathered at an "Earth Summit" in 1992 in Rio de Janeiro, Brazil.

Cause for Concern

There are many reasons for concern:

• People have transformed or manipulated ecosystems constituting about half the planet's ice-free land surface and have made a significant impact on most of the rest.

• They have appropriated to their own use about 40 percent of the photosynthetic energy produced by plants.

• They have steadily reduced the number of other species in the world through pollution, hunting and destruction of natural habitat. Now, as the inroads become deeper and more widespread, many biologists fear that human activity could bring about a mass extinction of epic scale, wiping out 25 percent of the world's remaining species in the next 50 years.

• By burning coal, oil, natural gas and trees they cut down, humans have altered the global flow of energy within the biosphere. Atmospheric concentrations of heat-trapping carbon dioxide have increased by 25 percent since pre-industrial times. That is well above levels recorded at any other time in the last 160,000 years, which is as far back as scientists have been able to track the trend. No end to the buildup is in sight. If it remains uncontrolled, scientists warn, a disruptive and possibly catastrophic warming of the earth could take place.

• Global population, which stood at 2.5 billion only 40 years ago, is expected to reach 6 billion by the year 2000 and swell to perhaps 10 billion 60 years from now. . . .

The question of limits to economic and population growth has come to the fore once again in connection with the summit. But this time it has been joined by the newer and more pressing question of the degree to which the biosphere is in jeopardy. Scientists are still struggling toward an answer in each case. . . .

Population: Pressure Is Building

Throughout most of history, humans have been a quite minor presence on the planet. Only 200 million people were alive at the time of the birth of Christ. By the time Europeans first settled in America 1,600 years later, the world population had grown to 500 million. But the human population spurted to 1 billion in 1850, more than doubled by 1950 and then more than doubled again, to 5.3 billion, in just the next 40 years. This post–Industrial Revolution expansion—and especially the last 50 years—is generally held responsible for most of the stress humans have put on the biosphere.

Demographers say that though women have been having fewer children since 1950, improved health and control of disease have caused death rates to plummet, so that global population increased. At the same time, population growth feeds on itself: more people means more women of childbearing age.

The United Nations now projects that if fertility ultimately stabilizes at a replacement rate of about 2.06 births per woman, the global population will reach 10 billion in the year 2050 before leveling off and stabilizing at around 11.5 billion soon after 2200. But those numbers could vary greatly if fertility rates turn out to be higher or lower. At a rate of 2.5 births per woman, the U.N. calculates, world population would reach 28 billion in 2150. At a rate of 1.7, which a few industrialized countries have achieved, it would reach 7.8 billion in 2050 but then fall to 4.3 billion a century later.

According to conventional wisdom, a country's population will stabilize as its economy develops and living standards rise. This "demographic shift," as it is called, has already taken place in industrialized countries, where the fertility rate is generally at or below replacement level.

But the shift is only starting in developing countries of the Southern Hemisphere, where fertility rates, while dropping in many instances, are still double and even triple those in the affluent countries of the North. As a result, the developing countries in 1990 accounted for 77 percent of the global population; by 2025, they are expected to account for about 85 percent. The U.N. projects that more than 60 percent of these will be urban dwellers, as compared with 37 percent in 1990.

Because the rural dwellers of developing countries rely for their direct sustenance largely on ready-at-hand renewable resources like trees, soil and water, growing population puts increasing pressure on the local biosphere. Forests are cut for wood, soil is depleted, water is withdrawn at ever-rising rates. In an anxious quest for income, many of these countries are also cutting some of their forests for commercial sale.

"WHAT WILL HAPPEN WHEN WE FINALLY AND IRREVOCABLY POLLUTE AND DESTROY OUR GOOD PLANET EARTH? THE MEEK WILL INHERIT IT I SUPPOSE.."

©Christian/©Impact Visuals. Reprinted with permission.

Perhaps a billion people remain desperately poor in these circumstances of mismatched resources and population, slowing the onset of the demographic shift. Many of these are moving to increasingly overcrowded and misery-racked cities in their search for sustenance. . . .

Agriculture: Revolution Has Slowed

Almost all prime agricultural land is now under cultivation. And although forests are being cleared at a rapid rate, scientists say, the land now being freed for farming is of marginal productivity and will have relatively little impact on future food production.

Moreover, since World War II, agriculture, deforestation and overgrazing have left an area about the size of China and India combined with moderately to severely diminished soil quality, reducing overall productivity.

The Green Revolution, based on higher-yield seeds and fertilizer, largely overcame these limitations starting in the 1960's and 1970's, enabling the world's farmers to sustain the doubling of the global population that began after World War II.

High-yield strains of wheat and rice bred in the world's agricultural laboratories doubled and tripled harvests in much of the developing world. So abundant did the harvests become that world food prices declined by more than 20 percent in the 1980's.

Sub-Saharan Africa is the main exception to the rule. It is the only region in the world with declining food production. It relies most heavily on imported food and a higher proportion of its people are malnourished than for any other region.

But out-and-out famine as a result of underproduction has largely disappeared. World hunger today is caused mostly by political upheaval, ineffective distribution of food and inability of the poor to buy it.

Yet the demand for basic food grains could double by 2020, and the ability of agriculture to keep pace with the demand is being called into question. . . .

Many scientists say that a variety of highly productive new strains of crops might be developed, but there are widespread fears that the natural genetic material from which they might be created is rapidly disappearing.

Farmers, as they embrace the Green Revolution, are abandoning traditional crop strains that constitute part of this genetic capital. And the United Nations Food and Agriculture Organization warned that global agriculture could be threatened by the extinction of 40,000 important plant species in the next 60 years unless conservation measures are immediately stepped up.

Species: The Signs of Danger

In the last 600 million years, the earth has experienced five big extinctions of life, usually linked to climatic change, in which 35 percent to 95 percent of all species then on the planet disappeared. Scientists know from fossil records that in each case it took 10 million years or more for the earth to regain its biological diversity.

Humans may now be precipitating an extinction of comparable scale, many biologists fear. Some economists argue that the fears are based on insubstantial evidence, and a few biologists say they may be exaggerated. But most biologists who have studied the situation believe the threat to species diversity is a clear and present danger.

As people alter or obliterate natural ecosystems to plant crops, harvest trees and build cities and towns, they destroy species habitat. Eventually a species that lives in a given kind of habitat will be doomed to extinction if enough patches of habitat disappear.

Globe-traveling humans have also introduced countless species into new habitats around the world, where they tend to choke out native species. Few areas on earth have been unaffected by this redistribution of plants and animals. Many animals have already been hunted to extinction. Others, like the rhinoceros and the African elephant, are threatened by hunting today. The Mediterranean Sea and parts of the Pacific and Indian Oceans are so heavily fished that fish populations can no longer withstand the pressure, the United Nations Food and Agriculture Organization says, and pressure is nearly as heavy in some other oceanic areas.

Diversity of Life

No one can say for sure how many species are being doomed. But Dr. E.O. Wilson, a Harvard University biologist, has determined on the basis of field observations that when a patch of habitat is reduced by 90 percent, the number of species living in it eventually declines by about half. Using this formula, Dr. Wilson has calculated that at the rate at which tropical rain forests are being destroyed, 10 percent to 22 percent of rain forest species will be lost in the next 30 years because of habitat destruction alone.

The rain forests contain about half the plants, animals and microbes on earth. A quarter or more of the planet's species could be eliminated in 50 years, Dr. Wilson said. . . .

What does it matter? Apart from the value attached to life in general, natural ecosystems provide the materials of human sustenance. That is where crops originally came from. Forests contain untapped riches in the form of medicines. But more than that, scientists say, natural ecosystems are such an essential part of the biosphere that mass extinctions could undermine its functioning. It is now widely recognized, for instance, that the diversity of life interacts with the oceans and the atmosphere in regulating climate, that it is essential in creating soils and holding them in place, that it cleanses waters of pollution and maintains a microbial standoff that keeps harmful pathogens under control.

Scientists do not know at what point a gradual loss of species results in the disintegration of ecosystems, or at what point the loss of ecosystems begins to affect the overall health of the biosphere. But many argue that it is dangerous to take chances.

Forests: Chain-Saw Progress

Of all the differences humans have made in the face of the earth, perhaps none is so striking as the disappearance of forests. People have long been cutting down trees, but only in recent decades have they become alarmed at the scope and rate of deforestation.

Trees play a vital role in the maintenance of the biosphere. They hold soil in place, preventing erosion and the silting of rivers. They absorb water and give off moisture, helping to recycle water. They absorb vast amounts of heat-trapping carbon dioxide and lock it up in their cells. And they contain a disproportionate share of the world's living species.

Estimating the extent of forest cover and of deforestation is chancy, since many forests regenerate and are in constant flux.

In fact, deforestation of temperate-zone forests in the industrialized countries has reversed in this century as marginal farm land is taken out of production and trees reclaim it. There were an estimated 7.7 million square miles of forest in the developed nations in 1900, and about 8 million in 1985.

But the population explosion in the developing countries has intensified the pressure on forests there, which are one of the last sources of fuel and of new pasture and arable land, however marginal. The advent of the chain saw, truck and tractor have made it immeasurably easier to clear trees. As a result, according to United Nations estimates, an area of tropical forest larger than the state of Florida is disappearing each year.

Scientists estimate that about half the forest cover of the developing world has vanished in this century, and the rate of tropical deforestation is believed to have increased by 50 percent in the 1980's.

Worldwide, scientists say, there has been a net loss of more than 3 million square miles of forest, an area roughly equal to the 48 contiguous states of the United States. About half the loss has come since 1850. Figures on deforestation vary somewhat, but experts agree that trees are being destroyed on a large scale, and many believe the rate in the tropics is accelerating.

Assuming that about 3 million square miles of forest have been lost, that would be 12 to 13 percent of the pre-agricultural worldwide total. Forests may therefore cover an area 85 to 90 percent as large as they did 10,000 years ago. Scientists nevertheless raise two main alarms.

First, some 25 percent of the heat-trapping carbon dioxide released into the atmosphere as a result of human activity has come from deforestation. While the burning of fossil fuels will continue to be the main source of carbon dioxide buildup, accelerating deforestation adds substantially to the atmospheric total.

Second, the tropical forests—which happen to be in the very developing countries where population pressures are greatest—harbor far more living species per acre than forests elsewhere. Their density, complexity and fertility allow many habitats to coexist in a small area, and the loss of even a tiny patch can doom numerous species.

As population expands and economies develop, humans are

pressing the world's freshwater resources hard, and some regions are starting to bump up against limits imposed by water supplies.

Only 3 percent of the water on earth is fresh. Most of that is locked up in ice caps and glaciers. If all the water in the world amounted to 25 gallons, about half a teaspoon would be available for human use.

Against this background of limitations, human use is 35 times what it was three centuries ago. People withdraw the equivalent of Lake Huron from the world's rivers, streams, lakes and aquifers each year, and withdrawals have been increasing by about 4 to 8 percent a year in recent decades. About 40 percent of the water withdrawn is returned quickly to the water cycle as waste water. The rest is consumed.

About two-thirds of the withdrawals are used for agriculture, about 25 percent for industrial use and the rest for domestic purposes. Experts expect withdrawals for farming to increase slightly by the end of this century and withdrawals for industrial use to double. Most of the increase will be in the developing countries. Water use is stabilizing in the industrialized countries and is actually expected to decline slightly in the 1990's.

The vagaries of rainfall make the distribution of water uneven related to human need. Water is chronically short in many areas of sub-Saharan Africa, threatening the ability of agriculture to keep up with population. Supplies of water are beginning to fall behind demand in northern China, and the World Resources Institute says shortages could reach crisis proportions in the Middle East before the end of the 1990's. Shortages have become a familiar and serious problem in the southwestern United States, particularly in California.

In their thirst, humans have greatly altered the distribution and quality of fresh water on the planet, most of which is found in river basins. They have submerged an area the size of France in reservoirs, disrupting the flow of rivers and transforming their ecosystems. They have polluted more than enough river water to fill Lake Superior. And typically, they have caused the amount of choking sediments to triple in large rivers and to increase eightfold in smaller ones in crowded regions. . . .

Atmosphere: Potential Disaster

Global warming is the most far-reaching transformation wrought by humans because it could catastrophically magnify other changes as well—if it develops as many scientists fear.

Atmospheric levels of some gases that trap heat in the atmosphere, mainly carbon dioxide and methane, are rising steadily as a result of human activity like the burning of fossil fuels. But scientists agree on little else beyond that. . . .

Warming, at least in the lower range of the prediction, could well benefit some people, scientists say. Higher concentrations of carbon dioxide, for example, stimulate crop growth. Some areas of the world would probably receive increased rainfall, making them more fertile. Some would enjoy longer growing seasons in regions where it is now too cold for maximum farm production. The cities of the industrialized North would experience a more salubrious winter climate, while still able to insulate themselves from summer's heat.

But there is also a long list of possible catastrophes, especially if warming develops in the high end of the predicted range. As glaciers and ice caps partially melt, according to the United Nations forecast, the level of the oceans would rise by about two feet by the end of the next century. This would place many coastal cities in jeopardy, inundate many low-lying, populous areas in countries like Egypt and Bangladesh and devastate coastal wetlands. . . .

While some areas would receive increased rainfall, others, particularly in the interior of continents, would probably get less. This global redistribution of water would subject some areas to disastrous flooding. In others, drought would devastate agriculture, and some studies show that drought generally would become more frequent. . . .

Even if humans were able to adapt, many scientists say, natural ecosystems would not easily be able to do so. While nature has adapted to climate change many times in the past, the rate of change was much slower then, taking place over hundreds or thousands of years. Global warming would take place over mere decades, and ecologists say that many ecosystems would be torn asunder as temperate-zone trees, for example, would be unable to migrate to friendly climes fast enough. Many climate-sensitive habitats could be destroyed, hastening the extinction of species. One study suggests that as much as 40 to 60 percent of the planet's vegetation could be disrupted, and the web of life with it.

How all of this might actually play out remains to be seen. But one conclusion seems inescapable: By altering the chemistry of the atmosphere, humans have launched out into unexplored territory.

"There is no scientific evidence to support the often heard claim that there is a global ecological crisis threatening humanity."

An Environmental Apocalypse Is Imaginary

Ronald Bailey

In the following viewpoint, Ronald Bailey asserts that there is no global ecological crisis and that there has been a solid record of environmental progress in recent decades. Bailey responds to seven "false doomsday predictions" regarding famine, pollution, ozone depletion, and other phenomena, and he discounts "doomsters' urgent siren calls" to head off an environmental apocalypse. Bailey is the author of *Eco-Scam: The False Prophets of Ecological Apocalypse* and the producer of the public television show *Think Tank*.

As you read, consider the following questions:

1. According to Bailey, what resources did the Club of Rome expect to become depleted?
2. What have satellite data revealed about global temperature trends, according to Bailey?
3. In the author's opinion, how do environmental organizations benefit from professing an environmental apocalypse?

Ronald Bailey, "Seven Doomsday Myths About the Environment," *The Futurist*, January/February 1995. Reproduced with permission from *The Futurist*, published by the World Future Society, 7910 Woodmont Ave., Suite 450, Bethesda, MD 20814.

As the author of *Eco-Scam: The False Prophets of Ecological Apocalypse*, I know by surprising experience that what I am about to say is going to make many people angry. But here goes.

The end is not nigh! That's right—the Apocalypse has been postponed for the foreseeable future, despite the gloomy prognostications by the likes of Paul Ehrlich, Lester Brown, Al Gore, Stephen Schneider, and Carl Sagan. There is no scientific evidence to support the often heard claim that there is a global ecological crisis threatening humanity and life on the entire Planet Earth.

There are local environmental problems, of course, but no global threats. Instead, there is a record of enormous environmental progress and much to be optimistic about. As far as the global environment is concerned, there is a brilliant future for humanity and Planet Earth.

Of course, millions of people believe that we have only a few more years before the end, and no doubt some such doomsters are among the readers of this viewpoint. But I would like to remind them of seven false doomsday predictions—many of which are still being peddled by unscrupulous activists—and take a hard look at what actually happened.

False Prediction No. 1: Global Famine

"The battle to feed all of humanity is over. In the 1970s the world will undergo famines—hundreds of millions of people are going to starve to death in spite of any crash programs embarked upon now," predicted population alarmist Paul Ehrlich in his book *The Population Bomb* (1968).

Two years later Ehrlich upped the ante by also painting a gruesome scenario in the Earth Day 1970 issue of the *Progressive*, in which *65 million* Americans would die of famine and a total of *4 billion* people worldwide would perish in "the Great Die-Off" between the years 1980 and 1989.

While the world's population *doubled* since World War II, food production *tripled*. The real price of wheat and corn dropped by 60%, while the price of rice was cut in half. Worldwide life expectancy rose from 47.5 years in 1950 to 63.9 years in 1990, while the world infant mortality rate dropped from 155 to 70 per 1,000 live births. Even in the poorest countries, those with per capita incomes under $400, average life expectancy rose spectacularly from 35 years in 1960 to 60 years in 1990.

And there's even more good news—for the last decade, grain output rose 5% per year in the developing world, while population growth has slowed from 2.3% to 1.9% and continues to fall. These figures strongly bolster University of Chicago agricultural economist Gale Johnson when he claims, "The scourge of famine due to natural causes has been almost conquered and could be entirely eliminated by the end of the century."

False Prediction No. 2:
Exhaustion of Nonrenewable Resources

In 1972, the Club of Rome's notorious report, *The Limits to Growth*, predicted that at exponential growth rates the world would run out of raw materials—gold by 1981, mercury by 1985, tin by 1987, zinc by 1990, oil by 1992, and copper, lead, and natural gas by 1993.

Humanity hasn't come close to running out of any mineral resource. Even the World Resources Institute estimates that the average price of all metals and minerals *fell* by more than 40% between 1970 and 1988. As we all know, falling prices mean that goods are becoming more abundant, not more scarce. The U.S. Bureau of Mines estimates that, at 1990 production rates, world reserves of gold will last 24 years, mercury 40 years, tin 28 years, zinc 40 years, copper 65 years, and lead 35 years. Proven reserves of petroleum will last 44 years and natural gas 63 years.

Now don't worry about the number of years left for any of these reserves. Just as a family replenishes its larder when it begins to empty, so, too, does humanity look for new mineral reserves only when supplies begin to run low. Even the alarmist Worldwatch Institute admits that "recent trends in price and availability suggest that for most minerals we are a long way from running out."

False Prediction No. 3: Skyrocketing Pollution

In 1972, *The Limits to Growth* also predicted that pollution would skyrocket as population and industry increased: "Virtually every pollutant that has been measured as a function of time appears to be increasing exponentially."

In 1969, Paul Ehrlich outlined a future "eco-catastrophe" in which he prophesied that 200,000 people would die in 1973 in "smog disasters" in New York and Los Angeles.

Since the publication of *The Limits to Growth*, U.S. population has risen 22% and the economy has grown by more than 58%. Yet, instead of increasing as predicted, air pollutants have dramatically declined.

Sulfur-dioxide emissions are down 25% and carbon monoxide down 41%. Volatile organic compounds—chief contributors to smog formation—have been reduced by 31%, and total particulates like smoke, soot, and dust have fallen by 59%. Smog dropped by 50% in Los Angeles from 1985 to 1995.

Water quality deteriorated until the 1960s; now, water pollution is abating. Experts estimate that up to 95% of America's rivers, 92% of its lakes, and 86% of its estuaries are fishable and swimmable. These favorable pollution trends are being mirrored in both western Europe and Japan.

But what about the developing countries and former communist countries? It is true that industrial pollution continues to rise in some poorer countries. But a study by two Princeton University economists, Gene Grossman and Alan Krueger, using World Health Organization data, concluded that air pollution typically increases in a city until the average per capita income of its citizens reaches $4,000–$5,000, at which point pollution levels begin to fall. This is what happened in the developed nations and will happen as developing nations cross that threshold. In other words, economic growth leads to less pollution—not more, as asserted by the doomsters.

False Prediction No. 4: The Coming Ice Age

The public has forgotten that the chief climatological threat being hyped by the eco-doomsters in the 1970s was the beginning of a new ice age. The new ice age was allegedly the result of mankind's polluting haze, which was blocking sunlight. "The threat of a new ice age must now stand alongside nuclear war as a likely source of wholesale death and misery for mankind," declared Nigel Calder, former editor of *New Scientist*, in 1975.

Global temperatures, after declining for 40 years, rebounded in the late 1970s, averting the feared new ice age. But was this cause for rejoicing? NO! Now we are supposed to fear global warming. Freeze or fry, the problem is always viewed as industrial capitalism, and the solution, international socialism.

False Prediction No. 5: The Antarctic Ozone Hole

There have been widespread fears that the hole in the ozone layer of the earth's atmosphere will wipe out life all over the world. John Lynch, program manager of polar aeronomy at the National Science Foundation, declared in 1989, "It's terrifying. If these ozone holes keep growing like this, they'll eventually eat the world."

In 1985, British scientists detected reduced levels of stratospheric ozone over Antarctica. Could the Antarctic ozone hole "eventually eat the world"? No. "It is a purely localized phenomenon," according to Guy Brasseur at the National Center for Atmospheric Research. It is thought that the "ozone hole" results from catalytic reactions of some chlorine-based chemicals, which can take place only in high, very cold (below –80° C, or –176° F) clouds in the presence of sunlight. It is a transitory phenomenon enduring only a bit more than a month in the austral spring. The polar vortex—that is, the constant winds that swirl around the margins of the ice continent—tightly confine the hole over Antarctica.

What about the southern ecosystems? Isn't the increased ultraviolet light threatening plants and animals there? U.S. Vice President Albert Gore credulously reports in his book that hunters are finding rabbits and fish blinded by ultraviolet light in Patagonia.

This is sheer nonsense. Scientists have found not one example of animals being blinded by excess ultraviolet light in the Southern Hemisphere.

What about the phytoplankton in the seas around Antarctica? Osmond Holm-Hansen, a marine ecologist at Scripps Institute of Oceanography, has been studying the effects of ultraviolet light on Antarctica's ecosystems since 1988. He found that the extra ultraviolet-B light reduces phytoplankton by less than 4%–5%, which is well within the natural variations for the region. Holm-Hansen concludes, "Unlike the scare stories you hear some scientists spreading, the Antarctic ecosystem is absolutely not on the verge of collapse due to increased ultraviolet light."

False Prediction No. 6: Ozone Hole over America

In 1992, NASA spooked Americans by declaring that an ozone hole like the one over Antarctica could open up over the United States. *Time* magazine showcased the story on its front cover (February 16, 1992), warning that "danger is shining through the sky. . . . No longer is the threat just to our future; the threat is here and now." Then–Senator Albert Gore thundered in Congress: "We have to tell our children that they must redefine their relationship to the sky, and they must begin to think of the sky as a threatening part of their environment."

On April 30, 1992, NASA sheepishly admitted that no ozone hole had opened up over the United States. *Time*, far from trumpeting the news on its cover, buried the admission in four lines of text in its May 11 issue. It's no wonder the American public is frightened.

But let's stipulate that there have been minor reductions in ozone over the United States due to chlorofluorocarbons in the stratosphere. So what?

Reduced stratospheric ozone over the United States was never going to be a disaster or a catastrophe. At most, it might have become an environmental nuisance in the next century.

But doesn't reduced stratospheric ozone severely injure crops and natural ecosystems? The answer is no. Ultraviolet levels vary naturally by as much as 50% over the United States. The farther south you go, the higher the ultraviolet exposure a person or plant receives. For example, an average 5% reduction in the ozone layer over the United States would increase ultraviolet exposure by about as much as moving a mere 60 miles south—the distance from Palm Beach to Miami. How many people worry about getting skin cancer as a result of moving 60 miles? Not many, I bet.

Alan Teramura, who is perhaps the world's leading expert on the effects of ultraviolet light on plants, says, "There is no question that terrestrial life is adapted to ultraviolet." His experiments have shown that many varieties of crops would be unaffected by reductions in the ozone layer. In fact, corn, wheat, rice, and oats all grow in a wide variety of ultraviolet environments now.

False Prediction No. 7: Global Warming

Global warming is "the Mother of all environmental scares," according to the late political scientist Aaron Wildavsky. Based on climate computer models, eco-doomsters predict that the earth's average temperature will increase by 4°–9° F over the next century due to the "greenhouse effect": Burning fossil fuels boosts atmospheric carbon dioxide, which traps the sun's heat.

The earth's average temperature has apparently increased by less than a degree (0.9) Fahrenheit in the last century. Unfortunately for the global-warming alarmists, most of that temperature rise occurred before World War II, when greenhouse gases had not yet accumulated to any great extent in the atmosphere.

The First Happy Earth Day

Most news regarding the environment conveys hope—hope for the planet and, possibly, hope for the human prospect itself. Two centuries ago, the thinkers of the European Enlightenment dreamed that one day the study of nature would reveal messages of enduring value to society. The environmental pessimism of the postwar era seemed to give up that promise: a weak, doomed nature could hardly find much worth knowing.

But perhaps if the environment is not doomed, it may be understood as a source of wisdom after all. The initial, halting attempts of Western society to create environment-protection programs suggest that mankind and nature eventually can become allies. That is the brightest and greatest hope of this, the first happy Earth Day.

Gregg Easterbrook, *The New York Times*, April 21, 1995.

And here's more bad news for doomsters: Fifteen years of very precise satellite data show that the planet has actually cooled by 0.13° C. Some years are warmer while others are cooler, according to NASA space scientist Roy Spencer, but the global temperature trend has been slightly downward. The satellites can measure temperature differences as small as 0.01° C. By contrast, the computer models of the doomsters predict that temperatures should have risen by an easily detectable 0.3° C per decade. They have not.

Even more bad news for the global-warming doomsters: One of the more robust predictions of the climate computer models is that global warming should be strongest and start first in the Arctic. Indeed, Albert Gore says in his book: "Global warming is expected to push temperatures up much more rapidly in the polar regions than in the rest of the world."

However, scientists did a recent comprehensive analysis of 40 years of arctic temperature data from the United States and the former Soviet Union. In an article in the prestigious scientific journal *Nature*, the scientists reported, "We do not observe the large surface warming trends predicted by the models; indeed, we detect significant surface cooling trends over the western Arctic Ocean during the winter and autumn." This is the exact opposite of what the doomsters are predicting is happening; the Arctic is becoming *cooler*.

Climate doomsters also predict that the ice caps of Antarctica and Greenland will melt, drastically raising sea levels and inundating New York, London, Bangladesh, and Washington, D.C. Recent scientific evidence shows that in fact the glaciers in both Antarctica and Greenland are accumulating ice, which means that sea levels will drop, not rise. Another false apocalypse averted.

Furthermore, over the past 100 years, winters in the Northern Hemisphere have become warmer. Why? Because the world is becoming cloudier. Cloud blankets warm long winter nights while long summer days are shaded by their cloud shields. This means longer growing seasons and fewer droughts for crops. This is decidedly not a recipe for a climate disaster.

Environmental "Crises"

Given the dismal record of the environmental doomsayers, why do so many people think the world is coming to an end? I think it's pretty clear. People are afraid because so many interest groups have a stake in making them afraid. "Global emergencies" and "worldwide crises" keep hundreds of millions of dollars in donations flowing into the coffers of environmental organizations. As environmental writer Bill McKibben admitted in *The End of Nature*, "The ecological movement has always had its greatest success in convincing people that we are threatened by some looming problem." That success is now measured at the cash register for many leading environmental groups. For example, in 1990, the 10 largest environmental organizations raised $400 million from donors. That pays for a lot of trips to international environmental conferences, furnishes some nice headquarters, and buys a lot of influence on Capitol Hill.

Crises also advance the careers of certain politicians and bureaucrats, attract funds to scientists' laboratories, and sell newspapers and TV air time. The approach of inevitable doom is now the conventional wisdom of the late twentieth century.

But despite the relentless drumbeat of environmental doomsaying, people have to want to believe that the end is nigh. How do we account for the acquiescence of such a large part of the public to a gloomy view of the future?

I conclude that the psychological attraction of the apocalyptic imagination is strong. Eric Zencey, a self-described survivor of apocalyptic environmentalism, wrote about his experience in the *North American Review* (June 1988): "There is a seduction in apocalyptic thinking. If one lives in the Last Days, one's actions, one's very life, take on historical meaning and no small measure of poignance. . . . Apocalypticism fulfills a desire to escape the flow of real and ordinary time, to fix the flow of history into a single moment of overwhelming importance."

To counteract the seduction of the apocalypse, scientists, policy makers, intellectuals, and businessmen must work to restore people's faith in themselves and in the fact of human progress. History clearly shows that our energy and creativity will surmount whatever difficulties we encounter. Life and progress will always be a struggle and humanity will never lack for new challenges, but as the last 50 years of solid achievement show, there is nothing out there that we cannot handle.

So what's the moral of the story? Please don't listen to the doomsters' urgent siren calls to drastically reorganize society and radically transform the world's economy to counter imaginary ecological apocalypses. The relevant motto is not "He who hesitates is lost," but rather, "Look before you leap."

"Conservation means preserving the world's natural resource base as the indispensable foundation for the future."

Sustainable Development Can Protect the Environment

Martin W. Holdgate

Sustainable development is the use of resources without depleting them or seriously damaging the environment. In the following viewpoint, Martin W. Holdgate argues that sustainable development can be achieved in the middle decades of the twenty-first century, but only through a process of international cooperation. Holdgate identifies six environmentally harmful trends that he says will continue into the early twenty-first century that must be addressed, slowed, and eventually reversed. The author contends that the burden of reaching sustainable development must fall on developed, industrialized nations, which should provide money and technology to developing nations to achieve sustainability. Holdgate served as director general of the World Conservation Union in Gland, Switzerland from 1988 to 1994.

As you read, consider the following questions:

1. According to Holdgate, why is population growth unstoppable?
2. In Holdgate's opinion, what four actions does the developing world expect from developed nations?
3. How can the environment be viewed as a nation's "natural capital," according to the author?

Excerpted from "The Environment of Tomorrow's World" by Martin Holdgate, the 1990 Annual Memorial Lecture of the David Davies Memorial Institute of International Studies. Reprinted by permission.

Earth is the scene of constant change. The summits of the Jura Mountains in Switzerland, more than 1,500 meters above present sea level, are formed of limestone laid down as soft sediments in the bed of a warm and shallow sea about 175 million years ago. There were once forests in Antarctica and dinosaurs and ice sheets in England. As Alfred, Lord Tennyson wrote, "There where the long street roars has been the stillness of the central sea."

Such changes will always occur. Some of today's seas will be squeezed out of existence by the collision of continents to form new mountain ranges, as the Himalayas are being shaped by the collision of India and Asia. The Arctic ice may well expand again, providing the ultimate solution to the architectural problems of Europe and North America. Life forms will continue to evolve and drive their predecessors toward the extinction that is the ultimate fate of every species. On a longer time horizon, as astronomer Fred Hoyle has put it, "we shall certainly be roasted" when the sun emerges from its present stable phase and expands to engulf and vaporize the Earth.

However, I am concerned with a more limited perspective. Throughout this viewpoint, I will use *tomorrow* to mean 2030, and the phrase *the day after tomorrow*, viewed through a haze of uncertainty and for that reason receiving less attention, as 40 years later, in 2070. I will address three simple questions:

- What will the world be like as a habitat for life if present trends continue?
- What are the implications of these changes for humanity and for the world of nature?
- What can we do about it if we would like tomorrow to be different? . . .

The Nature and Quality of Development

Most of the major changes on the planet today are very much acts of humanity, and they result from the cumulative impact of two linked processes: the growth in human populations and the process that we call development. . . .

Development, by permitting the dominance of our species, has inevitably altered the world both by the nature and the scale of the transformations involved.

Sustainable Development

In recent years, some so-called environmentalists in developed countries have spoken of development as if the word were dirty. That is nonsense, as the World Conservation Strategy, prepared in 1980 by the World Conservation Union (IUCN) in partnership with the World Wildlife Fund and the United Nations Environment Programme, makes plain. Development has been essential to the evolution and expansion of human civilizations, and more will be needed to help millions of people escape from today's poverty and squalor and to feed tomorrow's added billions. What we have to be concerned about is the nature and quality of development and the social and political structures needed to bring it about. It is clear from the destruction that has been the price of today's uneven and unsatisfactory development that the world cannot afford much more of the same. We need something different. To use today's catch-word, we need development that is sustainable—that is, it must not overcrop soil, pastures, forest, or fisheries or create products that spread from a beneficial activity, like industry, to blight other essential ones, like agriculture, the supply of drinking water, or the stability of the world's ecosystems.

When we demand that development should be sustainable, we must be clear about our meaning. We do not mean that the growth in a human activity, such as the cultivation of new land, must be capable of indefinite extrapolation—little such growth will be. Rather, we mean that the changes we make in our environment must not only improve the yield of a useful product today but also go on supplying that product tomorrow, without side effects or unforeseen consequences that undermine other essential environmental functions. If overuse has such an impact, we may have to accept adjustment to a lower level of sustainable production. To quote the World Commission on Environment and Development, sustainable development means "meeting the needs of the present without jeopardizing the ability of future generations to meet their own needs." For IUCN, conservation means preserving the world's natural resource base as the indispensable foundation for the future. . . .

Six Trends

If humanity is to have a sustainable future on this diverse planet with many environmental inequalities, it can only be through a process of international cooperation that transcends anything we see today. To state that is immediately to pose an immense challenge if we are to seek success in as short a time as 40 years. And we have to contend with certain trends arising from the nonsustainable nature of the current development process that aggravate our problems and are likely to prove unstoppable on a 40-year time scale. I am particularly concerned with six of these trends.

Population Growth

The first is population growth. [Consider] the dramatic increase in the world's population from around 1 billion people in 1800, to 2 billion in 1900, to over 5.2 billion today. Although the rate of population growth has slowed somewhat from a peak of nearly 2 percent per year in 1970 to around 1.66 percent now, a cautious medium projection suggests that by 2030 there will be more than 8 billion people in the world and that our descendants will be lucky if, by 2070, stability has been achieved at around 10 billion. The trend is unstoppable because in many countries half the population is still under reproductive age. Even if these people only have two children per marriage, a near doubling is inevitable. Forty years from now, most of those people presently under 16 years of age will still be alive and their children will be between 10 and 35 years old—and some of them will themselves have children. Common sense tells us that not all people will limit their family size to two children per couple by 2030, and it will obviously require an immense change in attitude for this to happen by 2070. The total population achieved in a number of countries will depend on how many children survive, as well as on how many are born. . . .

Deforestation and Land Degradation

The second trend is deforestation, which, I suggest, is also unstoppable because of the need to feed more people, especially in the developing world. Moreover, I do not think it is honest to present all tropical deforestation as an environmental disaster. There are parts of the tropics—including areas of the Amazon basin—where conversion of forests to well-managed agriculture, particularly agroforestry, could be a perfectly acceptable pattern of development, though the governments concerned are fearful about the damage caused by present methods. Further deforestation in the tropical regions of South America, central Africa, and Southeast Asia is virtually certain. The governments concerned should steer the process in the direction of sustainable agricultural systems, while halting destructive deforestation of areas that are especially valuable as reservoirs of biological diversity, that are essential to regulate local climate, or that protect the land from erosion. Looking beyond 2030 to 2070, my prediction is that the great forests of Earth will by then be concentrated in the boreal zone, in the more rugged and uncultivable mountains of the tropics, and in tracts of sparsely populated tropical lowlands, where the soils are poor. I also foresee significant but relatively small patches of natural forest in the temperate zones and in the densely populated and heavily utilized tropical lowlands. We may not like that pattern, but it is the one that I suspect our descendants will have to live with.

Another trend that is unstoppable is desertification, or land degradation. I do not refer to the advance of the Saharan dunes but, rather, to erosive soil loss, salinization, and declining fertility as a result of poor or inadequate irrigation—which has, for example, affected some 60 percent of the cropland in Pakistan. However, because of some good science in recent years, there are signs of a cure. In the Sahel, for example, food production has increased steadily since the early 1970s despite a lower average annual rainfall than in the preceding two decades. In Pakistan, measures to improve the quality of irrigation, to control salinization, and to plant crops that are resistant to salt are gaining ground. Accordingly, I do not expect the maps of the world to show more desert areas in 2030 than they do today, and by 2070 this phenomenon may have been brought under control or even reversed.

Biological Diversity

Fourth, I believe that the continuing loss of the planet's biological diversity is unavoidable. Before every conservationist starts jumping up and down and shouting, let me explain at once that I do not imply that destruction of biodiversity should continue at its present rate or that we should complacently accept this trend. We are, however, almost bound to lose a significant number of species from the Earth as a consequence of the development process impelled by the imperative of human need. Such loss is a logical necessity because, as I have said, it will be impossible to stop tropical deforestation. . . .

It is always better to maintain a system with the widest possible range of ecological functions and the greatest practicable reservoir of genotypes. But I suggest that some loss of biological diversity does not inevitably bring collapse. The problem is that we do not know how much loss of what kinds of organism is tolerable. Figuring that out is one of the real challenges to science.

Pollution and Climate Change

My final two unstoppable trends are quite different from the others. Trend five concerns pollution. Some kinds of damaging pollution are unstoppable over a 40-year time scale because they are already present in the environment and cannot be eliminated by 2030. For instance, polychlorinated biphenyls and other persistent chlorinated organic substances are widely dispersed in the ocean and in biological food chains, even though the most damaging kinds are no longer produced. Even if the production of chlorofluorocarbons (CFCs), which are responsible for depleting the ozone layer, ends by 2000, as many scientists wish, the persistence of these substances in the atmosphere is such that the ozone "hole" will not begin to fill in in less than 40 years, and the ozone layer will not be fully restored even by 2070.

The buildup of greenhouse gases is also most unlikely to be stopped by 2030; at best, the upward trend in carbon dioxide emissions will have been slowed, CFCs will no longer be released, and emissions of other greenhouse gases will be limited. Thus, the sixth and last unstoppable trend is climate change. Because of the many greenhouse gases already emitted, there is every reason to believe that by 2030 the world will be between 1° and 2° C warmer than it is now. . . . By 2030, sea level may rise by 10 to 20 centimeters. As for the climate in 2070, much depends on how successful people are in curbing greenhouse-gas emissions. If they are not—if politicians drag their feet—then the world could be 2° to 4° C warmer, and sea level could rise 20 to 40 centimeters, posing severe risks to burgeoning human populations, especially those in the coastal zones of the tropics. . . .

Unstoppable Trends

Why are these trends unstoppable over such a long time scale as 40 years? All six trends have two features in common. First, all are caused by the innumerable small actions of a very large number of people, who do not see their actions as detrimental. Second, there is a substantial lag time between cause and effect for each trend. . . .

Sharing Knowledge

Perhaps the first thing to do is to let facts about the world environment speak for themselves. This means openly sharing all available scientific knowledge and letting the professional community in each country evaluate the significance of those facts for itself. This is already happening to a considerable and increasing extent. There are internationally accepted compendia of environmental data, produced, notably, by the United Nations Environment Programme. There are many international bodies that bring together governments, nongovernmental organizations, and individual specialists from developing and industrialized countries. Some problems, such as climate change and ozone depletion, are accepted almost universally as serious and in need of concerted action. In both of these areas, the developing world wants and expects the developed countries to continue to share their knowledge; to help developing countries evaluate the unavoidable trends over the next 40 years; to take steps to reduce output of CFCs and greenhouse gases, which are already overtaxing the capacity of the environment and are leaving no room for development in the Third World; and to transfer alternative materials and technologies that will allow the Third World to develop without creating new environmental risks.

The costs of these four actions would all fall on the developed world. But is that unreasonable, when the causative agents of the ozone depletion and the greenhouse effect stem especially from the activities of developed nations? Unless the developed world shows itself willing to take these actions and shoulder a significant part of the costs, the credibility of its leaders as sincere advocates of action designed to benefit the whole world will be at stake. Any attempts by leaders of developed countries to sell the essential new technology at a profit or to transfer it on terms that add to the burden of debt that already hampers the capacity of the developing world to deal with other intense problems of sustainable development will be seen as proof of insincerity. Such attempts will make it more difficult to persuade the leaders of the Third World to treat the issues of population growth, deforestation, and loss of biological diversity with equal seriousness. Similarly, if the developing countries are going to conserve their biological diversity, promote sustainable use of forests and rangelands, and experience positive trends in economic and social conditions that will favor population stability, they will need money, which today is largely concentrated in the developed north.

Convincing world leaders that they must talk and think as one community is essential. . . . Indeed, given the burgeoning number of international bodies, the almost incessant conferences, and the more than 100 international conventions, agreements, and action plans that now deal with the world environment, it might be deduced that action was well in hand. The problem is, as one of my colleagues put it recently, that "thunderstorms of rhetoric are followed by droughts of inaction." Words are cheap and action plans are easy to put on paper. Because such agreements create the cozy, inexpensive illusion of a problem solved, they are dangerous.

Turning Words into Action

How do we turn the words into actions? Clearly, each international agreement must be the culmination of a process thoroughly built from within each nation so that, in signing the convention or plan, the leaders concerned know that they express the will of their people and can commit themselves to putting the agreement into operation—either by acting within their own territory or by giving aid to other countries where the need is greatest. How can such a process be ensured? Within any particular country there are three components of certainty: a sound understanding of the problems and of the means to solve them; good organization and administration; and the backing of a well-informed, committed public. None of these components can succeed without the others. Unfortunately, in many nations, environmental concerns have been grasped slowly and addressed half-heartedly through governmental measures that often lag behind public awareness and will. . . . If the environment is actually the fundamental resource base on which all development rests, then surely it is proper to see it as a country's "natural capital"—to use a term that is now widely used among economists. In other words, the environment is real national wealth, as precious or more precious than the manmade wealth guarded by treasuries and analyzed by finance ministers in annual budgets.

Managing the environment as a national treasure would unite science, economics, and government in a new way. Science would be needed to understand both the potential of using the natural environmental capital for sustainable development and the sensitivity of the environment to various impacts; the techniques for doing this already exist. Economics is needed to place financial value on the resource and to convert the material income yielded by the environment into cash terms. Again, the techniques for more precise economic evaluation of environmental assets and for evaluating the true costs and benefits of alternative options for their development are now well advanced. Government is needed to define how the state's managerial system then proceeds to get the best value for its money out of those resources. Government must also ensure that individual sectorial departments do not undermine the whole system by the pursuit of narrow and often traditional policies.

Use Resources Sustainably

In order for humanity to persist on the planet we have to use resources at a sustainable rate. Instead, we're exhausting critical and irreplaceable resources—fertile soils, fresh water, biodiversity. The global population is over 5.6 billion, and we're adding 90 million people each year. The UN's median projection is for 8.4 billion people by the year 2025, but nobody knows how high we can go without a dramatic increase in the death rate from famine, disease, or some combination of humanity's standard plagues.

Gretchen Daily, *Mother Jones*, November/December 1994.

However successful such national plans may be and however enlightened government administrations may become, . . . nothing will be accomplished without the support of the governed. This fact seems obvious in terms of the six unstoppable trends. For example, experience in China suggests that it is difficult for even an authoritarian and determined state to bring population growth rapidly under control. The power of governments to control pollution, desertification, deforestation and human-induced climate change is obviously limited, and it is expressed only by altering the behavior of individuals through education, training, incentives, help, and deterrence of those individuals who nonetheless insist on seeking their own ends, regardless of wider interests. In the end, the problem and the solution are matters of perception. . . .

Meanwhile, the chemicals we use, the gasoline we waste, the fumes we generate, the heat we let escape through poorly insulated walls and roofs, the litter we create, and the environmentally unfriendly pesticides we buy because they are cheap seem so trivial in proportion to the size of the problem that altering our behavior does not seem worth the effort—even if we can find alternatives to buy and places to send items for recycling. The perceived benefit is all too often of less value than the perceived cost. Yet, unless millions of people are helped, guided, and advised to alter their behavior, the unstoppable trends will not stop and the day after tomorrow will be dark. . . .

We need to devote great effort to slowing or reversing the damaging trends, but real changes in direction are also needed if we are going to build a world in which humanity lives in enduring harmony with nature. Willingly, or perforce, many people face life-style changes, and many industries may face a smaller profit margin. But unless we begin to travel with hope we shall certainly never arrive, and unless we start quickly, we shall face regression rather than progress. Let us, therefore, begin to develop practical measures that will enlist the aid and inventiveness of all the world's peoples to make their contribution to tomorrow's world.

"Government ownership and control of resources is a recipe for economic collapse and environmental degradation."

Sustainable Development Will Harm the Environment

Thomas J. DiLorenzo

Sustainable development pursued by government control of resources and international bureaucracies will ruin the environment, Thomas J. DiLorenzo argues in the following viewpoint. DiLorenzo supports his opinion by describing what he contends was the vast environmental damage inflicted by formerly communist nations. DiLorenzo maintains that the best way to protect the environment is through private ownership of natural resources rather than government regulations. DiLorenzo is an economics professor at Loyola College in Baltimore.

As you read, consider the following questions:

1. What did NASA satellite photographs reveal in Africa, according to DiLorenzo?
2. How does DiLorenzo compare the protection of elephants in Kenya and Zimbabwe?
3. Why is government development aid ineffective, in the author's opinion?

Thomas J. DiLorenzo, "The Mirage of Sustainable Development," *The Futurist*, September/October 1993. Reproduced with permission from *The Futurist*, published by the World Future Society, 7910 Woodmont Ave., Suite 450, Bethesda, MD 20814.

There is no precise definition of sustainable development. To some, it simply means balancing economic growth with environmental-protection goals, a relatively uncontroversial position. But to others, it means something different: dramatic reductions in economic growth in the industrialized countries coupled with massive international income redistribution.

According to advocates of the latter viewpoint, there are not enough resources left worldwide to sustain current economic growth rates, and these growth rates are also too damaging to the environment. Consequently, these advocates argue for government regulation of virtually all human behavior on a national and international scale and for governmental control of privately owned resources throughout the world. Such controls may be enforced by national governments or by international bureaucracies such as the United Nations. The "lesson" to be learned from the tragic failures of socialism, the sustainability advocates apparently believe, is that the world needs more socialism.

Such views would be dismissed as bizarre and irrational if they were not held by someone as influential as Norway's Prime Minister Gro Harlem Brundtland, who also chairs the United Nations World Commission on Environment and Development. This Commission published its views in a 1987 book, *Our Common Future*, which laid the groundwork for the June 1992 "Earth Summit" held in Rio de Janeiro.

But the policy proposals advocated by *Our Common Future* and the Earth Summit fail to recognize the many inherent flaws of governmental planning and regulation, and they ignore the important role of private-property rights, technology, and the market system in alleviating environmental problems.

The Communist Legacy

The final collapse of communism in 1989 revealed a dirty secret: that pollution in the communist world was far, far worse than virtually anywhere else on the planet. In theory, this should not have been the case, for it has long been held that the profit motive and the failure of unregulated markets to provide incentives to internalize external costs were the primary causes of pollution. Government regulation or ownership of resources was thought to be a necessary condition for environmental protection.

But that was just a theory. The reality is that, in those countries where profit seeking was outlawed for decades and where government claimed ownership of virtually all resources, pollution and other forms of environmental degradation were devastating. According to the United Nations' Global Environment Monitoring Program, pollution in central and eastern Europe "is among the worst on the Earth's surface."

In Poland, for example, acid rain has so corroded railroad

tracks that trains are not allowed to exceed twenty-four miles an hour. Ninety-five percent of the water is unfit for human consumption, and most of it is even unfit for industrial use, so toxic that it will dissolve heavy metals. Industrial dust rains down on towns, depositing cadmium, lead, zinc, and iron. Half of Poland's cities do not even treat their wastes, and life expectancy for males is lower than it was twenty years ago.

Market Institutions for the Environment

We don't have to choose between promoting industry and protecting the environment, because capitalism is not the cause of environmental problems. People are strongly motivated to conserve and protect that which they own. Private spaces almost always are better managed and cared for than public spaces. The goal of environmental policy, therefore, should be to extend market institutions—private property rights, freedom of contract, common law liability rules—to the widest possible array of natural resources.

Malcolm Wallop, *Competitive Enterprise Institute UpDate*, November 1994.

The landscape is similar in other parts of central and eastern Europe, in the former Soviet Union, and in China. Eighty percent of the surface waters in former East Germany are classified unsuitable for fishing, sports, or drinking. One out of three lakes has been declared biologically dead because of decades of dumping untreated chemical waste. Some cities are so polluted that cars must use their headlights during the day. Bulgaria, Hungary, Romania, the former Yugoslavia, and the former Czechoslovakia suffered similar environmental damage during the decades of communism.

These sad facts teach important lessons that the sustainable development theorists have not learned. The root cause of pollution in the former communist world, and worldwide, is not the profit motive and unregulated markets, but the absence of property rights and sound liability laws that hold polluters responsible for their actions. The environmental degradation of the former communist world is an example of one massive "tragedy of the commons," to borrow the phrase coined by biologist Garrett Hardin. Where property is communally or governmentally owned and treated as a free resource, resources will inevitably be overused with little regard for future consequences.

But when people have ownership rights in resources, there is a stronger incentive to protect the value of those resources. Furthermore, when individuals are not held liable for damages

o mention was made of the role of property rights
entives.

Sustainable Delusions

development—as it is defined by the Brundtland
nd the planners of the Earth Summit—can best be
a euphemism for environmental socialism—grant-
nts more and more control over the allocation of
he name of environmental protection. But if any
learned from the collapse of socialism in the for-
st countries, it is that government ownership and
ources is a recipe for economic collapse and envi-
gradation. Socialism is no more effective in pro-
vironment than it is in creating wealth.

t ownership of natural resources inevitably leads
of the commons, but that is all too often the "solu-
by the Brundtland Commission. The Commission
government control of everything from outer space
ich is supposedly "too important for its develop-
ue in such a manner" as the free market allows.

top priority of sustainable development theorists is
international welfare state by agitating for wealth
n "the rich" countries to the developing. But the
y of development aid is government-to-govern-
f it is typically used to finance the expansion of
bureaucracies in the recipient countries—which
e to economic development. Even if most of the aid
to the hands of the citizens of the recipient coun-
ble development theorists do not explain how that
into savings, investment, capital formation, and en-
activity—the ingredients of economic development.

theory of sustainable development commits in
the mistake of what Nobel laureate Friedrich von
"the pretense of knowledge." The detailed and
anging "information of time and place" required to
the simplest of items efficiently is so immense
y dispersed that no one human mind or group of
e largest computer in existence could imitate to
e efficiency of a decentralized market system.
l, is the principal lesson to be learned from the
llapse of socialism.

Guess Work

he larger and more complex an economy becomes,
note the likelihood that governmental planning
hing but guess work. As Hayek states in his 1988
l Conceit,

150

---

inflicted on others—including environmental damages—then
there is little hope that responsible behavior will result. Needless to say, the state did not hold itself responsible for the environmental damage it was causing in the former communist
countries. Thus, far from being the answer to environmental
problems, pervasive governmental control of natural resources
was the cause.

Our Common Future's Misinterpretations

Our Common Future neglects the role of property rights, and,
consequently, it grants entirely too much credence to the effi-
cacy of greater governmental controls and regulations as solutions to environmental problems. Several examples stand out.

Deforestation. International economic relationships "pose a
particular problem for poor countries trying to manage their environments," says *Our Common Future*. For example, "the trade
in tropical timber . . . is one factor underlying tropical deforestation. Needs for foreign exchange encourage many developing
countries to cut timber faster than forests can be regenerated."

But the need for foreign exchange is not unique to people in
developing countries. All individuals prefer more to less, but
they do not all cut down and sell all the trees in sight for economic gain. Deforestation was also a massive problem in the
former communist countries, but the main reason was that the
forests were communally owned. Consequently, anyone could
cut them down, and there were virtually no incentives to replant because of the absence of property rights.

Deforestation has also taken place in democratic countries,
primarily on government-owned land that is leased to timber
companies who, since they do not own the land, have weak incentives to replant and protect its future value. Some of these
same timber companies are very careful indeed not to overhar-
vest or neglect replanting their own private forest preserves.
They do so not so much out of a desire to protect the environment as to protect the value of their assets. Well-enforced property rights and the existence of a market for forest products will
assure that forests are likely to be used wisely, not exploited.

Desertification. The sustainable development theorists also mis-
diagnose the problem of desertification—the process whereby
"productive arid and semiarid land is rendered economically un-
productive," as *Our Common Future* defines it. They blame capitalism for desertification, particularly "the pressures of subsistence food production, commercial crops, and meat production
in arid and semiarid areas." Their "solution" is greater governmental controls on agriculture.

Desertification is undoubtedly a problem throughout the
world—including parts of the United States. The primary cause

147

is not commercial agriculture, however, but the tragedy of the commons.

A particularly telling example of the importance of private property to desertification was reported in *Science* magazine in a 1974 article on desertification in the Sahel area of Africa. At the time, this area was suffering from a five-year drought. NASA satellite photographs showed a curiously shaped green pentagon that was in sharp contrast to the rest of the African desert. Upon investigation, scientists discovered that the green blotch was a 25,000-acre ranch, fenced in with barbed wire, divided into five sectors, with the cattle allowed to graze only one sector a year. The ranch was started at the same time the drought began, but the protection afforded the land was enough to make the difference between pasture and desert.

Endangered Species

Wildlife management. The Earth Summit advocated a "biodiversity treaty" whereby national governments would establish policies aimed at slowing the loss of plant and animal species. The type of policies most preferred by sustainable development theorists include prohibition of commercial uses of various plants and animals, such as the ban on ivory from African elephants, and the listing of more "endangered species," which may then be "protected" by governments on game preserves or elsewhere.

There is growing evidence, however, that the best way to save truly endangered species is not to socialize them, but to allow people to own them. As conservationist Ike Sugg has written:

> [W]here governments allow individuals to reap the economic benefits of conserving and protecting their wildlife stocks— wildlife flourish. Where individuals are denied the opportunity to profit from wildlife legally, they do so illegally and without the sense of responsibility that comes with stewardship.

One particularly telling example that illustrates Sugg's point is the African elephant. Kenya outlawed elephant hunting in the 1970s; its elephant population quickly *dropped* from 140,000 in 1970 to an estimated 16,000 today as illegal poaching proliferated.

In contrast, Zimbabwe had only 30,000 elephants in 1979 but has over 65,000 today. The main reason for these differences, according to Sugg, is that in 1984 the government of Zimbabwe granted citizens ownership rights over elephants on communal lands—a large step in the direction of defining property rights. As expressed by one tribal chief who implicitly understood the value of property rights and the commercialization of elephants:

> For a long time the government told us that wildlife was their resource. But I see how live animals can be our resources. Our wealth. Our way to improve the standard of living without waiting for the government to decide things. A poacher is only stealing from us.

The preservation of enda[ ] property rights and free mar[ ] United States in the form of [ ] volves "exotic" or nonnative a[ ] berger of Texas, for example[ ] thirty-one remaining bloodlin[ ] rare antelope that is virtually [ ] such successes, several states [ ] cause the notion of privatizing[ ] gion" of environmentalism ([ ] which holds that markets and [ ]

The Soviet Env[ ]

Before its demise, the Soviet [ ] most detailed environmental re[ ] forced, says RAND researcher [ ]

In his book, *Troubled Lands*, Pe[ ] 1950s, once the Soviet econom[ ] environmental degradation ir[ ] passed a number of laws aimed [ ] wildlife. But the regulations an[ ] stacles in the Soviet Bureaucra[ ] thing, responsibility for carryin[ ] environmental protection was d[ ] and state committees, all with o[ ] the environment.

The Futurist, September/October 1993.

The principle of using property [ ] protect global resources and the [ ] range of problems, including the [ ] in the American West, the mis[ ] owned forest lands, the overfishin[ ] and even the ocean commons: Th[ ] the United States has thus far re[ ] the oceans as the largest gover[ ] commons on Earth—and, inevita[ ] commons.

This elementary principle, howe[ ] by the United Nations' sustainab[ ] answering the question, "How a[ ] suaded or made to act in the comm[ ] Commission answered with "edu[ ] forcement," and eliminating "dispa[ ]

cal power." [ ] in shaping in[ ]

Sustainabl[ ] Commission [ ] understood a[ ] ing governm[ ] resources in[ ] lesson can b[ ] mer commu[ ] control of r[ ] ronmental [ ] tecting the [ ]

Governm[ ] to the trage[ ] tion" offere[ ] recommenc[ ] to energy, [ ] ment to co[ ]

Perhaps [ ] to expand [ ] transfers f[ ] whole his[ ] ment—mo[ ] governme[ ] can be ad[ ] did make [ ] tries, sust[ ] will trans[ ] trepreneu[ ]

Finally [ ] grand fas[ ] Hayek c[ ] constantl[ ] produce [ ] and so w[ ] minds w[ ] any deg[ ] This, af[ ] worldwi[ ]

Morec[ ] the mo[ ] could b[ ] book, T[ ]

By following the spontaneously generated moral traditions underlying the competitive market order . . . we generate and garner greater knowledge and wealth than could ever be obtained or utilized in a centrally directed economy. . . . Thus socialist aims and programs are factually impossible to achieve or execute.

The theory of sustainable development calls for myriad varieties of *international* central planning of economic activity. If the "pretense of knowledge" is fatal to attempts at governmental planning at the national level, the belief that international or global planning could possibly succeed is untenable.

The Brundtland Commission's recommendation that every government agency in the world engage in economic planning and regulation in the name of environmental protection would lead to a massive bureaucratization of society and, consequently, a sharp drop in living standards. The image of millions of "green" bureaucrats interfering in every aspect of our social and economic lives is frightening.

The irony of it all is that the wealthier economies are typically healthier and cleaner than the poorer ones. By impoverishing the world economy, "sustainable development" would, in fact, also be harmful to the environment. Private property, free markets, and sound liability laws—anathemas to the theory of sustainable development—are essential for a clean environment and for economic growth.

"The world [c]ould simply go on warming, placing a viable future for human and animal life on the planet at risk."

Global Warming Could Be Disastrous

Jeremy Leggett

Global warming is a phenomenon that could potentially alter the earth's biosphere and harm plants and animals. In the following viewpoint, Jeremy Leggett argues that the pumping of greenhouse gases—carbon dioxide, methane, ozone, and others—into the atmosphere could result in a worst-case scenario of runaway global warming in the twenty-first century. Leggett contends that in this scenario, most of the earth would suffer ecologically and economically because of the damage to animals and vegetation. Leggett is the director of science for Greenpeace International's Atmosphere and Energy Campaign based in Cambridge, England.

As you read, consider the following questions:

1. What is albedo, according to Leggett?
2. What would be the effect of melting ice around the Arctic ice cap, in Leggett's opinion?
3. According to the author, what did the April 1991 report from Japan's Advisory Panel on Environment and Culture warn about "expansionism"?

Jeremy Leggett, "Global Warming: The Worst Case," *The Bulletin of the Atomic Scientists*, June 1992. Reprinted by permission of *The Bulletin of the Atomic Scientists*, copyright ©1992 by the Educational Foundation for Nuclear Science, 6042 S. Kimbark Ave., Chicago, IL 60637. A one-year subscription is $30.

As recently as 1990, it looked as if world leaders would soon agree on a far-sighted course of action to insure cutbacks in the production of "greenhouse" gases, to make certain that future generations would not suffer from excessive global warming.

Many of us, in fact, thought the ceremonial signing of a global warming treaty would be the centerpiece of the U.N.-sponsored "Earth Summit," in 1992 in Rio de Janeiro.

Political and economic issues that lie beyond the scope of this viewpoint help explain why the compromise treaty failed to commit governments to a limitation of greenhouse gases. But there is also the matter of scientific uncertainty. Although the world's scientists share a broad consensus that the human-enhanced "greenhouse effect" will lead to potentially dangerous global warming, profound uncertainty remains as to the exact response of the climate system to an atmosphere overloaded with greenhouse gases, most of them long-lived.

Formulating a policy response to global warming is, at heart, an exercise in risk assessment. Perhaps the world's policy-makers have not been able to agree on a plan of action partly because we scientists have not fully explained the nature of the threat—particularly the possibility that a worst-case scenario might develop.

Early Warning

Scientific consensus on global warming was formalized in May 1990 in a scientific assessment by the Intergovernmental Panel on Climate Change (IPCC). Its authoritative early warning set most of the world's governments negotiating for a Global Climate Convention in February 1991. Amid rapid advances in scientific research, the IPCC was asked to prepare an updated report by January 1992.

When climate scientists gathered in Guang-zhou, China, to complete the second IPCC report, the political scrutiny was intense. Progressive governments (like Germany and Austria) looked for confirmation that their policies of cutting carbon dioxide emissions—the gas is modern civilization's major contributor to global warming—were sound. Foot-dragging governments (like the United States and Saudi Arabia) sought evidence for their arguments that uncertainties about global warming permitted delays in efforts to cut emissions.

The central question the 300-plus scientists who collaborated on the 1992 IPCC report had to tackle was whether the "early warning" in the 1990 report could be confirmed. The scientists, from 44 governments, concluded that it could. However, the subsequent February session of the climate negotiations in New York City ended in deadlock, primarily because the United States refused to concede the need for setting targets and deadlines for limiting carbon dioxide emissions.

Foot-dragging governments, by definition, advocate go-slow approaches to global warming issues. They argue that the science is uncertain, and that global warming is an unproved process. This view is a travesty of the science behind global warming. Climate models on which future warming estimates are based attempt to simulate a complex interactive system. They are not perfect, but they give us a clear warning that business-as-usual emissions of greenhouse gases means taking an appalling gamble with the environmental security of the generations to come.

A Poll of Scientists

Many experts' concerns go beyond the ecologically dangerous rates of warming now forecast by all the world's climate modeling centers. Many scientists ask if the abundance of greenhouse gases might lead to a worst-case scenario with runaway warming in the next century. How close are we to a self-sustaining warming that would be beyond human control? Recently, Greenpeace collected scientists' gut feelings (something that would never find their way into an institutional document).

In a poll of 400 climate scientists conducted by Greenpeace International during January and February 1992, almost half (45 percent) said that a runaway greenhouse effect is possible if action is not taken to cut greenhouse gas emissions. And more than one in ten of those polled believe that such a scenario is probable.

The poll included all scientists involved in the 1990 study of the Intergovernmental Panel on Climate Change, and others who have published on issues relevant to climate change in *Science* or *Nature* during 1991. A total of 113 scientists had responded to the questionnaire by the time of the February negotiations.

The worst-case hypothesis is viewed as a serious consideration by many of the world's best climate scientists, but they have been unable to communicate that to policy-makers. Meanwhile, best-case advocates have become regular fixtures in the global media simply by advocating the minority view—rejected in the IPCC's reports—that natural climatic dampening mechanisms will suppress the heat-trapping abilities of the greenhouse gases.

It is vital that policy-makers appreciate the risks associated with global warming. And policy-makers need to understand what we know—and what we don't know—about feedbacks involved in the climate system.

The Feedback Factor

A feedback is a natural component of the climate system that is activated by other system components. The extent to which climate models can simulate and predict reality depends on their ability to simulate these feedbacks. In a warming world, negative feedbacks can act to suppress warming. (An example might be the formation, in a warming atmosphere, of cloud types that reflect more solar radiation back into space than other types.) Positive feedbacks amplify the warming—the release of now-trapped greenhouse gases from melting tundra in the far north would be an example.

The feedbacks generated by water vapor and clouds are incorporated in all modern global circulation models. Water vapor concentrations are generally projected to increase in a warming atmosphere: a positive feedback. Clouds, according to the IPCC, can provide positive or negative feedbacks, and it is in simulating clouds that most of the current variance in climate models is found. The ice-albedo feedback (the reflection of solar radiation back to the atmosphere) is also included in global circulation models. In most, it is positive: a warmer world will involve shrinking ice cover, lowering albedo, and reflecting less solar radiation. But many feedbacks, especially biological feedbacks, are simply omitted from climate models because they are too difficult to quantify, given the extent of our ignorance of the climate system.

As policy-makers assess risks, they need answers to several vital questions. To what extent are the feedbacks accurately simulated in these climate models? What is the best-case analysis of global warming? What is the worst-case analysis? Between extremes, what is the best-estimate analysis? And if the best-estimate analysis is wrong, on balance, is it more likely to be wrong on the worst-case side or on the best-case side?

Best-Case Advocates

A minority of world-class atmospheric scientists subscribe to the best-case analysis of feedback interactions. Their analysis suggests that the human-enhanced greenhouse effect is a nonproblem. Advocates of this view do not question the buildup of greenhouse gases in the atmosphere, unprecedented since humans first appeared on earth, which is measured and proven. Neither do they question the heat-trapping capacity of the gases, which is based on simple physics. Rather, the best-case advocates ask policy-makers to place faith in the expectation that negative feedbacks will work to cool the planet.

According to Richard Lindzen of MIT [Massachusetts Institute of Technology], for instance, a warming troposphere will not produce more water vapor in the way anticipated by global warming models. Instead, water vapor will be wrung from the lower atmosphere by the increased vigor of atmospheric circulation. Lindzen and other advocates of this view ask policy-makers to commit the environmental security of future generations to a theoretical negative feedback concept, which has been rejected by a majority of their peers.

Global warming risk assessment is complex, unlike risk assessment associated with the ozone depletion problem. Ozone depletion is represented by one main variable: chlorine and bromine from halocarbons. The higher these chemical concentrations, the lower the ozone concentrations. It is a proven process, and the thinning ozone layer can be measured. Measurements in recent years, in fact, have shown that atmospheric scientists have consistently underestimated the pace and extent of ozone depletion. What if the scientific community's underestimation of ozone depletion proves to apply to global warming as well? Bad as the broad-consensus, best-estimate IPCC prognosis is, what might the worst-case analysis of global warming be?

The Worst Case

The main worry is that a coalescing pattern of positive feedbacks might be awakened and continue unchecked by negative feedbacks. Some of nature's carbon reservoirs are so huge that they could become involved, in principle, in a runaway greenhouse effect. The world would simply go on warming, placing a viable future for human and animal life on the planet at risk.

Consider the following: the world warms at the accelerated rates predicted by the IPCC, and concentrations of carbon dioxide and other greenhouse gases continue building up in the atmosphere. As the oceans warm, they are not able to absorb as much carbon dioxide from the atmosphere as they do today. This is a safe bet; the IPCC warns that this will be a positive feedback, since carbon dioxide is less soluble in warmer water.

Luck is not with us; a "plankton multiplier" effect begins. This is a drop in net productivity (the creation of biomass by photosynthesis) in the phytoplankton. It results from a reduced deep ocean nutrient supply to the stabler-than-normal upper levels. Therefore, one of the two major carbon dioxide "sinks" suffers a drop in its capacity to absorb carbon dioxide. (Many scientists believe the plankton multiplier appeared suddenly at the end of the last ice age, boosting average temperatures in the North Atlantic region by as much as five degrees centigrade within as little as a century.)

This time, the effect worsens. Increased fluxes of ultraviolet radiation penetrating the depleted ozone layer above the highly productive waters of the Antarctic and sub-Arctic have seriously weakened the phytoplankton, thus further shrinking the ocean's capacity for carbon dioxide absorption and allowing more of the gas to accumulate, by default, in the atmosphere. This is a major fear, now that ozone depletion has been found to extend into the spring, when phytoplankton bloom.

156

By now, ecosystems are responding to warming temperatures with increases in soil and plant respiration in excess of normal photosynthesis, causing further carbon dioxide accumulation in the atmosphere and boosting temperatures above currently predicted rates. This excess respiration, like all the foregoing feedbacks, was flagged as a positive feedback by the IPCC in its 1990 report.

A Climate of Extremes

Among many scientists, there is growing concern that the world may have entered a period of dangerous climatic extremes. Although we are still in the early stages of human alteration of the atmosphere—greenhouse gas concentrations are rising at a record pace—computerized climate models suggest that these gases are likely to warm the atmosphere in the decades ahead.

Christopher Flavin, *World Watch*, November/December 1994.

As temperatures rise, the tundra begins to melt faster than expected. More carbon dioxide and now huge quantities of methane, a more potent greenhouse gas, are emitted from the spreading wetlands and the increased oxidation of organic matter. However, much depends on the behavior of water tables, for flooded soils are capable of releasing 100 times more methane than dry soils.

Now the reorganization of global cloud cover also works against us, creating a new positive feedback factor. More high-altitude clouds form than do at the present time. They contain ice crystal distributions that trap more heat in the atmosphere. According to the IPCC, this feedback could go either way in a warming atmosphere, as much depends on the physics of ice in clouds. In the worst-case analysis, luck is not with us.

Meanwhile, profound aridity has begun to develop at many latitudes. Though one might expect that vegetation would prosper from the carbon dioxide "fertilization effect," in fact it suffers because of other factors such as decreasing soil moisture, increasing forest fires, multiplying plant pests, and increased exposure to ultraviolet-B radiation. Hence, land plants are less able than expected to absorb carbon dioxide from the atmosphere. Even higher concentrations of the gas build up, driving temperature levels higher than previously projected. (A depressing possibility is that the northern forests have already prospered as a result of this process.)

By now, today's children are in their 50s and 60s, some of them the policy-makers of the day. Some regions, as would be expected from the variability of climate, have warmed only slightly.

Most, however, are suffering profound ecological trauma. Warming effects are such that the "short-term winners"—areas where the climate has become more temperate and crop yields have risen—are now deteriorating as a result of a drastically blighted world economy. Cuts in greenhouse gas emissions have long since been internationally implemented, but they are still not deep enough to stabilize atmospheric concentrations. Net economic savings from energy-saving measures and enhanced energy independence have been lost in the bill for environmental damage.

Under Stress

Bad luck continues. Tropospheric chemistry has started to work against humankind. The hydroxyl reservoir (the atmosphere's cleansing agent, oxidizing a host of polluting gases) has come under stress from excess quantities of methane, hydrochlorofluorocarbons, hydrofluorocarbons, carbon monoxide, and nitrogen oxides in the atmosphere. The quantities of these gases increase by default, as do their lifetimes, boosting global warming still further. Meanwhile, the pollution assault continues. Still more carbon monoxide and nitrogen oxides are emitted by the ever-expanding global automobile fleet. These gases are precursors for tropospheric ozone, a powerful greenhouse gas.

By now, the Arctic is appreciably warmer. The ice around the fringes of the ice cap is beginning to retreat, reducing the Arctic's albedo and providing more positive feedback. The Arctic ocean warms still further and the ice cap begins to show signs of thinning. At this stage, one of the worst feedbacks is awakened. On the Arctic continental shelf, submarine methane hydrates start to destabilize. Methane hydrates are ice-like solids comprising a network of water crystals with methane gas trapped under pressure. Geologists have shown that an unspecified but apparently huge quantity of methane is isolated from the atmosphere in these hydrates. Warming can destabilize them under the permafrost and in shallow high latitude seas. (The IPCC reserves judgment on the magnitude of this problem.)

The measurements of the World Climate Monitoring System detect unprecedented acceleration of atmospheric methane concentrations. In emergency session the United Nations votes sweeping measures for worldwide greenhouse-gas reductions. But it is too late. A runaway greenhouse effect has been generated.

The point is not that a worst-case scenario will happen, but that it could happen. Consider some of the reservoirs in the planet's carbon cycle. The pre-industrial atmosphere contained around 580 billion tons of carbon for thousands of years. Now it contains 750 billion tons. The coal and oil reserves waiting to be burned total 4,000 billion tons of carbon. We cannot afford to burn more than a small fraction of this, yet oil and coal companies are looking for still more. Carbon in soils amounts to 1,500 billion tons, a good proportion of it at risk of positive feedback. Nearly 90 billion tons is exchanged each year between the atmospheric reservoir and the 39,000 billion-ton reservoir in the oceans. Approximately 100 billion tons of carbon circulates between the atmosphere and the approximately 750 billion-ton reservoir in land plants. Almost a quarter of all atmospheric carbon is cycled down into the terrestrial and marine biota each year. Even small changes in this quantity could have huge implications for atmospheric concentrations.

Policy by Worst Case

Though not yet addressed in the IPCC science-advisory process, the worst-case scenario is central to formulating a policy response. In evaluating military threats throughout history, policy response has been predicated on a worst-case analysis. The standard military yardstick must also apply to environmental security.

The Japanese government's report, "Action Program to Arrest Global Warming," released in October 1990, refers on its first page to the potential magnitude of the stakes. "It is essential," it says, "to steadily promote feasible measures so that damage from global warming may not become prominent and give birth to irreversible situations." The tension here between the "feasible" and the "irreversible" is clear, and it reflects the fact that 13 ministries and agencies are represented by the committee planning the Japanese government's response to climate change.

What seems "feasible" to the Ministry of International Trade and Industry is not very far outside the present energy-industrial status quo. In contrast, what seems "irreversible" to scientists of Japan's environment agency is made clear in several of its publications. For example, the April 1991 report from Japan's Advisory Panel on Environment and Culture notes "expansionism consists of damaging the environment without replenishing it. If we refuse this definition of expansionism, we run the risk of creating a crisis which will not stop with the ruin of one country, but will cause the destruction of the entire planet and every living thing on it." Worst-case analyses can creep into the language of governments, not just the language of environmentalists.

But such examples are far fewer than the instances of governmental rhetoric stressing the difficulties and economic costs involved in cutting emissions. Unfortunately, policy-makers see the risks of responding to the threat of climate change as equal to, or even greater than, simply waiting to see what happens in a business-as-usual world. A sad potential epitaph for humankind thus emerges: "We wanted to save the world. But our leaders told us it would be too expensive."

"We are not on the edge of an abyss and the human race is not facing destruction from the accumulation of greenhouse gases."

Global Warming Would Not Be Disastrous

Wilfred Beckerman and Jesse Malkin

Global warming, even if it increased significantly in the twenty-first century, would present no cause for alarm, Wilfred Beckerman and Jesse Malkin assert in the following viewpoint. Beckerman and Malkin maintain that the environmental and economic effects of global warming would not be severe and that the harm from global warming can be reduced by developing alternative energy sources and reducing the use of fossil fuels. Beckerman is a fellow at Oxford University's Balliol College in England. Malkin is a doctoral fellow at the RAND Graduate School in Santa Monica, California.

As you read, consider the following questions:

1. Why would global warming have little impact on the U.S. economy, in the authors' opinion?
2. According to Beckerman and Malkin, how could coastal cities be protected from a rise in sea level?
3. What renewable energy sources could compete with fossil fuels in the twenty-first century, according to the authors?

Excerpted from Wilfred Beckerman and Jesse Malkin, "How Much Does Global Warming Matter?" Reprinted with permission of the authors and *The Public Interest*, no. 114, Winter 1994, pp. 3–16; ©1994 by National Affairs, Inc.

More than a billion people in developing countries have no access to safe drinking water, and at least twice that many have no access to adequate sanitation. Consequently, between 1 and 1.5 billion people suffer from water-related diseases such as schistosomiasis, hookworm, and diarrhea. Infant mortality attributable to diarrhea is estimated to be about 5 million per year.

But the environmental problems that dominate the media, that are given the most attention by environmentalist pressure groups, and that capture the imagination of the public, are the melodramatic issues. The myth of "scarce resources" is one, and was exposed in the *Public Interest* by Stephen Moore (Winter 1992). Another is global warming—"the highest-risk environmental problem the world faces today," according to Vice President Al Gore. The public is bombarded by television images showing the earth surrounded by a layer of "greenhouse gases" (GHGs) that allow the sun's energy to penetrate, but block much of the outgoing radiation from the earth's surface. These images are accompanied by dire predictions that we shall all frizzle up and that the world will become a desert—despite concurrent predictions that rainfall will increase and sea levels will rise. Such scenarios of global warming are much more exciting for the viewer than pictures showing that what the world's population needs most are more lavatories and better sewage systems.

Climate Modeling of the Greenhouse

The "consensus" opinion on climate change, as embodied in the 1990 report of the International Panel on Climate Change (IPCC), is that a doubling of equivalent carbon dioxide (an index that summarizes the effect of all man-made GHGs), is likely to occur within the next fifty years if nothing is done to reduce CO_2 emissions. Because of the time lags in the dynamics of climate change—notably those caused by the inertia introduced into the system as a result of the absorption of carbon dioxide by the oceans—the temperature increase associated with this warming commitment would not be realized until approximately 2100. At that point, the global mean surface temperature is predicted to increase by between 2° and 5° Celsius.

This conclusion has not gone unquestioned. To be sure, the scientific work that has gone into climate modeling represents a major intellectual achievement. Yet it is widely recognized that these estimates have a wide margin of error and that there are still great gaps in our understanding of how the climate is determined. The IPCC report itself contains hundreds of pages of misgivings about the potential temperature increase, and many climatologists have expressed skepticism about the reliability of the global climate models that forecast significant warming.

For example, equivalent CO_2 levels have increased by over 40 percent during the past 100 years, yet the climate has not responded in the manner predicted by the models. Consider the following anomalies:

- The amount of global warming that has occurred over the past century—roughly .45°C—is at least a factor of two less than that predicted by the most sophisticated models.
- The Northern Hemisphere, which the models say should have warmed more rapidly than the Southern Hemisphere, is no warmer than it was a half century ago.
- The models say warming should occur as a result of GHG buildup, but most of the warming during the past 100 years occurred prior to World War II—*before* most of the GHGs were emitted.

Clearly a dose of skepticism is warranted. But let us suppose that the skeptics are wrong—suppose the earth's temperature does rise by somewhere between 2°C and 5°C. How damaging is this likely to be?

Rapid Climate Change and Population Movement

There is one simple piece of evidence, which does not require vast computerized models of the world's climate or economy (our understanding of both being extremely limited), and which does at least refute the widespread notion that the human race is some tender plant that can only survive in a narrow band of plus or minus 3°C. This is the present dispersion of the world's population throughout widely different temperature zones. For example, taking the average temperatures in the coldest month in the countries concerned, 32.3 percent of the world's population lives in a band of 0°C to 3°C, whereas 18.8 percent live in a band of 12°C to 15°C, and 14.6 percent live in a band of 24°C to 27°C. Furthermore, across the world as a whole there appears to be no correlation at all between average temperatures and income levels (even excluding the Middle Eastern oil states).

Of course, it will be argued that such cross-country comparisons do not adequately take into account the difficulty of adjusting to relatively rapid changes in temperature. There is some truth in this. But as the distinguished economist Thomas Schelling has observed, the sort of rapid climate changes experienced throughout history by vast migratory movements of population were far greater than those predicted to occur during the next century as a result of global warming. The human race has always been a highly adaptable species, and is likely to become increasingly so, since most of its adaptability comes from its accumulation of technical knowledge.

Similar back-of-the-envelope calculations show that, for the United States at least, global warming could hardly have a significant impact on national income. For the sector most likely to

162

be affected is agriculture, which constitutes 2 percent of U.S. gross domestic product (GDP). Most other sectors of economic activity are not likely to be affected at all, and some, such as construction, will probably be favorably affected. So even if the net output of agriculture fell by 50 percent by the end of the next century, this is only a 1 percent reduction in GDP.

No Significant Warming

Weather satellites have been measuring temperature with great precision on a truly global scale since 1979 with a single, well-calibrated microwave radiometer instrument. As is widely known, but rarely mentioned, the satellite record from 1980–1995 shows no significant global temperature increase. While mathematical models predict a "best" temperature rise of 0.3 degrees C (0.5F) per decade, the satellite data indicate, at most, one-fifth of that. If extrapolated to the next century, the feared global warming may not even be detectable above the "noise" of natural climate fluctuations.

S. Fred Singer, *The San Diego Union-Tribune*, March 12, 1995.

Anyway, the net effect on U.S. agriculture is more likely to be negligible. In the northern states, growing periods would be longer and there would be less disruption by frosts. Further, the predicted rise in carbon dioxide—the most important green-house gas leading to global warming—is actually good for plant growth. Authoritative estimates put the impact on the net output of U.S. agriculture at somewhere between plus and minus $10 billion. Even the worst end of this range, minus $10 billion, is a trivial part of a U.S. GDP of about $6 trillion.

The Global Economy

Similar estimates for the world as a whole (which, as far as we know, were not done on the back of an envelope) also show that agricultural output in some countries will be favorably affected by global warming, whereas others will lose; and that, on balance, the net effect is likely to be negligible. Of course, the effects depend partly on how climate change affects the regional distribution of rainfall. But this is even more difficult to predict than is the global climate change.

All in all, such estimates as have been made of the overall effect of a doubling of the CO_2 concentration on the world economy suggest that world output would be reduced by about 1 or 2 percent. Suppose that these estimates are much too conservative—as they may well be given that the models on which they are based are extremely shaky. Suppose instead that world output would be reduced by 10 percent by the end of the next century below what it otherwise would be.

Well, what would it otherwise be? Over the whole period 1950 through 1985, the annual average compound rate of growth of world output *per head* has been 1.9 percent. Given that the rate of growth of world population is slowing down and that, at the same time, there has been a rapid increase in the proportion of the world's population receiving higher education or engaged in scientific research—the mainsprings of technical progress—there is good reason to believe that this growth rate will be at least maintained, if not increased. But suppose that it is only, say, 1.5 percent a year. This means that by the year 2093 world output per head will be 4.4 times as great as it is now. If global warming cuts world GDP by 10 percent, then instead of it being 4.4 times as great as it is now, it would be only 3.96 times as great. Would this be such a disaster? Would it justify imposing vast costs on the present generation rather than devoting more resources to helping developing countries overcome the environmental problems that they are facing today?

Sea Level Rise

So far we have limited our discussion to the effect of global warming on agriculture, since this is the most vulnerable sector. But what about sea level rise, the other eco-catastrophe most frequently associated with global warming?

In 1980 scientists predicted that global warming would lead to a sea level rise of as much as 8 meters. In early 1989 the prevailing estimate was down to about 1 meter. By 1990 (as in the IPCC report) the predicted sea level rise was about 65 centimeters, and current authoritative estimates put it as low as about 30 cm by the end of the next century, assuming a 4°C rise in average temperature by then. (If one were to extrapolate from trends in these estimates, the sea level would be predicted to fall, with consequences for many seaside resorts that would be as serious as sea level rises!)

But even if sea levels did rise appreciably, the economic consequences would not be disastrous. A few years ago, when the sea level was still predicted to rise by 1 meter, the U.S. Environmental Protection Agency estimated that it would cost about $100 billion to protect U.S. cities by building sea walls. Applying a 1.5 percent a year annual growth rate to the present U.S. GDP of $6 trillion gives a GDP of $26.2 trillion in 2093; so as a fraction of GDP in the year 2093, the once-and-for-all capital cost of the sea walls would be about .38 percent. As a fraction of cumulative GDP over the whole of the next 100 years—the time during which the work would have to be carried out—the amounts involved are, of course, trivial.

What about the rest of the world? Estimates by William Cline of the Institute for International Economics, also assuming a 1 meter rise in the sea level and that the costs of sea walls for other threatened coastal cities are comparable to those of the United States, show costs of adaptation, plus the value of land lost in coastal areas, of about $2 trillion. On the above assumption concerning the growth rate, world GDP in the year 2093 will be about $115 trillion—so the one-time capital cost of the sea walls would still be only about 1.7 percent of one year's GDP. As a fraction of cumulative GDP over the whole period it would still be negligible. Given that the latest predictions of the rise in the sea level are about one-third of those assumed in these estimates and that a given reduction in the estimated sea level rise implies more than a proportionate reduction in the costs of adaptation or the damage done through land loss, the costs for the world as a whole would be insignificant even if the above estimates are way off. . . .

Technological Change

Fossil fuels will probably continue to be used well after the year 2100, so it is likely that there will be greater atmospheric build-up of CO_2 and more global warming than that indicated by century-long models. William Cline, for example, has shown that over a period of three centuries, atmospheric concentration of CO_2 might increase eight-fold and temperatures might rise 10°C to 13°C or more unless action is taken to reduce carbon dioxide emissions. This, he argues, could lead to a reduction of world GDP on the order of 10 percent.

Of course, the further one projects into the future the more uncertain the already shaky projections become. There have been vast technological changes in energy use in the last century. And these will probably be dwarfed by the changes that will take place in the next three centuries, during which an incomparably greater number of people will be engaged in technological and scientific research all over the world. Hence, nobody can suppose that the world of the 23rd century will bear much resemblance to the world that we know today. It is most unlikely that energy will still be produced on a large scale by the use of dirty and polluting substances such as coal.

One need only look at the past to see how difficult it is to make predictions over hundreds of years. Who could have predicted three centuries ago that sources of power would shift from wind, water, and wood to coal, oil, natural gas, and nuclear energy? Who could have imagined that modern gas-fired, combined-cycle power plants would be about ten times as energy efficient as power stations built at the beginning of the century, or that the thermal efficiency of steam engines would be about forty times that of the earliest engines, or that the most advanced fluorescent lights would be 900 times more energy efficient than the original kerosene lamp?

Renewable Energy

And progress is now being made in developing viable forms of renewable energy that emit no carbon at all. These include the photovoltaic cells that convert sunlight directly into storable electricity. They are regarded as having great promise for local power generation in developing countries. During the past twenty years the cost of photovoltaic-generated electricity has fallen from about $60 per kilowatt hour to about 30–50 cents, and is expected to fall to about 12–16 cents within the next few years as a result of further efficiency improvements that are already in the pipeline. Industry analysts say costs could go as low as 6 cents per kilowatt hour by 2020, little more than the price of electricity from a coal-fired station.

More Carbon Dioxide Benefits Plants

Plants grown in air enriched with CO_2 are generally larger than similar plants grown in ambient air. They are usually taller, have more branches or tillers, more and thicker leaves containing greater amounts of chlorophyll, more and larger flowers, more and larger fruit, and more extensive root systems. The bottom line, however, at least in terms of economic productivity, is the harvestable yield produced; and . . . comprehensive reviews of this subject indicate that for all of the many plant species which have been studied in this regard, the mean increase in harvestable yield produced by a 330 to 660 ppm [parts per million] doubling of the air's CO_2 content is approximately 33 percent.

Sherwood Idso, *Carbon Dioxide and Global Change: Earth in Transition*, 1989.

Similarly, the cost of wind-generated electricity has dropped from 50 cents per kilowatt hour in 1975, to 25 cents in 1980, to 7–9 cents in the best locations today. A new wind turbine under development is expected to bring costs down to 5 cents or less. The U.S. Department of Energy projects that over the next twenty years, costs in moderately windy sites could fall to 3.5 cents per kilowatt hour. Wind power's contribution will ultimately be limited by the number of suitable sites. The German Future Energies Forum, an energy research group, estimates that wind power can meet no more than 15 percent of the world's energy requirements.

Then there is always the possibility of a breakthrough in geothermal, solar thermal, hydrogen fuel, or nuclear fusion technology. It is impossible to determine the ultimate potential of technologies that are barely off the drawing board, but it would be foolishly pessimistic to assume that none of these carbon-free technologies will ever become cost-competitive with fossil fuels. . . .

No Cause for Alarm

Global warming may be a problem, but it is no cause for undue alarm or drastic action. There is plenty of time to improve our understanding of the science and scrap policies that encourage economically inefficient uses of fossil fuels. It does not justify diverting vast amounts of time, energy, and funds from more urgent environmental problems, particularly those in developing countries. Nor does it justify a massive diversion of resources from high-yield projects in the private sector. We are not on the edge of an abyss and the human race is not facing destruction from the accumulation of greenhouse gases. There is far less danger of the human race being wiped out on account of the conflict between Man and the Environment than on account of the conflict between Man and Man (or Woman and Woman). Global warming is far more glamorous and telegenic, of course, than the need for better toilets and drains in the Third World. But if we truly care about the welfare of our fellow world citizens, it is these kinds of environmental issues upon which we must focus our attention.

"A world where everyone eats as much meat as Americans is a recipe for ecological disaster."

Meat Consumption Damages the Environment

Alan Thein Durning

In the following viewpoint, Alan Thein Durning argues that the production of red meat and poultry in America is contributing to numerous ecological problems. Durning warns that these problems, including intensive use of crops, energy, and water, as well as soil erosion and air and water pollution, could spread to other countries that duplicate America's method of meat production. Durning is a senior researcher specializing in the relationship between social and environmental issues for the Worldwatch Institute in Washington, D.C.

As you read, consider the following questions:

1. According to Durning, what is the difference between the role of livestock in the United States and abroad?
2. In Durning's opinion, what is the cause of world hunger?
3. How many people worldwide eat a meat-centered diet, according to the author?

Alan Thein Durning, "We Can't Keep Eating the Way We Do," *USA Today* magazine, November 1992; ©1992 by the Society for the Advancement of Education. Reprinted with permission.

When most Americans sit down to dinner, they're only a bite away from unwittingly worsening the environment. The over-looked offender lurking on their plates—between the potato and the vegetables—is a steak, pork chop, or chicken breast. The un-paid ecological price of that meat is so hefty that Americans, if they aren't careful, could end up eating themselves out of plane-tary house and home.

Putting half a pound of red meat or poultry on the table each day rings up quite a tab. The industry that supplies the world's leading nation of meat-eaters is associated with environmental ills ranging from depleted and contaminated underground water to an atmosphere pumped full of greenhouse gases. Even mod-ern egg production participates in the ecological wrongdoing.

There is nothing anti-ecological about cows, pigs, and chick-ens themselves. Rather, American-style animal farms are a bur-den on nature because they have outgrown their niche. In the United States, livestock stand at the center of agriculture, ab-sorbing much of the country's crop harvest along with vast quantities of energy and water. Elsewhere, most livestock are raised as they always have been—as a sidelight to crops, turning plants people cannot eat into food that people can.

Every nation in the world that is wealthy enough is taking notes from the United States and starting to shower resources on raising animals for meat. American-style animal farms seem to be the wave of the future.

Putting farm animals back in their place won't be easy. It will take a one-two punch of political and personal change—new farm policies in Washington and new diet policies in the kitchen.

Shifts in Diet

Some shifts in national dining habits already are apparent. Fresh fruit and vegetable sales are climbing. Many restaurants feature meatless selections and there is a booming trade in vege-tarian and low-meat cookbooks, but Americans are not yet fat-shunning herbivores. While beef consumption per person has declined slowly since 1976 and per-capita egg consumption peaked decades ago, poultry has more than taken up the slack.

Americans have been jumping from one animal product to an-other, eating fewer burgers and more chicken nuggets, fewer eggs and more turkey. Annual consumption of red meat and poultry together is at an all-time high of 178 pounds per person, up from about 137 in 1955. Each year, they eat approximately 65 pounds of beef and veal, 63 pounds of poultry, and 49 pounds of pork, plus 139 eggs and dairy products made from 70 gallons of milk. For a family of four, that works out to half a steer, an en-tire pig, and 100 chickens a year.

Churning out those quantities of animal products takes all the ingenuity agriculturalists can muster. Consequently, modern meat and egg production bears little resemblance to the family farm idyll that still colors the imagination of most Americans. In the United States, animal foods are produced in concentrated agro-industries, not cow barns or chicken coops.

In fact, where animals are raised are as much factories as farms. Of all farm animals in industrial countries, only cattle spend most of their lives in daylight. Broiler chickens live exclusively in gigantic, darkened sheds where thousands of birds are fed carefully measured rations of grain. Eggs come from similar installations, with hens crowded into stacked cages, eating from one conveyor belt and laying onto another. Pork comes from warehouse-size sheds built over sewage canals that sluice away manure.

Beef cattle graze a year before ranchers truck them to vast outdoor feedlots to be "finished" for slaughter. Their last months are spent gorging on rich rations of corn, sorghum, and soybean meal that fatten them. Dairy cows, though, continue to be raised in something like the old-fashioned farm life, often grazing outdoors part of each day.

Regardless of animal type, though, modern meat production involves intensive use—and often misuse—of grain crops, water resources, energy, and grazing areas. In addition, animal agriculture produces surprisingly large amounts of air and water pollution. Taken as a whole, livestock rearing is the most ecologically damaging part of the nation's agriculture.

A Waste of Resources

Animal farms use mountains of grain. Nearly 40% of the world's total and more than 70% of U.S. production are fed to livestock, according to U.S. Department of Agriculture data. In 1990, 162,000,000 tons of grain—mostly corn, but also sorghum, barley, oats, and wheat—were consumed. Millions of tons of protein-rich soybean meal rounded out the diet. Were all of that grain consumed directly by humans, it would nourish five times as many people as it does after being converted into meat, milk, and eggs, points out the Iowa-based Council for Agricultural Science and Technology, a nonprofit research group.

Such calculations don't mean that, if Americans ate less meat, hungry people would be fed. Worldwide, 630,000,000 people are hungry today—because they are too poor to buy food, not because it is in short supply. The more immediate problem with raising animals on grain is the waste of resources.

The effectiveness with which animals turn grains such as corn into food products varies enormously. Nearly seven pounds of corn and soy are needed to put one pound of boneless, trimmed pork on the table in the United States. Cattle require less—4.8

pounds of grain and soy per pound of meat—because, unlike pigs, they eat grass most of their lives. Dairy cows are more efficient. Because most of their nutrition comes from grass, they provide enough milk to make a pound of cheese for each three pounds of grain and soy they consume. Chickens eat 2.8 pounds of feed per pound of meat, and egg layers do better at 2.6 pounds.

American feed takes so much energy to grow—counting fuel for farm machinery and for making fertilizers and pesticides—that it might as well be a petroleum byproduct. Cornell University's David Pimentel, a specialist in agricultural energy use, estimates that 14,000 kilocalories are required to produce a pound of pork—equivalent to the energy in nearly half a gallon of gasoline. His data show that energy use, like grain consumption, declines from pork to beef, chicken, and eggs and cheese.

Almost half the energy used in U.S. agriculture goes into livestock production, the majority of it for meat. Producing the red meat and poultry eaten each year by a typical American takes energy equal to 50 gallons of gasoline. Supplying vegetarians with nourishment requires one-third less energy on the farm than supplying meat-eaters.

Guzzling Water

Feed grain guzzles water, too. In California, the nation's leading dairy-producing state, livestock agriculture takes nearly one-third—the largest share—of irrigation water, indicates independent water analyst Marc Reisner of San Francisco. Animal raising accounts for similar shares across the western states, including areas irrigated with water from dwindling underground aquifers. The beef feedlot center of the nation—Colorado, Kansas, Nebraska, and the Texas panhandle—relies on crops raised with water pumped out of the Ogallala aquifer, a depleting underground water source.

Jim Oltjen, professor of animal science, University of California, Davis, calculates that it takes approximately 390 gallons of water, mostly for irrigation, to produce one pound of beef. While chicken and pork production involve much less water, to supply Americans with meat requires nearly 100 gallons per person per day, roughly equal to what typical people use at home for all purposes.

The livestock industry uses half the territory of the continental United States for feed crops, pasture, and range. On the cropland growing animal feed and hay, soil continues eroding at a frightful pace, despite recent progress in conservation. For each pound of red meat, poultry, eggs, and milk, farm fields lose about five pounds of prime dirt.

The vast majority of land devoted to livestock is not fertile cropland or pasture, but arid public range in the West that the govern-

171

ment leases to ranchers for grazing. Although the 270,000,000 acres so used—an area larger than the 14 eastern seaboard states—supply less than five percent of the beef Americans consume, damage to the land is acute.

The worst harm was done in the great cattle drives of the 19th century. An Environmental Protection Agency (EPA)-sponsored study describes the shameful history: The land was grazed so ruthlessly that "native perennial grasses were virtually eliminated from vast areas and replaced by sagebrush, rabbitbrush, mesquite, and juniper." The exposed soil "was quickly stripped from the land by wind and water. . . . Unchecked flood flows eroded unprotected streambanks. . . . Water tables lowered. Perennial streams became intermittent or dry during most of the year."

Harold Dregne, professor of soil science, Texas Tech University, estimates that 10% of the arid West has been turned into desert by livestock. The U.S. Bureau of Land Management (BLM), which is responsible along with the U.S. Forest Service for overseeing public rangeland, reported in 1990 that nearly 70% of its expansive holdings in the West were in unacceptable condition.

Animal Wastes

With such colossal quantities of food, water, and energy going into the livestock industry, other things are bound to come out. The most distinctive is animal waste, which, after it is dried, amounts to 158,000,000 tons a year. Most comes from cattle in pastures or on the range, where waste management simply means letting natural decomposition take its course. However, about one-fourth is from stockyards, chicken factories, and other feeding facilities. There, disposal is a vexing task—it must be moved, stored, and spread without polluting water supplies.

Congress first instructed the EPA to regulate animal wastes in the Clean Water Act of 1972, but the effectiveness of that legislation is contested hotly. In the Chesapeake Bay basin, EPA reports that manure from livestock contributes about one-tenth of nitrogen and phosphorus water pollution from all sources. Nitrogen and phosphorus overfertilize algae, which grow rapidly and disturb the balance of aquatic ecosystems.

Fertilizers running off feed-crop and pasture fields also deserve an entry in animal products' environmental ledger. Adding them to animal wastes, livestock agriculture probably accounts for 40% of the nitrogen and 35% of phosphorus released into U.S. bodies of water, according to a computer model devised by Resources for the Future, an environmental research center in Washington, D.C.

As animal wastes and feed-growing chemicals contaminate the

water, animals themselves pollute the air. Cattle and other ruminants such as goats and sheep emit methane, a potent greenhouse gas, as they digest grass and other fibrous plants. Each head of beef cattle belches out about one-third of a pound of methane per pound of beef it yields. Add the carbon released from fuels burned in animal farming, and every pound of steak has the same greenhouse-warming consequences as a 25-mile drive in a typical American car.

Meat and Health

The first line of defense against animal agriculture's ecological side effects is individual action—eating less meat. The health benefits alone are compelling, since the saturated fats in animal products increase one's risk of heart disease, stroke, and even certain types of cancer.

Results of a comprehensive study of diet and health in China suggest that the healthiest range for fat consumption is 10–15% of calories, about one-third of the current U.S. rate. For Americans to lower their fat intake that much, they would have to treat meat as a delicacy instead of a staple, eating it perhaps twice a week, rather than most days.

Personal decisions to consume foods lower on the food chain won't suffice without corresponding changes in governmental codes that allow the livestock industry to deplete and pollute resources without bearing the costs. What is needed is enough citizens demanding that lawmakers take aim at the ecological side effects of meat production.

There is a lot to do. Overgrazing on public land in the West, for example, continues largely because the BLM and Forest Service subsidize and mismanage cattle grazing. This is readily apparent where fences divide public from private land. On the public side, where the government charges just $2 per head of cattle per month, ranchers run as many cattle as they can, and the land is in various stages of becoming desert. On the private side, grazing charges are typically five times higher, and the land is in far better condition, with denser and more diverse vegetation.

Furthermore, revenues the government gets from its bargain-basement prices cover scarcely one-third the costs of its present, inadequate management. They are far too meager to support such necessary efforts as vigilant monitoring of range conditions, fencing off degraded areas, and ensuring that ranchers keep their herds moving to lighten the burden on the land.

The Federal government also takes the blame for some waste of irrigation water through what Congress estimates is a $2,200,000,000 annual subsidy to western water projects. Between $500,000,000 and $1,000,000,000 of that goes to feed and fodder growers.

While western water and grazing subsidies are classic pork-barrel politics, prospects never have been better for change on both fronts. With public awareness of the issues higher than ever before, environmentalists in Congress are optimistic about ending grazing subsidies and recasting long-term public water contracts, which are coming up for review across the West.

Shifts in Consumption

From there, environmental reformers might move on to animal farms' pollution of water and air, as well as their excessive reliance on fossil fuels. If such efforts succeed, the full ecological cost of meat and egg production will show up clearly in the price of a pork chop or chicken breast. Then, people's pocketbooks will guide them down the food chain.

A low-meat diet may sound bizarre to Americans, but it is the norm for most of the Earth's population. Worldwide, only about one in four people eats a meat-centered diet, though that is changing rapidly as incomes in others nations rise. For example, the Japanese diet of rice and fish is succumbing to the onslaught of high-fat fast food. Per-capita consumption of red meat in Japan has doubled since 1975.

The logical extension of this trend—a world where everyone eats as much meat as Americans—is a recipe for ecological disaster. Supporting just the world's *current* population of 5,300,000,000 on a U.S.-style diet would require two and one-half times as much grain as all the world's farmers produce. How many planets would it take to feed the world's projected future population of 10,000,000,000 on the American ration of eight ounces of grain-fed meat a day? If the global food system is not to destroy its ecological base, the onus will be on rich nations to shift from consumption of resource-intensive foodstuffs toward modest fare.

"Beyond Beef alleges that cattle destroy the environment and cause world hunger. The scientific evidence does not support these views."

Meat Consumption Does Not Damage the Environment

Kathleen Meister

In the following viewpoint, Kathleen Meister disagrees with claims by the Beyond Beef Coalition that beef consumption contributes to environmental degradation and hunger. Meister argues that cattle graze primarily on poor quality land that is unusable for crops and that rather than destroying grasslands, cattle enrich them with their manure. Meister contends that grain constitutes only 15–20 percent of the feed that U.S. cattle consume and that such grain would not necessarily become available to the world's hungry people if it were not fed to cattle. Meister is a freelance science writer and a former research associate for the American Council on Science and Health in New York City.

As you read, consider the following questions:

1. What have been the causes of most major famines in the twentieth century, according to Meister?
2. In Meister's opinion, what are the major sources of methane?
3. How much beef does the United States import from rain-forest areas, according to the author?

At lunchtime today, you will have the opportunity to devastate the environment, promote world hunger, and wreak havoc on your own health, according to a group of activist organizations. All you have to do is eat a hamburger.

The group making these claims is the Beyond Beef coalition, headed by Jeremy Rifkin, author of the book *Beyond Beef: The Rise and Fall of the Cattle Culture*. The stated goals of Rifkin's group are to "reduce individual beef consumption by at least 50 percent; replace beef in the diet with organically raised grains, legumes, vegetables and fruits; and reform current cattle industry practices and promote humanely and organically raised beef as an alternative for those who include some beef in their diet."

In this viewpoint, the American Council on Science and Health (ACSH) critically examines the charges raised by the Beyond Beef coalition.

Beef Production and Consumption

Beyond Beef alleges that cattle destroy the environment and cause world hunger. The scientific evidence does not support these views.

With good management, cattle production need not ruin land or pollute the environment. Well managed grazing can actually improve the quality of pastureland and rangeland. Manure, when properly handled, is a valuable fertilizer rather than a damaging pollutant. The methane produced by cattle is only a very minor contributor to the so-called greenhouse effect. Cattle graze primarily on poor quality lands that cannot be used for crop production. On a worldwide basis, grazing more than doubles the land area that can be used to produce food for humans.

Reducing beef production would lead to a decrease in the demand for feed grain, but it does not necessarily follow that the grain would become available to the world's hungry people. The more likely outcome is that farmers would not grow the grain because there would be no market demand for it, or it would be diverted to other uses. Grain typically constitutes only 15 to 20 percent of the total feed consumed by beef cattle in the United States. The remainder consists of grasses and other cellulose-rich materials that humans and nonruminant animals cannot digest. The raising of ruminant animals is the only way to transform these plant materials into food for human consumption.

Contrary to allegations made by Beyond Beef and others, there is little relationship between fast-food hamburger consumption in the United States and the destruction of rainforests in Central and South America. Only about 0.6 percent of the beef consumed in the United States comes from Latin American rainforest areas, and much of that is imported as cooked, canned products rather than as ground beef.

There was a 30 percent decrease in per capita beef consumption in the United States between 1976 and 1991. If Beyond Beef's arguments were valid, one would expect that this decline would already have produced demonstrable benefits for the environment and world hunger. Yet Beyond Beef has presented no evidence of any beneficial effects.

Lean beef, in reasonable serving sizes, can be included in a healthful diet that meets current dietary guidelines. Beef makes positive nutritional contributions to the diet; its iron and zinc content is especially important.

Residues of pesticides, antibiotics and hormones in beef are well within acceptable limits and do not pose a risk to the health of the American public.

Raising Cattle Without Clearing Forests

Lately, the Greens [environmental activists] have begun to condemn the raising of beef cattle as a threat to the rain forest. Seldom have forests been cut to pasture cattle, however, for a very good reason: Cattle don't generate more profit than trees. It is true that rain forest has been cut to pasture beef cattle in Brazil, but because of an ill-advised government subsidy (now withdrawn) rather than free economic forces. Ironically, Brazil didn't even need the rain forest for pasture; its new acid-tolerant forage crops will support ten times the cattle population on the 200 million brushy acres of the Cerrados Plateau.

Dennis T. Avery, *Hudson Institute Briefing Paper*, July 1992.

As with all raw foods of animal origin, raw beef can be contaminated with bacteria that cause foodborne diseases. Adequate cooking kills these bacteria, making the meat safe to eat. With current technology, it is not possible for producers to guarantee that all meat sold to the public will be free from disease-causing bacteria. Therefore, food service personnel and consumers must do their part to prevent foodborne illness by handling foods in a sanitary manner and cooking them properly.

The U.S. Department of Agriculture intends to require new labels on all packages of meat and poultry which will give instructions for safe handling and cooking. This labeling program is worthwhile, but it should be extended to include eggs, fish and shellfish, as well as meat and poultry. All of these foods require thorough cooking to destroy microorganisms that may be present in the raw products.

The Beyond Beef coalition has raised a wide variety of arguments in support of its goal of drastically reducing beef consumption. Some, including animal rights issues and the desirability of small- versus large-scale agricultural operations, are matters of personal philosophy and are outside the scope of this scientific report. Other arguments, to be described in detail below, focus on the effect of beef production on the environment and the world food supply.

Desertification

During most of their lives, beef cattle graze on pastureland and rangeland. Beyond Beef claims that cattle are "hoofed locusts" that destroy millions of acres of grazing land in the United States each year.

It is true that uncontrolled grazing can damage grasslands. Properly managed grazing, however, is not destructive. In fact, because cattle fertilize land by depositing manure, they can enrich grasslands rather than destroy them.

Most of the 600 million acres of pastureland and rangeland in the United States are unsuitable for crop cultivation. Their only possible agricultural use is the grazing of ruminant animals (cattle or sheep). The same is true in other parts of the world. . . . If the demand for ruminant animal products ceased, these vast lands would make no contribution to feeding the people of the world.

No Contribution to Hunger

Perhaps the most disturbing charge raised by Beyond Beef is that cattle production is a major contributor to world hunger. The coalition contends that a billion people go hungry because "precious grain" is fed to cattle and other livestock. It claims that if everyone stopped eating beef, this grain could be used to feed the world's hungry people.

Beyond Beef apparently assumes that the problem of world hunger could be solved simply by increasing the amount of food available for consumption. This is an oversimplified, outdated view. The best current evidence indicates that world hunger is not caused by a simple scarcity of food. Experts believe that hunger is attributable primarily to economic and political factors and problems of distribution, rather than to an insufficient food supply. Hunger is caused by a lack of access to adequate food, rather than a shortage of food *per se*.

Even emergency situations of widespread starvation, such as the crisis in Somalia, are generally not due to a simple lack of food. Most of the major famines in this century have been caused by war, political or economic disruption or unwise government policies, rather than by acts of nature such as drought, flood or disease. Efforts to provide food aid to victims of modern famines have been hampered not by a shortage of food, but by the difficulties of wartime intervention and by problems of distribution that prevent food from reaching the people who need it most.

If people stopped eating meat, the grain now fed to livestock would not necessarily become available to the world's hungry people. Those very poor people cannot afford to buy the grain or transport it from the United States to their homes. Farmers might donate a small amount of the grain to relief organizations, but they would not be able to stay in business if they gave away a substantial proportion of their crops. The more likely outcome is that farmers would not grow the grain if there were no market demand for it, or it would be diverted to other uses, such as the production of alcohol for fuel.

It is also important to point out that only a small proportion of the feed consumed by beef cattle consists of grain. In the system of beef production currently used in the United States, cattle consume grain only during the latter part of their lives, when they are housed in feedlots. Grain typically constitutes 15 to 20 percent of the total feed consumed by the animals at all stages of their life cycle. Less than five pounds of feed grains are used to produce one pound of beef. The remainder of the animals' intake consists of grasses and other cellulose-rich materials that humans and nonruminant animals cannot digest. The raising of ruminant animals is the only way to transform these plant materials into foods for human consumption.

Cattle can be raised entirely on grass, with no grain at all. This is the custom in many developing areas. In the United States, however, it makes good economic sense to "finish" cattle on grain because it is readily available at a reasonable price. Despite Beyond Beef's frequent references to "precious grain," there is a surplus rather than a shortage of grain in the United States. Many American farmers who could not otherwise make a profit by growing grain are able to stay in business because they can sell their crops to livestock producers.

Cattle: Not a Source of Pollution

Beyond Beef argues that organic waste from livestock is a massive source of pollution. But as with the destruction of grasslands, this is a matter of management rather than an inevitable consequence of meat production. Manure is indeed a harmful pollutant if it ends up in the wrong places. But in the right places, it is a valuable fertilizer.

The manure produced by grazing cattle is recycled naturally into the soil and plants of the grazing lands. Most of the manure produced in feedlots is removed and applied to soil as a fertilizer. When used in this way, animal wastes are not a source of pollution; instead, they replenish the organic matter and nutrients in soil and enhance plant growth. Federal and state laws prohibit the discharge of livestock manure into surface or groundwaters.

Beyond Beef also contends that cattle production is responsible for the release of large quantities of methane, a greenhouse gas which is thought to contribute to global warming, into the atmosphere. Cattle do produce methane as a byproduct of their ruminant digestion, but the impact of cattle flatulence on global warming is far smaller than Beyond Beef claims. One expert has calculated that driving six miles each way to buy a hamburger would result in 100 times as much greenhouse gas as the production of the hamburger. Another has pointed out that the amount of methane emitted by one cow in a year has the same effect on global warming as the fuel burned to power a single 75-watt light bulb. The major sources of methane are wetlands, rice paddies, biomass burning, drilling for oil, landfills and coal mines, not cattle. In fact, the National Academy of Sciences has calculated that all ruminant animals, both wild and domesticated (including sheep, goats, deer, buffalo, giraffes and camels, as well as cattle) account for only five percent of total greenhouse gas production.

Destroying Nature?

Beyond Beef argues that cattle are causing "the extinction of plant and animal species" and "the purposeful extermination of millions of predators." More succinctly, they claim that cattle are destroying nature.

The problem here is not with the facts but with their interpretation. In discussing these issues, Beyond Beef ignores the needs of people and the ways in which people must modify nature if they are to earn a living and feed themselves. The productive use of land inevitably changes the types of plants and animals that live on it. If humans left all of the earth's land in its natural state, there would be no food for the human population.

In his book, Rifkin claims that "the elimination of beef will be accompanied by an ecological renaissance, a grand restoration of nature on every continent. . . . Ancient rivers will flow. . . . Streams and springs will come to life. . . . Predator species will thrive. . . . Buffalo will once again roam the West." This is a romantic view, not a realistic one.

The destruction of tropical rainforests is an issue of concern to many Americans. The idea, raised by Beyond Beef and others, that Americans can help to preserve the rainforests by reducing their consumption of beef (particularly fast food hamburgers) has great emotional appeal. In actuality, however, there is little relationship between U.S. beef consumption and the fate of Central and South American rainforests.

The United States is not dependent on foreign sources for its beef supply. About 94 percent of the beef consumed in the United States is produced domestically; only six percent is imported. Central America and Brazil account for only about 10 percent of the imports. Thus, about 0.6 percent of all beef consumed in the United States comes from rainforest areas. No beef from Brazil ends up in fast food hamburgers, because Brazil exports only cooked or canned beef products (such as canned corned beef) to the United States. Central American beef may be used in hamburgers, but it constitutes no more than 0.35 percent of all beef consumed in the United States. Most hamburger imports come from Australia and New Zealand, rather than from tropical rainforest areas.

The Missing Evidence

It is important to make one final point. Beyond Beef envisions that if American consumers substantially decreased their beef intake, there would be vast improvements in the environment and drastic decreases in world hunger and poverty. There has already been a substantial decrease in per capita beef consumption in the United States—from the peak level of almost 90 pounds per person per year in 1976 to about 63 pounds in 1991. So where is the evidence of benefits? Nowhere in the 353 pages of Rifkin's book or in the extensive literature published by his organization is there any documentation of environmental or world health improvements attributable to this decline in beef intake. Evidence of such improvements would be the best possible argument in favor of the Beyond Beef campaign. Yet the coalition is strangely silent on this subject.

Periodical Bibliography

The following articles have been selected to supplement the diverse views presented in this chapter.

Stephen Budiansky — "The Doomsday Myths," *U.S. News & World Report*, December 13, 1993.

Gregg Easterbrook — "The Good Earth Looks Better," *New York Times*, April 21, 1995.

Economist — "Biology Meets the Dismal Science," December 25, 1993–January 7, 1994.

Final Frontier — Special section on monitoring the earth from space, May/June 1995. Available from PO Box 534, Mt. Morris, IL 61054-7852.

Christopher Flavin and Odil Tunali — "Getting Warmer," *World Watch*, March/April 1995.

Daniel Glick — "The Alarming Language of Pollution," *National Wildlife*, April/May 1995.

Al Gore — "Global Climate Change: Protecting the Environment," *U.S. Department of State Dispatch*, April 3, 1995.

Robert M. Lilienfeld and William L. Rathje — "Six Enviro-Myths," *New York Times*, January 21, 1995.

Lester W. Milbrath — "Climate and Chaos: Societal Impact of Sudden Weather Shifts," *Futurist*, May/June 1994.

Thomas Gale Moore — "Why Global Warming Would Be Good for You," *Public Interest*, Winter 1995.

National Geographic World — Special issue on sustaining the earth, April 1995.

G.T. Pope — "The Hole Truth," *Popular Mechanics*, April 1995.

Peter H. Stone — "Forecast Cloudy: The Limits of Global Warming Models," *Technology Review*, February/March 1992.

T. Tamkins — "Ozone Crisis?" *American Health*, May 1994.

Michael Weber — "Oceans at Risk," *Popular Science*, May 1995.

World Press Review — Special section on global warming, July 1995.

What Will Be the Future of International Relations?

21ST CENTURY EARTH

Chapter Preface

The history of humanity is replete with armed and violent conflicts—wars, insurrections, coups, and terrorism. But many authorities consider the twentieth century, marked by two world wars, to be the most violent era ever. Analysts debate whether the world will become increasingly turbulent or more peaceful during the twenty-first century.

However, some of the world's regions, such as Africa and the Middle East, are more conflict-ridden than others. In their book *The Real World Order: Zones of Peace/Zones of Turmoil*, authors Max Singer and Aaron Wildavsky separate world regions into two categories: zones of peace and democracy (North America, Western Europe, Japan, Australasia, and parts of South America) and zones of turmoil and development (Africa, Asia, and Central America). The latter category contains 85 percent of the world's population, the authors note.

Many analysts, including Robert D. Kaplan, author of *The Coming Anarchy*, maintain that in the early twenty-first century much of the world—including the zones of peace—will suffer from conflict and violence. According to Kaplan, this turmoil will be generated by

> disease, overpopulation, unprovoked crime, scarcity of resources, refugee migrations, the increasing erosion of nation-states and national borders, and the empowerment of private armies, security firms, and international drug cartels. . . . The map of the world . . . will be an ever-mutating representation of chaos.

Other political scientists and experts are more optimistic and contend that more regions will become zones of peace during the twenty-first century. For example, Yale professor Bruce Russett argues that an increase in democracy worldwide (following the demise of many communist regimes in the late 1980s and early 1990s) will contribute to international peace: "The more democratic a nation is, the more peaceful its relations with other democracies are likely to be. The chance for wide democratization now offers a new policy of building democratic peace." Defense and intelligence expert Henry S. Rowen of Stanford University envisions the spread of zones of peace as regions "within which international conflict has such a low probability that it can be considered nearly impossible."

The likelihood of increased conflict or peace in the twenty-first century is one of the aspects of the future of international relations debated in this chapter.

"Despite all their domestic troubles, an open-ended club of democracies is already forming."

Democratic Nations Will Govern World Affairs

Harlan Cleveland

Harlan Cleveland is the president of the World Academy of Art and Science in Vienna, Virginia, a former U.S. assistant secretary of state, and the author of *Birth of a New World: An Open Moment for International Leadership*. In the following viewpoint, Cleveland argues that a "club of democracies" can cooperate to maintain world peace in the "new world disorder." Cleveland maintains that over the next generation these democratic nations will consult on decisions concerning U.N. affairs, peacekeeping, economic growth, and social development.

As you read, consider the following questions:

1. What two values does Cleveland believe will collide with cultural diversity?
2. According to the author, what are the two tiers of international cooperation?
3. How has the club of democracies influenced world affairs, according to Cleveland?

Harlan Cleveland, "Ten Keys to World Peace," *The Futurist*, July/August 1994. Reproduced with permission from *The Futurist*, published by the World Future Society, 7910 Woodmont Ave., Suite 450, Bethesda, MD 20814.

In a talk to the World Future Society in 1991, I voiced my worries about the global collision of cultural diversity—which President John F. Kennedy pledged to make the world safe for—with two other values on which the twenty-first century will also have to be built.

One of these collisions is clearly the clash of group rights, asserted by ambitious cultural and ethnic communities, with the contrasting ideology of individual and inalienable human rights—the idea that a person has rights not because he or she belongs to a nation, religion, gender, ethnic category, economic class, or even family, but by virtue of having been born into the human race.

The other collision with cultural diversity comes from the outward push of modern science and technology, which makes it possible, and therefore necessary, to think of the world as one—as a global market for goods, services, and money, as a biosphere to be monitored and protected, and as a community in which nuclear war might be outlawed and human hunger eliminated.

The community gives each of us part of our valued identities; it is an important component of reality. But so, too, is the value of each person as an individual, and so, too, is the need to shape more-inclusive communities and institutions that are made possible by modern knowledge.

So, while celebrating cultural diversity and the political change it's bringing about on four continents, we need to think hard about reconciling it with both individual human rights *and* global human opportunities. That's the triple dilemma—the trilemma—of the 1990s. How do we formulate the principles and fashion the institutions that will reconcile with each other these lively ambitions in the new world disorder?

A Third Try for Peaceful Change

There are many new opportunities for international leadership in this time of world disorder. In the mid-1980s, thirty-one of my colleagues from twenty-four countries began doing what we called "postwar planning without having the war first."

Because there had already been two tries at world order in this century, our work together became a first draft of "the third try." But the aim of the third try cannot be "world order." That phrase has too often meant the defense of the status quo by those who were, temporarily, the most powerful. The object of this new try must be to ensure peaceful change in a world made safe for diversity. The future always has to be grafted onto the past. So for a third try, the United Nations Charter is the obvious starting point.

Years ago, a diplomat assigned to U.N. headquarters in New York gave me an important clue. "There's nothing wrong with the first five pages of the Charter," he said. "It's those following fifty pages that get in the way."

It is true that the elaborate procedural architecture of the United Nations as an organization has often obstructed the pursuit of the common purposes set forth in the first few policy paragraphs. What's interesting and suggestive for the future is that, during the past half century, the agencies and processes that have worked pretty well in practice are those that remained loyal to the Charter's purposes and principles, but played fast and loose with its procedures.

A Concert of Major States

The nations of the world need a more orderly and efficient means to address international problems. At the same time, the United States needs a more structured means of fulfilling its role of leadership—one that will serve both national and universal interests. If structured carefully, a "concert of major states" might serve both needs.

This *concert* would include states with a legitimate claim to a major international role. It should represent the majority of the world's peoples, military forces, and economic products and thus should at least include the United States, the United Kingdom, France, Germany, Italy, Russia, Japan, Brazil, and India.

Although the political systems in several of these countries remain shaky, all are functioning democracies. . . .

The concert of major states will redefine what it means to be a world leader. Nations seeking acceptance into this informal, collegial club will realize the need for adherence to, or at least movement toward, universal democratic norms. It is hoped that association with the concert will strengthen and stabilize democracy in *all* member countries, but particularly in Russia and its neighboring states.

Raymond D. Gastil, *The Futurist*, July/August 1994.

For example, the United Nations' peacekeeping role (stepping in between belligerents) is not spelled out in the Charter's fifty pages of procedure. Yet, it has won a Nobel Peace Prize and is clearly consonant with the Charter's purposes to ensure, as the Preamble says, "that armed forces shall not be used, save in the common interest."

As another example, the Charter describes voting procedures but does not require voting. Most of the successful actions taken by agencies of the United Nations have been agreed on by consensus. When votes have been taken, it is mostly to confirm what has already been agreed on by consensus, or to record what hasn't yet been fully agreed upon—as in the Law of the Sea Treaty.

A third example is that the Charter's procedures describe an organization of governments and sees the parties to a dispute as being only governments. Not until the Charter drafters got to Article 71 did it occur to them that nongovernmental organizations might need to be consulted, and then only on matters of economic and social relevance. Even the chapter on the secretary-general assumes that international staff work would be done only by U.N. employees.

Yet, the history of the last half century is replete with examples of nongovernmental organizations taking the lead in carrying out international policies, with the United Nations' official members catching up late, if at all.

Most of the systematic training for U.N. peacekeeping has been done by the nongovernmental International Peace Academy. Much of the mediation and conciliation efforts undertaken by the secretary-general have been done by people loaned to him or engaged by him outside the "international civil service," or even sometimes by volunteers with no formal U.N. affiliation. And most of the useful fact-finding and publishing on violations of human rights guaranteed by the Charter have been done by such nongovernmental gadflies as Amnesty International.

So strengthening the United Nations for the years ahead means taking its purposes and principles very seriously, but building fresh institutions within the framework of the Charter that reflect the probable realities of the future. Viewed this way, the United Nations is needed more than ever, but new work-ways must be developed to bypass not the Charter's stated purposes but its outdated processes.

Uncentralizing Global Power

A clear distinction should be made between the two tiers of international cooperation: (1) the more centralized public-policy decisions with universal participation, where debate is encouraged and agreement reached on standards, norms, goals, and codes of ethics, and (2) the more operational, *uncentralized* processes, where many different enterprises and authorities "do their own thing," acting within the framework of the agreed standards and norms. In some cases, especially in the world economy, this operational level will be a market system.

This distinction between the collective establishment of standards and the dispersed bargaining, sharing, and clearing is not well described by the much misused word "decentralization." In a decentralized system, the control is still in a central office. It's

188

the center that decides how partial controls will be exercised by subordinate authorities and keeps track of them through a central accounting system. This is why I use the word "uncentralized" for a system in which "many flowers" are encouraged to bloom, "many points of light" stimulated to shine. Learning works from the bottom up.

In such a two-tier system, setting norms and standards is everyone's business. That is not unrealistic. In practice, the world community has already made quite a lot of global policy.

Guidelines for Managing Peace

Here are ten guidelines for managing peace in a pluralistic world:

1. No nation, region, race, or creed is going to be in general charge.

2. Nations and their citizens, without homogenizing their cultural identities, can and will pool their collective learnings in win-win systems for shared purposes.

3. For much of what needs to be done, people can agree on next steps to be taken together without having to agree on *why* they are agreeing.

4. Some common norms are already widely accepted:
- Territorial integrity. Iraq's 1990 [invasion of Kuwait] provoked a worldwide coalition in defense of this principle.
- The inviolability of diplomatic missions. The violations are dramatic because they are rare.
- The nonuse of nuclear, chemical, and biological weapons.
- The immunity of civilian aircraft and ships. A few brutal attacks and tragic accidents have served to strengthen norms against hijacking or firing on innocent craft.
- An international obligation to help refugees.
- The inadmissibility of colonial rule.
- The unacceptability of officially sanctioned racial discrimination.
- The undeniable equality of women.
- And the full menu of human rights described in the Universal Declaration of 1948, reinforced in the Helsinki Final Act of 1975.

5. In a third try, most of the world's people, and even their governments, might now agree on some even more far-reaching norms:
- A third World War is wholly impermissible.
- Nuclear weapons are militarily irrelevant—and should be made irrelevant to political conflict.
- Local conflicts should be insulated whenever possible from outside involvement to prevent any kind of escalation.
- Growth with fairness, not "equilibrium" or "balance," is the

purpose of economic policy.

- The lives of innocent bystanders should not be used as political bludgeons.
- The quality of human life worldwide must be protected from catastrophic degradation of the atmosphere and the biosphere.
- And this above all: No child in the world should go to bed hungry.

6. A review of what works best in the new world disorder drives us to belated recognition of the crucial role played by major nongovernments. These include corporations whose decisions affect people's lives and fortunes, professional associations whose expertise educates and informs, religious movements with their unique capacities for love or hate, the distinctively international scientific community, and advocacy groups that mobilize people for behavioral change.

7. Some global issues require actions by millions of individuals, families, and small groups. There is an increasingly important role for the communications media in spreading the word and developing wide consensus as a basis for political cooperation.

8. When governments have to work together to make something different happen, they increasingly decide from the outset to act by consensus. In the many cultures accustomed to practicing decision making by "consensus," that word does not mean "unanimous consent." It means something more like *the acquiescence of those who care* about a particular decision, *supported by the apathy of those who don't.*

9. Almost nothing in world affairs needs to involve everyone. What's needed to handle each problem is a community of the concerned, what my MIT [Massachusetts Institute of Technology] colleague Lincoln Bloomfield was the first to call a "coalition of the willing." Those who can and will act have to take whatever action is to be taken. If a collective task is to be accomplished, it cannot be subject to acquiescence by the least relevant or least cooperative member of the world community—nor by the most apathetic one.

10. But in matters affecting the globe we all share, those who do act have an inescapable obligation to explain to the rest of the world what they are doing together and why. So we also need to open consultative forums where stakeholders not able or willing to act can nevertheless be heard.

The Club of Democracies

Who is both able and willing to work hard in this global workshop?

Three of the leading clusters of advanced information societies are already closely associated as the nucleus of an emerging,

190

open-ended "club of democracies": the United States and Canada, the European Union, and Japan. The parts of Europe outside the European Union and a good many of the larger or more successful developing countries will qualify as influential states and will join the club whether the more established democracies like it or not.

This expanding fellowship, acting in shifting patterns of cooperation and competition, will decide over the next generation what the formal organs of the United Nations will be empowered to do. They will decide what to do together within the U.N. Charter, but outside its procedures. They will decide how stability and fairness are to be reconciled in peacekeeping and peacemaking, economic growth and social development, and in using and protecting the global commons. In sum, this club of democracies will decide whether and how to work together worldwide for what the U.N. Charter called "better standards of life in larger freedom."

The politics of this club of democracies will be consultative. Writing about American local communities, public philosopher John Gardner described consultative politics in world affairs: "The play of conflicting interests in a framework of shared purposes is the drama of a free society. It is a robust exercise and a noisy one, not for the fainthearted or the tidy-minded. . . . Wholeness incorporating diversity is the transcendental goal of our time."

Despite all their domestic troubles, an open-ended club of democracies is already forming. It is a consultative group of those willing and able to act together—in different guises, with differing leadership for different problems—on issues requiring an unusual degree of international cooperation to get anything done.

The club of democracies was at the core of the resistance to Iraqi aggression in the Persian Gulf. Its economic core is visible, if anemic, in the periodic summits of the "Group of Seven" [the seven largest industrialized nations] on trade and money issues. It is the guts of U.N. peacekeeping, the determined majority in the U.N. Security Council, the main source of support for the World Bank and the International Monetary Fund, the moving force behind such disparate events as the treaties to protect the global ozone shield and the 1990 "children's summit."

The Center of Action

The club of democracies is not a new organization, complete with secretariat and a permanent headquarters somewhere. It is a confederation of the concerned, a center of initiative, a habit of consultation. It coordinates government policies where governments are the main actors. And it will increasingly have to bring nongovernments into consultation where they, too, are major actors—as they obviously are on the world economy, international development, and the global environment.

If you bring together the nations that are now governed by consent and add those that are trying in their fashion to get that way, you have the bulk of the world's economic output, communication lines, science and technology, financial resources, and military power. Those who have a stake in a thoroughly democratic world have the resources, if they work together, to make change peaceful and prosperous, and thereby help democracy itself to flourish in its own diverse patterns.

"Nation-states such as Germany, Italy, Denmark, the United States, and Japan will no longer be the most relevant socio-economic entities."

City-Regions Will Supersede Nations in World Affairs

Riccardo Petrella

Riccardo Petrella heads the European Community's Forecasting and Assessment of Science and Technology division in Brussels, Belgium. In the following viewpoint, Petrella predicts that by the middle of the twenty-first century, "technologically highly developed city-regions" will replace nation-states as the world's predominant socioeconomic and political entities. Petrella contends that these city-regions—Orange County, California; Osaka, Japan; Lyon, France; and others—will exert their influence in an alliance with transnational companies in the future global economy.

As you read, consider the following questions:

1. What is the triadic approach to development, according to Petrella?
2. How could the vast majority of the world's population be relegated to a "disintegrating wasteland," in the author's opinion?
3. According to Petrella, why is the triadic approach the least effective way of using global resources?

Riccardo Petrella, "World City-States of the Future," *New Perspectives Quarterly*, Fall 1991. Reprinted with permission.

The new world order taking shape is not the one imagined by obsolete statesmen of the cold-war era. Rather than an order of nation-states weighing in on a new global balance of power, an archipelago of technologically highly developed city-regions—or mass-consumer *technopoles*—is evolving. These city-regions are linked together by transnational business firms that bypass the traditional nation-state framework in their ceaseless pursuit of new customers, as well as by thousands of local and transnational Non-Governmental Organizations that are active in the promotion of customer protection and citizens rights.

A New Web

If present trends continue, for better or for worse, by the middle of the next century nation-states such as Germany, Italy, Denmark, the United States, and Japan will no longer be the most relevant socio-economic entities and the ultimate political configuration. Though the nation-state entity will not disappear, *national identities* and cultures will survive or new ones will emerge. Areas like Orange County, Osaka, the Lyon region, or the new Ruhrgebiete [Germany's Ruhr River district] will acquire predominant socio-economic and political status. Already within Europe, a new web of cooperative programs has mushroomed between Barcelona, Lyon, Milan, Strasbourg, and Stuttgart—all without passing through a national hierarchy of capitals or central ministries. Lyon, which already is home to Europe's largest intercity airport, recently established direct service to and from the U.S.

Evidence shows a strong movement toward the emergence in the next few decades of a Europe of city-regions.

At the world level, the real decision-making powers of the future, it appears, will be a network of transnational companies in alliance with city-regional governments. Today the decision-making powers are already the networks of transnational companies, with the support of declining nation-state governments.

The High-Tech Hanseatic League

On a global scale, this new order will resemble the flourishing fourteenth- and fifteenth-century European economy, which was governed by the Hanseatic [northern European] cities and intercity alliances that hosted trading guilds and their networking merchants. The postnational economic geography of the future will look very much like that of prenational times.

As the urbanist John Friedmann has sketched it, today's global economy is principally organized through a system of some thirty world-city regions—nodes of the world capitalist system. These are London, New York, Tokyo, Toronto, Chicago, San Francisco, Los Angeles, Houston, and Miami; Mexico City and Sao Paulo;

Seoul, Taipei, Hong Kong, Singapore, and Bangkok; Paris, Zurich, Vienna, Milan, Madrid, and more or less the whole of Holland [Randstadt].

This trend toward a new Hanseatic phase of the world economy, with its multiplication of interfirm consortia and networks between U.S., Japanese, and European firms—especially in high technology—has been intensified by the *triadic approach* to development. This business strategy, backed up by government policies, is based on the idea that in order to remain competitive, any internationally oriented firm or economy must be present simultaneously in the largest, increasingly integrated, consumer market comprising America, Japan, and Europe. Kenichi Ohmae, the Japanese management guru, calls this the "global insider" strategy; Sony's Akio Morita calls it "global localization."

The aim of such a strategy is to attain global technological and industrial supremacy by capturing the allegiance of those with the means to be consumers; that is, about seven hundred to eight hundred million people worldwide.

Future Political Entities

Some forecasters see a future world not with today's 150–200 states, but with hundreds, even thousands of mini-states, city-states, regions, and noncontiguous political entities. The decades to come will see even stranger possibilities emerge as existing national boundaries lose their legitimacy.

Alvin Toffler and Heidi Toffler, *War and Anti-War*, 1993.

I call this approach "myopic utilitarian opportunism" because it excludes—save for the tiny fraction of elites in such world cities as Sao Paulo, Mexico City, and Hong Kong, or in places like Caracas, Cairo, and Bombay—any concern with development among what, by the year 2020, will be the world's other seven billion–plus inhabitants. Even if sixty to eighty million Indians, for example, were linked to the prosperous archipelago of the privileged territories fifty years hence, ten times as many Indians would be excluded. And, estimates suggest, by the year 2020, more than twenty mega-cities in the poor world, with populations of twenty-five million each, will appear.

A Growing Gap

Obviously, committing the vast majority of the world's population to a global underclass is not only unjust but unsustainable in a well-armed world that is ecologically interdependent and exposed to unstoppable waves of mass migration.

Absent a strategy to use science and technology constructively in the global interest—rather than in the competitive interest of becoming Number One—the future, I fear, will be characterized by a prosperous network of transnational firms and revitalized capitals of innovation that will grow dynamically together in what is basically a G-7 [the world's seven largest industrialized nations] club, leaving behind the great mass of humanity that doesn't qualify as customers.

By absurdly redefining humanity as *customers*, the population of the planet in such a new world order would be conveniently reduced from an order of eight to one! Imagine how this *order* would redraw the world map: on one side we would see a dynamic, tightly linked, fast-developing archipelago of technopoles comprising less than one-eighth of the world's population; on the other side would be a vast, disconnected and disintegrating wasteland which is home to seven out of every eight inhabitants of the earth.

Every day, this disarticulated world—what Alvin Toffler refers to as the growing gap between the fast and slow worlds—is being formed before our eyes. As universities are closing all across Africa, every week the European Community [EC], Japan, and the U.S. (as well as Korea) are building new research parks and university facilities. As new *airtropolises* are being constructed in Japan and Singapore, and a new High Speed Train network is developing in Western Europe, the transportation infrastructure in Africa is worse than it was in 1981, and is continuing to deteriorate. While Mercedes and Mitsubishi are joining up to capture world markets, famine and malnutrition are catching up with millions in sub-Saharan Africa. The EC budget for one research program—the Esprit microelectronics consortium—is fourteen times the total EC aid to the entire continent of Latin America.

Triadic Techno-Nationalism

When Europeans, Americans, and Japanese talk about globalization, they always seem to talk as if the world beyond their borders didn't exist. And they increasingly tend to speak about each other in the terminology of *technonationalism* or *technological patriotism.*

People are told they are soldiers in an open technological war; that their countries are fighting for survival; that they must be more and more skilled and educated if they want to find and keep a job. They are told that their future is linked with the mastery and use of high-tech products and systems, combined with good management and new organizational models. Productivity, efficiency, effectiveness, flexibility, reliability, and quality are the new by-words in the vocabulary of commercial war.

Individuals and masses of people have been promoted from the *factors of production*, as they were known during the industrial age, to *human resources*.

Commercial performance has become the whole point of national policy under the triadic approach; it has become the primary objective of national ingenuity and action. Over the past twenty years, the ideology of competitiveness, based on technological innovation and nourished by scientific advance, has overshadowed all other objectives.

In Europe this has meant that national priority in the development of science and technology has been given to measures that favor and facilitate successful integration of domestic firms into triadic consortia and networks.

The Rise of the Region-State

The noise you hear rumbling in the distance is the sound of the late 20th century's primary engine of economic prosperity—the region-state—stirring to life. . . .

It is through region-states that participation in the global economy actually takes place, largely because they are the only human-scale political entities whose economic policies put the global logic of individual well-being ahead of cheap nationalism and the interests of national political elites. These region-states may in fact stretch across national borders: Hong Kong and southern China, for instance, or San Diego and Tijuana.

Kenichi Ohmae, *The Wall Street Journal*, August 16, 1994.

Not surprisingly, such an approach favors the most developed regions of the EC, where the potential and capability to compete in the global markets are considerably more developed. The robotics industry in Italy is a good example.

The production of robots and their diffusion into Italian manufacturing are characterized by strong regional inequalities between the north and south of that country, with the southern region participating to a very modest degree in this new technology. The intensification of triadic power will thus largely benefit the already developed urban regions of London, Frankfurt, Paris, and Zurich; it will mean little for Naples or Sicily. For Italy the same applies to the development of financial services. And, naturally, to the extent serious competition remains between countries in Europe, the worse the consequences for regional development. . . .

The rise of the new high-tech Hanseatic network has eroded

the basis of democracy that was associated with the development of the nation-state. Territorial accountability has been radically diminished. City councils may spend weeks debating the allocation of $200,000 for housing rehabilitation, while the British financial houses transfer $120 billion from one market to another within minutes, fundamentally affecting the currency balances, exchange rates and terms of industrial finance. Where's the democracy?

Globalization Process

The globalization of technological innovation is not a new phenomenon. The chemical industry (particularly pharmaceuticals), the steel industry, and car manufacturing have been globally organized for decades. A few examples: Through joint ventures, personnel exchanges, cross-licensing research, and production partnerships, or through shares of ownership, Chrysler is linked to Mitsubishi, Samsung, and Fiat as well as Volkswagen; GM is linked to Toyota, Isuzu, and Suzuki; Ford is linked to Mazda and BMW; Nissan is linked to Volkswagen as well as Daewoo; and Mitsubishi with Hyundai.

Globalization today is accelerating at the heart of the technological revolution—in semiconductors and computers, robots, telecommunications, and biotechnology. There is increasing integration, cooperation, and strategic links between multinationals, who are in turn allied with local manufacturers. Such alliances, for example, link Motorola with Nippon Electric Company and, in turn, to Hitachi; Nippon Telephone and Telegraph is linked to IBM as well as to Mitsui and Hitachi; Sony is linked to RCA; the Swedish Ericsson company to Honeywell and Sperry; Ricoh is tied to Rockwell.

In the electronics industry, strategic partnerships have been established between Hitachi and Hewlett-Packard, between Fujitsu and Texas Instruments, and between Siemens and Intel.

Many factors are pushing this globalization—high R&D [research and development] costs that must be shared, the limited pool of high-quality skilled scientists and engineers, and the multinational corporate system itself, which requires telecommunications, organized research, coordinated production, and financial infrastructure on a global scale.

In fifteen to twenty years' time many believe that there will remain only eight to ten large world consortia in telecommunications, five to eight in the automobile industry, three to five in tire manufacturers, and so on.

The presence of these global companies, with their global markets and quests for advanced communication infrastructures and socio-cultural services, is reshaping the functions, the internal organization, and the image of cities for better and for worse. As hosts to corporate divisions, universities, research labs, and sophisticated consumers—as well as large pools of low-wage labor, often immigrants—cities have become the real loci of the innovation process.

Rather than going global, one alternative to the widely shared triadic strategy gaining appeal is "going European in an open world economy." In this way, Europe as a whole could pay more attention to its internal regional inequalities as a matter of policy—gaining scales of efficiency by sharing R&D and joint projects, like the successful Airbus—and to the definition and implementation of the proper conditions for a new European social contract.

However, the absence of a large enough internal market (purchasing power in the East is still paltry) and—more significantly—the weakness of European common socio-economic projects limit the possibilities for European firms to develop strategic capabilities strong enough to take on their world competitors. Since economic globalization, driven by the market, is happening much faster than the politically managed economic integration of Europe, European firms risk remaining prisoners of a vicious, limiting circle if they chose *going European* only.

There is yet another, in my view preferable, option of global common development. Aware of the pernicious influence of the competitiveness metaphor and of the long-standing dangerous effects of the war for triadic power, the most highlighted and inspired sectors of society from Europe, the U.S., and Japan should give priority to science and technological development—not in order to compete for global leadership of a market of seven hundred million people, but to seek development for the entire eight billion inhabitants of the planet fifty years from now.

The World at Risk

The triadic approach, if it remains dominant, will result in so widening the gap between the privileged archipelago and the sea of impoverished peoples that the whole world system will be at risk. Moreover, the competitive triadic approach also is the least effective way of using global resources, particularly the opportunities associated with science and technology, because their chosen challenges primarily concern how to find new products for the market rather than how to resolve the most pressing problems of humanity.

Obviously, competition between economic powers is not going to stop. It would be naïve to expect such a thing. But, its importance can be lessened and brought into greater balance with the logic of cooperation organized around projects that focus on reversing the disintegration of Africa, Arab countries, Latin America, or the Indian subcontinent and linking them to the fast world.

"At no time in this century have the prospects of collective violence been . . . stronger than they are today."

Conflict Among Nations

Joseph F. Coates

In the following viewpoint, written prior to the demise of the Soviet Union, Joseph F. Coates argues that a variety of factors is contributing to economic, ethnic, and religious conflict worldwide, increasing the chances of violence or war in the decades ahead. Coates maintains that although the United Nations will expand its role to ensure peace, many types of "collective violence" among ethnic groups and nations will become more commonplace. Coates is the president of Coates and Jarratt, a future forecasting firm in Washington, D.C.

As you read, consider the following questions:

1. What have been the effects of decolonization in the Third World, in Coates's opinion?
2. What two new forms of violence does the author identify?
3. In Coates's opinion, what is the likelihood that economic prosperity will deter ethnic and religious conflict?

Reprinted by permission of the publisher from Joseph F. Coates, "The Future of War," *Technological Forecasting and Social Change*, vol. 38 (1990), pp. 201–205. Copyright 1990 by Elsevier Science Inc.

Were Major Barbara's father, Undershaft [an arms manufacturer in George Bernard Shaw's play *Major Barbara*], with us today, he would chortle with delight at the prospects of war over the next decades. At no time in this century have the prospects of collective violence been more universal, diversified, and stronger than they are today. Consider:

- The drivers of change giving new vigor to violence.
- The various forms of collective violence.
- Implications of that surge of violence for people and nations of goodwill.

Throughout the world, America has been and continues to be the promised land, the standard of human success, and the embodiment of the fulfillment of a broad range of human aspirations for prosperity, health, freedom, mobility, and the good things in life. That expanding image of American culture has been augmented today by television and by films. American culture is the dominant culture in the world. English is the universal language of the world's middle class and, increasingly, of business, industry, and diplomacy. One result of the U.S. dominance in entertainment and its delivery of culturally oriented messages are the comparisons, in most parts of the world, with what could be—the U.S. situation, and what is—the local situation. Information technology has led to a rise in global expectations and promoted a global homogenization of values and expectations.

Trends Promoting Violence

Low-cost transportation allows the direct cultural injection of values into people, as tourists and, more deeply, as students. One consequence of American cultural imperialism we see was pathetically illustrated in June 1989 in Tiananmen Square [when Chinese troops shot and killed hundreds of student demonstrators]. The plan of the old-guard Chinese leadership was to have their students go abroad and selectively pick up only the economically and technologically useful lessons from the West. Instead, the inevitable happened, they picked up the cultural messages as well, and on returning home became unacceptably culturally disruptive. The Tiananmen Square response is a classic, at least 150-year-old, Chinese response to the inability to separate the cultural from the techno-economic intrusion of the West.

Together telecommunications and transportation have another more negative implication for collective violence. Cheap worldwide telecommunication makes planning, plotting, orchestration, and execution of plots simpler and flexible. Transportation costs are so low that not only the materials, but the men of violence can move with ease from place to place. This is the core base of the expansion of terrorism.

Expanding arms sales and the associated attempt to build alliances and, in the case of the United States, to dump obsolescent weapons to make room for new ones has made the U.S.A., U.S.S.R. [the Union of Soviet Socialist Republics, which collapsed in 1991], and Israel the world's biggest armories. The notorious Krupp [a longtime German arms manufacturer] pales in comparison to what we alone have done to arm the world. The availability of arms at ridiculously discounted prices leads inevitably to their use and abuse.

©Kemchs/Rothco. Reprinted with permission.

Declining legitimacy of governments and other authorities is pandemic. The situation in the Soviet Union and in Eastern Europe today is the clearest most recent example of this trend.

Ethnic conflict continues and will expand, as there is relaxation of authoritarian constraints, which have held incompatible people in tolerable cooperation. The opportunities for ethnic conflict will grow, whether this is the Russians oppressed by the Estonians, Turks by the Bulgarians, or the Turks and the Greeks by each other in Cyprus. Related but distinctly different is the continuing acculturation to perpetual ethnic violence in several parts of the world—notably, Northern Ireland, Lebanon, and Israel.

Decolonization and the failure to resolve structural conflicts at the time of independence are now coming home to roost throughout most of the excolonies of Africa and of the Pacific Islands.

The governments already shaky at the time of liberation have now gone into decades of steady decline, corruption, and, in many cases, ethnic and racial favoritism in the distribution of government largess. Many Third World governments have frank policies of oppression. The excolonies are generally in a state of declining public administrative capability. Democracy has not caught on, and the greatest number of them are not enjoying any benefits of economic growth. The declining prospects of these countries is the single most important factor promoting internal ethnic and racial conflict and violence.

Divisions along the religious, ethnic, and income lines continue throughout much of the world. This closely correlates with, and promotes the rise of, religious fundamentalism. We see this in the relatively benign form in the United States and in the progressively vicious forms in Northern Ireland, Indonesia, Israel and Iran.

Reluctance to Intervene

The increasing reluctance of big powers to intervene should be clear. The U.S.S.R.'s adventures in Afghanistan in the 1980s and the United States' not so recent adventures in Vietnam make each of them reluctant to undertake any aggressive commitments anywhere in the world. Other colonial powers, such as Britain, are facing stringent budgetary constraints, and reluctance to act except under the most extreme provocations, as with the Falkland Islands episode. [Argentina invaded the British-owned islands in 1982, but surrendered to British forces.]

The simple rise in the number of nations—some 163 in 1990—alone makes clashes more likely. The border promotes two kinds of movements—movements toward further scission, with dissident internal groups wishing to split off, and the irredentist movements pushing groups overlapping national boundaries to come together.

The rise of the United Nations as a positive peace-keeping force will expand and in the 1990s, in my judgment, move to a peace-making role, which it is very unwilling to assume. But as it learns to deal better with peace-keeping and the negotiations sides of conflict, it will undertake relatively minor peace-making ventures, at first. As with any successful enterprise, it will expand.

Relaxation of central Moscow control both of the Russian satellites and, more recently, the entire Soviet Socialist Republic will unleash several forms of internal, collective violence within and among the various ethnic groups. Liberation can rarely be administered or accepted in moderate and measured doses. It almost inevitably goes to the head of the extremists and destroys any possibility or expectations of modest, stepwise expansion of liberty.

Poor economic prospects in individual countries, particularly those in population explosion, will lead to extreme measures along borders or internally that, in turn, will evoke extreme measures for control or containment.

Forms of Collective Violence

Nine kinds of traditional, collective violence will become increasingly popular. Irredentist and balkanizing movements directed at the same goal of putting ethnic groups in closer cohesion with greater independence will flourish. There will be border conflicts, either skirmishes or outright wars between nations. Coup d'état, the relatively peaceful turnover of head of state with little or extremely limited violence, will be common. Ethnic conflicts and civil war resulting from the expansion of either the coup d'état, balkanizing and irredentist movements, or ethnic conflict will flourish. Terrorism, both internal and transnational, and civil unrest with substantial collective violence . . . will be widespread. Finally, insurrection—collective violence to change some policy of the central government, and different from civil war—will be seen in five continents.

There will also be two new forms of violence. We anticipate that in the 1990s several countries will go into a form of international receivership. Utter chaos with the total failure of central legal authority will force international collective action to move in to stabilize the situation. The likely and obvious candidates for this are Haiti, numerous minor South Pacific republics, and, most interesting to speculate about, Colombia.

The second form of a new collective violence will involve some novel applications of nuclear materials. We see this in three distinct forms: The first is the distribution of radioactive materials in nonnuclear explosive devices by techniques varying from traditional bomb blasts to the equivalent of crop dusting to contaminate a population or a region. Second, we see an occasional weapon being lobbed by one small power at another small power. Since about a dozen countries now have nuclear weapons and materials, the abuse potential will shift from U.S.A.–U.S.S.R.–China to one of the other bomb holders. Finally, one can anticipate terrorist action destroying either a civil (nuclear power plant) or military (weapons facility) installation, thereby releasing large amounts of nuclear material.

Sites of Collective Violence

This brief viewpoint is too limited to go into the details on a country-by-country or even region-by-region basis, so let me use a tabulation of emerging conflicts and allow the reader to work out the details. On the left of Table 1 is a sample of regions and individual countries. Across its top are the eleven forms of

Table 1. The Future of Collective Violence, 1990–2010

	Receivership	New Nuclear Violence	Terrorism	Insurrection	Civil Unrest	Civil War	Ethnic/Racial Violence	Coup d'Etat	Border Conflict	Balkanization	Irredentist Movements
USA			•		•		•		•		•
Canada				•						•	
Mexico				•		•		•	•		
Central Am.				•	•	•		•	•		
Brazil											
Argentina											
Carib. Islands	•		•	•	•	•	•	•		•	
Union S. Af.			•	•	•	•	•	•	•	•	•
Blk. W. Africa	•		•	•	•	•	•	•	•	•	
E. Africa			•	•	•	•	•	•	•	•	•
N. Africa			•	•	•	•	•	•	•	•	•
UK			•	•			•		•		
Germany			•				•		•		•
France			•		•		•				
Spain			•	•	•		•	•		•	
E. Europe	•		•	•	•	•	•	•	•	•	•
USSR			•	•	•	•	•	•	•	•	•
Saudi Arabia			•	•			•	•			
Emirates			•	•			•	•			
Iran			•		•	•		•	•	•	•
India		•	•	•	•	•	•	•	•	•	
China				•	•			•	•	•	•
Indonesia			•	•	•	•	•	•	•	•	
Philippines			•	•	•	•	•	•			
Korea				•	•			•	•	•	•
Japan							•				
Bangladesh				•	•			•			
Australia					•		•				

conflict. This table deals with the high probability of collective violence, not the very low probability of general war or nuclear strategic war.

There is no universal remedy. Many of the remedies to the conflicts are, themselves, extremely unsatisfactory since they convert collective violence into individual violence and ambiguous personal fear. For example, in several Latin American and African nations, a fascistic takeover by the military can carry many of those countries into the situation of Haiti under Papa Doc [dictator François Duvalier, 1957–71]. In other cases, the resolution will come from a definitive resolution of a conflict—one side or the other will win the war.

We can expect a number of border conflict situations. For example, the emerging conflict between the United States and Mexico will result from the uncontrollable population growth in Mexico and its dismal economic prospects, which will create a flood of pressure for illegal movement into the United States. Ultimately, the U.S.A. will close the border violently and effectively, and keep it closed. Early and effective peaceful control of the U.S.A.–Mexico border is unthinkable in the present political climate.

Water: Rising Source of Violence

Water will replace oil as the primary reason for international conflict over the next half century, according to researchers at the Indiana Center on Global Change and World Peace.

Countries such as Israel, Jordan, Turkey, Iran, Bangladesh, and even the United States and Mexico contain the potential for disputes over access to water, according to Jack Hopkins, the associate director of the center. Severe water pollution in eastern Europe and the former Soviet Union may also contribute to the problem.

The Futurist, July/August 1994.

The happy prospect of economic prosperity washing out the bases of many kinds of recent ethnic and religious conflict is possible in some areas, but not likely in many. For example, with the rise of the European economic community, the Protestant-Catholic conflict in Northern Ireland may be alleviated should that region become economically prosperous. Similarly, the conflicts of the Spaniards with the Basques [of northern Spain] could be relieved by prosperity. The probability is not high, but, on the other hand, is not so low as to leave us without hope.

Some positive collective intentional action may also occur as suggested earlier in the case of countries that are in receivership. The situation in Haiti may reach such desperate proportions that the United States unilaterally, or the United States with Canadian-European forces, may move in to impose peace and even bring some reforms in government. [In September 1994, the United States sent twenty thousand troops to dismantle Haiti's military government.] It is unlikely that Latin Americans would cooperate with the Haitian intervention, since so many of them would be candidates for a similar kind of intervention and, hence, would balk at the prospect. Haiti and the South Pacific Islands are likely candidates for that kind of intervention. International intervention in the South Pacific would use more Asian forces, such as the Indians. We might even find ourselves collectively resorting to rearming the Gurkhas [an ethnic group in Nepal] as an international peace-keeping force. That would be a revived source of revenue for that strapped, small country.

World government will grow over the next decades. This growth will be primarily driven by the needs of high-technology systems of value and will be of use to many international partners that require stability. When some international systems are challenged, collective action will protect it.

One of the brightest prospects for collective action may follow one of the nuclear events discussed above. The major powers may pull themselves together to disarm the nuclear capabilities of all the lesser powers. The world opinion can move in only one direction after a true nuclear disaster. This trigger would not be a trivial difficulty like Three Mile Island [Pennsylvania, 1979], or the modest difficulty with Chernobyl [Ukraine, 1986], but the kind described above.

Undershaft lives.

"The chance for wide democratization now offers a new policy of building democratic peace."

Peace Among Democracies

Bruce Russett

The demise of many communist regimes and the emergence of new democracies provides the chance for increased democracy and peace among the world's nations, Bruce Russett maintains in the following viewpoint. Russett contends that cultural and institutional restraints among democracies prevent such countries from engaging in war and foster a belief in peaceful resolution of conflict. Many nations, the author argues, are making successful transitions to democracy and can serve as models for nondemocracies. Russett is the Dean Acheson Professor of Political Science at Yale University in New Haven, Connecticut, and the author of *Democratic Peace: Principles for a Post–Cold War World*.

As you read, consider the following questions:

1. How many wars have been fought between democracies in the twentieth century, according to Russett?
2. In Russett's opinion, what can a nation expect in a dispute with a democracy?
3. According to Freedom House, cited by the author, how many nations in 1991 were democracies or in transition to democracy?

Bruce Russett, "Peace Among Democracies," *Scientific American*, November 1993; © 1993 by Scientific American, Inc. All rights reserved.

A vision of peace among democratically governed nation-states has long been invoked as part of a configuration of institutions and practices that reduce war. In 1795 [German philosopher] Immanuel Kant spoke of perpetual peace based in part on states that shared "republican constitutions." Woodrow Wilson expressed the same conviction in his 1917 war message to Congress when he asserted that "a steadfast concert of peace can never be maintained except by a partnership of democratic nations." This vision once sounded utopian. But now, at the end of the 20th century, it is newly plausible.

The research of social scientists points to an irrefutable and tantalizing observation: stable democracies are unlikely to engage in military disputes with one another or to let any such conflicts escalate into war. In fact, they rarely even skirmish. Democracies are more likely to accept third-party mediation, to reciprocate one another's behavior and to settle their disputes peacefully. At the same time, they are about as prone to violence in their relations with authoritarian states as authoritarian states are toward one another.

What a Democracy Is

In the modern world, a "democracy" means a country in which nearly everyone can vote, elections are freely contested and the chief executive is chosen by popular vote or by an elected parliament. The more democratic a nation is, the more peaceful its relations with other democracies are likely to be. Since 1946, pairs of democratic states have been only one-eighth as likely as other kinds of states to threaten to use force against each other and only one-tenth as likely actually to do so. Established democracies fought no wars against one another during the entire 20th century. (Although Finland, for example, took the Axis side against the Soviet Union in World War II, it nevertheless engaged in no combat with the democracies.)

Moreover, the fairly tranquil relations among democracies are not spuriously caused by some other shared influence such as high levels of wealth or rapid growth or ties of alliance. Peace reigns among democracies even when these other favorable conditions do not apply. These peaceful relations are not limited just to the rich industrialized countries or to NATO [North Atlantic Treaty Organization] members. During the cold war, the phenomenon was not maintained simply by pressure from a common adversary, and it is outlasting that threat.

Peace among democracies derives in part from cultural restraints on conflict, primarily from the belief that it would be wrong to fight another democracy. This view extends into the international arena the norms of live-and-let-live and peaceful resolution of conflict that operate within democracies. Institutional

An Emergence of Democracies Could Reduce Conflict and Increase Peace

Several political analysts, including Samuel Huntington, observe that democracy has advanced in waves from the early nineteenth century, with each wave followed by reversals and then new gains. Happily, each reversal did not undo all previous gains; on Huntington's accounting . . . the net number of democracies went from zero before 1828 to fifty-nine in 1990. Reversals of democracies can happen again, and several in the former Soviet Union, Latin America and Africa look shaky.

The long-term trend, however, is clearly up, and an estimate of future incomes provides a basis for estimating future freedom levels. . . . Assuming a 3% average annual growth rate, and assuming that additions to income will add to freedom as much as in the past, the number of "free" countries goes from sixty-seven in 1990 to eighty-five in 2020, while the number of "not free" shrinks from fifty-three to forty-one. (If one believes that growth will be slower, but also believes in the wealth/democracy nexus, then this political evolution will take longer.)

In 1990, of the sixteen most populous non-rich nations, only Brazil, South Korea and Bangladesh were rated as politically "free." In the next generation, allowing for increases in wealth and education, eight of these nations are likely to be rated "free," six "partly free" and two (down from five in 1990) as "not free." [The organization Freedom House rates nations by these three categories.]

The spread of democracies would have several major consequences, one of which might be a decline in international conflicts. Many scholars have called attention to the fact that democracies do not war with each other, although there are, naturally, marginal cases; at most, it is a rare event. Michael Doyle credits Immanuel Kant with the key idea: republics rest on the consent of citizens; this induces prudence but not abhorrence of war, for wars must be fought for liberal purposes. Liberal states tend to be morally integrated; free speech and communications yield a more accurate perception of foreign peoples and their politics and this, in turn, leads to understanding and respect. But because nonliberal governments are in a state of aggression with their own people, relations of liberal states with them are suspect. Bruce Russett offers two explanations: the more plausible is that cultural norms of live-and-let-live that operate within democracies are extended internationally to other democracies; the other is that democratic political processes give time to resolve conflicts. In short, democracies have domestic constraints, are cautious about conquest, and have many shared values with other democracies.

Henry S. Rowen, paper titled "World Wealth Expanding: Why a Rich, Democratic and (Perhaps) Peaceful Era Is Ahead," 1994.

constraints also play an important role: it is a complicated procedure to persuade the people, the legislature and other independent institutions that war is necessary. Consequently, in a dispute with a democracy another nation can expect that there will be ample time for conflict-resolution processes to be effective and virtually no risk of incurring surprise attack.

Culture: A Stronger Influence

Evidence supports both the cultural and the institutional explanations; they reinforce each other. The cultural explanation may be somewhat more powerful, however. A culture of democracy, manifested in the absence of violence in domestic politics and the duration of stable democratic regimes, seems to exert a somewhat stronger influence on peace among democracies than do particular institutional constraints.

Nonindustrial societies, studied by ethnographers and anthropologists, also show less war among democratically organized polities. These units lack the institutional constraints of a modern state. Nevertheless, groups that are organized democratically fight one another significantly less often than do groups that have more authoritarian rule. The relation between democracy and peace is weaker and less consistent in preindustrial societies than in the modern international system, but to find it there at all shows that the pattern of peace among democracies is not limited to contemporary Western countries.

The more democracies there are in the world, the fewer potential adversaries the United States and other democratic nations will have and the wider the zone of peace will spread. The emergence of new democracies with the end of the cold war presents a chance for change in international relations more fundamental even than the opportunities created by the end of the Napoleonic Wars and World Wars I and II. Freedom House, a New York City–based research organization, has for more than 20 years graded countries by their types of political systems. At the end of 1991, for the first time ever, close to a majority of states (91 of 183) approximated reasonable standards employed for judging whether or not a country is a democracy; another 35 were in some form of transition to democracy.

Aid to the Former Soviet Union

The real possibility for widespread peace provides a compelling reason to strengthen democracy in the successor states of the former Soviet Union. There is no massive American Marshall Plan, and outside influence will be limited in any case. Yet a favorable international environment can make a difference. Western states can offer some economic help. International organizations can promote human rights and democracy.

Newly Free and Partly Free Nations

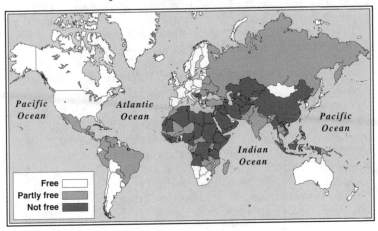

Free	Partly Free
Bulgaria	Armenia
Czech Republic	Belarus
Estonia	Cambodia
Germany (East)	Croatia
Latvia	Georgia
Lithuania	Haiti
Poland	Kyrgyzstan
Slovakia	Moldova
South Africa	Romania
Slovenia	Ukraine

Source: Freedom House, 1994.

Successful transitions to democracy in some countries can supply a model for others. A stable and less menacing international political environment can assist the emergence and consolidation of democratic governments.

Democracy in many of these nation-states may not prove stable. This global wave of democratization may crest and fall back, as earlier ones have done. But states probably can become democratic faster than they can become rich. The cold war policy of containment succeeded. The chance for wide democratization now offers a new policy of building democratic peace. If it can be grasped and consolidated, world politics might be transformed.

Periodical Bibliography

The following articles have been selected to supplement the diverse views presented in this chapter.

Arnold Beichman	"By the Year 2020, Will the World Be Rich and Free?" *Insight*, May 30, 1994. Available from 3600 New York Ave. NE, Washington, DC 20002.
Boutros Boutros-Ghali	"A New Departure on Development," *Foreign Policy*, Spring 1995.
Lester R. Brown	"Who Will Feed China?" *World Watch*, September/October 1994.
Marvin J. Cetron and Owen Davies	"The Future Face of Terrorism," *Futurist*, November/December 1994.
Nicholas Colchester	"Goodbye, Nation-State. Hello . . . What?" *New York Times*, July 17, 1994.
Brian Crozier	"The New World Disorder," *National Review*, December 19, 1994.
Terry L. Deibel	"Internal Affairs and International Relations in the Post–Cold War World," *Washington Quarterly*, Summer 1993. Available from 1150 15th St. NW, Washington, DC 20071.
Larry Diamond	"The Global Imperative: Building a Democratic World Order," *Current History*, January 1994.
Michael W. Doyle	"Forcing Peace: What Role for the United Nations?," *Dissent*, Spring 1994.
David Fromkin	"The Coming Millennium: World Politics in the Twenty-first Century," *World Policy Journal*, Spring 1993.
John F. Hillen III	"Peacekeeping Is Hell," *Policy Review*, Fall 1993.
Thomas F. Homer-Dixon	"Environmental Scarcities and Violent Conflict," *International Security*, Summer 1994.
Journal of Democracy	Special section on the future of democracy, January 1995.
Robert D. Kaplan	"The Coming Anarchy," *Atlantic Monthly*, February 1994.
Charles W. Kegley Jr. and Gregory A. Raymond	"Preparing Now for a Peaceful Twenty-first Century," *USA Today*, September 1994.

Catherine M. Kelleher — "Soldiering On," *Brookings Review*, Spring 1994.

Lewis H. Lapham — "Pax Economica," *Harper's*, April 1995.

Edward D. Mansfield and Jack Snyder — "Democratization and War," *Foreign Affairs*, May/June 1995.

Riccardo Petrella — "A Global Agora vs. Gated City-Regions," *New Perspectives Quarterly*, Winter 1995.

Psychology Today — "Apocalypse Right Now?" Interview with Alvin Toffler and Heidi Toffler, January/February 1994.

David K. Shipler — "Four Futures for Russia," *New York Times Magazine*, April 4, 1993.

Social Justice — Special issue on Japan in the twenty-first century, Summer 1994.

Thomas G. Weiss — "New Challenges for UN Military Operations: Implementing an Agenda for Peace," *Washington Quarterly*, Winter 1993.

What Are Projected Trends and Wild Cards?

21ST CENTURY EARTH

Chapter Preface

For centuries, scholars and scientists have wondered precisely what causes human beings to age. Today, researchers who are investigating aging in lower organisms (and its similarities with human aging) predict that this enigmatic process could be fully understood in the twenty-first century.

Some scientists argue that human longevity can be pushed far beyond current limits, primarily by controlling the genetic mechanisms which inevitably halt cell division and cause cells to die. In the words of evolutionary biologist Michael Rose, "I don't think there is any predefined limit to life span in flies or humans. Aging can be changed, since it is something that we can manipulate, analyze, and understand." Geneticist Michael West adds, "For the first time in history, we have the power to manipulate aging on a very profound level."

Others, however, are apprehensive about the prospect of extending human longevity. As Robert Butler, author of *Why Survive? Growing Old in America*, points out, "Supposing we wound up having the 'terrible twos' for fifteen years, or a teenage crisis that went on for twenty years? Some interesting dangers await our inventiveness." Longevity researcher Leonard Hayflick warns, "If somebody does find a way of tampering with the aging process, God help us. We've had other medical advances that have gone far beyond people's abilities to deal with them."

Extended longevity is just one example of a wild card that may become reality in the twenty-first century. The viewpoints in the following chapter examine other wild cards and trends that could forever alter the human species.

"It's possible that some people alive now may still be alive 400 years from now."

Human Longevity May Become Greatly Extended

Brad Darrach

Since 1850, the life span of the average American has increased from approximately forty-five to seventy-five years. In the following viewpoint, Brad Darrach argues that molecular biologists are making remarkable discoveries about the aging process that could increase human longevity by one hundred years or more. Darrach is a staff writer for *Life*, a monthly general interest magazine.

As you read, consider the following questions:

1. What feature of cancer cells do researchers hope to control, according to Darrach?
2. According to the author, why are nematodes ideal for studying aging?
3. How does human growth hormone affect the body, according to Darrach?

Excerpted from Brad Darrach, "The War on Aging," *Life*, October 1992; ©1992 by Time Warner, Inc. Reprinted with permission.

For more than a decade, with increasing success, molecular biologists all over the world have been struggling to answer a question as old as death: Why do we age and what—if anything—can we do to slow the process down? Theorizing on the basis of current experiments, a number of these scientists, including many pioneers in the study of the genes that control aging, now envision that within a generation or two mankind's maximum life span of 120 years—which probably hasn't changed since the Stone Age—could be extended by decades, possibly by centuries.

A Revolt Against Aging

There is an irresistible fascination in the idea of living to an enormous age. It figures in a thousand tales and legends, but to most contemporary scientists the notion that people can live for many centuries sounds more like sci fi than science. Biologists and gerontologists usually place such expectations on a scale between premature and preposterous. But the researchers who are now asserting that life can be greatly extended insist that they are on to something more than the high concept for a mad scientist movie and that there is scientific evidence to prove it. Extrapolating from the results of their own experiments and from those of other experts in the field, they have framed a startling new vision of the shape of things to come. Yet what they are saying all but defies belief.

Dr. Edward Masoro, 67, physiologist, University of Texas Health Science Center in San Antonio:

> If dietary restriction has the same effects in humans as it has in rodents, then human life span can be extended by at least 30 percent—which would give us an extra 30 to 35 years. But once we understand the mechanisms that control aging, we may find it possible to extend life span considerably more, perhaps by 100 percent—which would give us an extra 100 to 120 years.

Dr. Thomas Johnson, 48, University of Colorado, the leading investigator of aging in roundworms: "I think we may well be able to lengthen human life far beyond anything we ever dreamed possible. Based on what has been achieved in animal studies, it's conceivable that we may achieve human life spans in excess of twice the current norm."

Dr. Michal Jazwinski, 45, Louisiana State University [LSU] Medical Center, the foremost authority on aging in yeast: "Possibly in 30 years we will have in hand the major genes that determine longevity, and will be in a position to double, triple, even quadruple our maximum life span of 120 years. It's possible that some people alive now may still be alive 400 years from now."

Dr. Michael Rose, 37, University of California, Irvine, the top expert on fruit fly aging:

If we're willing to spend enough money on research, and if we spend it intelligently, I believe that in 25 years we could see the creation of the first products that can postpone human aging significantly. This would be only the beginning of a long process of technological development in which human life span would be aggressively extended. The only practical limit to human life span is the limit of human technology.

Dr. William Regelson, 67, professor of medicine at the Medical College of Virginia:

With the knowledge that is accumulating now about the nutritional and neuroendocrine aspects of aging, and if we develop ways to repair aging tissues with the help of embryonic cells, we could add 30 healthy years to human life in the next decade. And beyond that, as we learn to control the genes involved in aging, the possibilities of lengthening life appear practically unlimited.

Even with the conditions these scientists attach to their predictions, the prospect they portray is astonishing. It sounds as if a group of scientific visionaries, taking over where the God of Genesis left off, is heralding the dawn of the Eighth Day of Creation—and in fact they are proposing nothing less than a revolt against the one-billion-year tyranny of the genes.

Could they possibly be right? Given the status of those who make the claim and the swiftly developing state of the art they practice, the question has to be taken seriously. . . .

Fascinating Discoveries

There have already been some fascinating findings. A scientist in California has identified the genes that make skin age and is now researching substances that reverse the process and may open the way to a wrinkle-free future for the human race. A team in Dallas found a way to make human cells live up to 100 percent longer and then figured out another way to make them immortal (able to replicate indefinitely)—a discovery they believe prefigures the possibility of extending human life span. Treating a group of elderly men with a potent hormone, one scientist temporarily reversed some symptoms of aging by up to 20 years in less than six months. Several teams have identified genes that extend the life of simple organisms and genes that cut it short. Still others have learned to tweak the molecular switches that turn genes on and off. Biologists have managed to double and triple the life spans of insects. A team working in Canada and on Long Island found a genetic clock that measures the rate at which human beings age—and a team member isolated an enzyme that opens a promising line of research that could lead to a new cancer therapy. Dr. John Shepherd, a biophysicist at the University of Sussex, in Brighton, England, exults: "For the first time, after years of evolution, we are on the verge of influencing our fate.

Nothing, nothing is impossible.". . . .

The idea of an hourglass that measures the sands of life as they run out has been around for centuries. To poets it offered a metaphor, but to biologists it presented a challenge. For the past 40 years, ever since the structure of DNA was discovered, they have wondered if human cells contained a clock of aging. . . .

Not a Biological Impossibility

Many of the studies of aging point toward the same question: Can it be stopped? Theory says yes. The fact that humans do not live for three hundred years does not reflect a basic biological impossibility; it reflects the working of natural selection, which operates according to the logic of the genes. But people may choose to alleviate natural selection by making the environment benign and, if necessary, sacrificing reproductive success. In principle, that way lies an increased lifespan.

The Economist, January 7, 1995.

At the University of Texas Southwestern Medical Center at Dallas, Dr. Woodring Wright, 43, and Dr. Jerry Shay, 46, discovered two separate genetic programs, Mortality 1 and Mortality 2, that cause human cells to become senescent. When Mortality 1 is activated, the cell begins gradually to age; when Mortality 2 kicks in, the cell swiftly decays and soon dies. By inactivating the Mortality 1 program, Wright and Shay were able to extend the life span of cells in culture between 40 and 100 percent. Nevertheless, sooner or later the Mortality 2 program kicked in, and at that point the cells, as expected, rapidly began to decline. What would happen, Wright and Shay wondered, if they inactivated Mortality 2? To their astonishment, the cells became immortal—like cancer cells, they continued to replicate indefinitely. Pressing on, Wright and Shay found a way to make cells shuttle between the senescent and immortal states simply by manipulating a single gene. Next step: to find out if the endless replication of cancer cells can be stopped in the same way. . . .

Studying Organisms

Working with whole organisms, biologists have made interesting advances:

• Evolution is thrifty. Once it solves a problem, the solution is preserved from species to species in the vast library of the genes. Aware of this miserly trait, LSU's Michal Jazwinski launched a research program designed to discover the genes that cause aging in yeast—and then to find the same genes in human cells.

Yeast is easy to work with because it reproduces rapidly. Yet Jazwinski spent years in painstaking study before he zeroed in on a gene that can extend the life span of a yeast cell by 30 percent. He named it Longevity Assurance Gene-1, and after sequencing and cloning it he went looking for an identical gene in humans. In 1992 he found a piece of human DNA that resembles the longevity gene in yeast, and since then he has been studying the human counterpart. Meanwhile Jazwinski's team has discovered three more longevity genes in yeast, one of which can nearly double the life span of a cell and at the same time causes the cell to retain its youthful ability to replicate. "Each longevity assurance gene we discover potentially adds to the life span of the yeast cell," Jazwinski says. "The same should be true of longevity genes in humans. As we find them we can manipulate them, one by one, and ultimately perhaps add hundreds of years to our lives.". . .

• A biologist's best friend is a roundworm the size of a comma. It is called a nematode, and it is a perfect subject of study for scientists interested in how a whole organism works. A nematode's flesh is as clear as glass, and under a microscope every one of its 959 cells is glowingly visible. Though conveniently simple, it contains many of the basic human structures: nerves, muscles, blood vessels, digestive tract, reproductive system. It comes in two sexes (male and hermaphrodite), matures in three days, lays 250 to 300 eggs, defecates every 50 seconds and dies as if on schedule after 20 days.

Is the schedule set by death genes and enforced by killer proteins? After 12 years of dogged research, molecular gerontologist Tom Johnson and his team have found the answer: yes. They have discovered and mapped a gene they call AGE-1 that begins to age nematodes when they are only three days old and can produce proteins that may flip the little worms into a fatal decline. When the gene is inactivated, the worms live as much as 110 percent longer. Johnson plans to test AGE-1—and AGE-2, which he isolated in 1992—in yeast, fruit flies and mice. "Within a few years," he says, "we could nail the aging mechanism in mice. After that, research in humans should go rapidly. We hope to find the genes that shorten life and one by one knock them out. Or we'll tailor drugs to inactivate the destructive proteins that finish us off. The drug companies are good at that."

Turning Back the Clock

It was the biggest surprise in the history of aging research. While all those molecular biologists were struggling to slow the clock of aging, a 65-year-old endocrinologist at the Medical College of Wisconsin found a stunningly uncomplicated way to turn the clock back. What the devil did for Faust in the medieval legend, Dr. Daniel Rudman did for real human beings: In a 1990 experiment that lasted six months he reversed some symptoms of aging in a group of men in their sixties and seventies.

Rudman accomplished this with the help of human growth hormone, a potent secretion of the pituitary gland that surges through the body healing wounds, bolstering the immune system, building bones, muscles and internal organs and helping the body break down fats. . . .

The results were startling. Some members of the control group lost muscle, bone and organ mass more rapidly than Rudman had expected. But the men injected with human growth hormone regained 10 percent of their muscle mass, had a 9 percent increase in skin thickness and lost 14 percent of their body fat. Their liver and spleen also substantially regained mass. A few reported pain in their hands produced by expanding muscles that compressed the nerves in their wrists. "In effect," says Rudman, "the treatment reversed body composition changes that would occur in 10 to 20 years of aging."

When the experiment was over, every man in the hGH group rapidly lost the youthful characteristics he had regained. . . .

Living to 400

Tom and Mary Wright took the longevity injection on their 10th wedding anniversary, May 20, 2041. He was 34 and a junior partner in a Kansas City law firm. She was 31 and had just been made assistant manager of the local center for the arts. They had two children, Billy, six, and Ellen, four. A thoughtful couple, they had struggled with the decision. The idea of tampering with the natural order of things made them uneasy, and the prospect of living 500 or 600 years was almost frightening. At first the injection had been banned, but immortality mania swept the planet, and bootleg ampoules were soon available. By 2030 the injections were legal in most developed countries, and 70 percent of U.S. adults had "taken the needle." Feeling left out, Tom and Mary went for their shots, then broke out the champagne and wished themselves "many happy returns."

Physically, the Wrights felt no different, but emotionally they sensed a gradual easing of the pressure of time. Seeing their lives in a longer perspective, they felt less driven to accomplish. A certain tension and excitement were missing, but they enjoyed life more as it went by—enjoyed each other and the children, enjoyed their work, enjoyed just being alive. . . .

Family and Work

In 2120 Tom was 113 and Mary was 110, but they still looked and felt like a lively couple in their early thirties. Billy and Ellen, 85 and 83, could have passed for 20. But the world had changed, and so had the way people lived. Expecting to run through a score of careers in the course of several centuries, many people took four or five graduate degrees before starting their first jobs at 45 or 50. Very few got married before 60, and nobody expected marriage to last a lifetime. Even the happiest relationships wore out after 40 or 50 years, and in a society where everybody looked young and felt lusty there were plenty of attractive alternatives. People still wanted children, but with menopause postponed for centuries there was no need to hurry. Most women had their first child at 80 or 100. . . .

By 2357 Tom and Mary had each gone through more than a dozen careers and were now horse breeders in northern California. He was 350, she was 347, and they had just celebrated the birth of a great-great-great-grandchild. Yet both were still as active sexually as they had been at 35. The year she turned 365, Mary had the first indications of menopause, and about 30 years later they began to have trouble transferring information from short-term to long-term memory—a common difficulty for people entering their fifth century. The problem, neurologists said, was that their memory banks had filled. More storage space would be needed, and science had recently learned how to create it. Tom and Mary took hormone treatments that stimulated the growth of new memory cells, and in about four months the problem disappeared.

Another problem remained and grew steadily worse: boredom. Most people over 400 had a constant droning sense that they had done it all. Millions asked for euthanasia, recently legalized, or died in headlong pursuit of thrills. A 423-year-old friend of the Wrights was killed in a motorcycle accident on the way to an Elvis sighting.

Technology, it was true, provided spectacular entertainments: virtual-reality orgies, computer-controlled mystical experiences, war games with cyborgs and, for the very rich, mountaineering expeditions on Mars. After 200 years of atmospheric engineering, the little planet was ready for human habitation, and Ellen had actually been there. When she was 346 she won a vacation at the Billionaire's Club on the shore of the red planet's brand-new ocean and came back raving about the pure air and the bright yellow sunsets. But Tom and Mary had lost interest in such things. To pass the time, they curled up with 100,000-page novels and 1,000,000-piece all-white jigsaw puzzles. One night they talked about euthanasia and felt so relieved they made love for the first time in two years.

The next morning Mary had an inspiration. "Let's have ourselves cloned. Then we can raise ourselves as our own children. When we die, we'll go right on living. Maybe forever." And that's just what they did.

"I am quite pessimistic that, in the next century, we will . . . accelerate the processes that drive our increasing life span."

Human Longevity Will Not Become Greatly Extended

Leonard Hayflick

In the following viewpoint, excerpted from his book *How and Why We Age*, Leonard Hayflick argues that it will not be possible to achieve major increases in human longevity with existing or foreseeable medical technology. Hayflick asserts that the scientific objective should not be to slow or stop the aging process, but to strive for maximum human life expectation by eliminating the present leading causes of death, such as cancer and cardiovascular disease. Hayflick is a professor of anatomy at the University of California at San Francisco School of Medicine.

As you read, consider the following questions:

1. According to Hayflick, what would be the economic impact of eliminating cancer and cardiovascular disease?
2. How long would it take to reach a maximum life span of 120 years, in Hayflick's opinion?
3. What optimal scenario for increased aging does the author present?

Excerpted from *How and Why We Age* by Leonard Hayflick. Copyright ©1994 by Cell Associates, Inc. Foreword copyright ©1994 by Robert N. Butler, M.D. Reprinted by permission of Ballantine Books, a division of Random House, Inc.

Today people in developed countries can, for the first time in history, expect to live long enough to become old. The enormous medical, social, and economic progress made in these countries in the twentieth century has added about twenty-five years to life expectation at birth. This dramatic rate of change will not continue into the next century—annual gains have declined and in some years not appeared. . . .

Resolving Causes of Death

Resolution of the leading causes of death would add more than a decade to our life expectation, but even eliminating all of them would not make us immortal. When all of the goals of biomedical research have been achieved, the limit in extending life expectation will be reached: we will die, not from heart disease, stroke, or cancer—the causes now written on death certificates—but from the effects of the normal decrements of old age. We will then have to coin succinct terms to say that death was caused by a normal loss in physiological function, ultimately resulting in the failure of the kidney, heart, liver, nervous system, or some other vital organ. Our fate will be to die only from "natural causes."

Resolution of the two leading causes of death, cardiovascular diseases and cancer, would increase our life expectation by about seventeen years. To extend our longevity by significantly more than that, we would have to perturb the processes that determine longevity or produce age changes. However, any benefits of increasing human life expectation—whether by eliminating disease, manipulating longevity-assurance genes or slowing the rate of aging—might be tempered by the economic impact that the achievement could have.

For example, if we were able to eliminate cardiovascular diseases and cancer, people would live longer and thus be exposed to an increased incidence in the remaining causes of death. Economists at the Office of Management and Budget calculate the increase in social security, medicare, medicaid, retirement benefits, and other costs would be profound. If cardiovascular disease were eliminated, the additional annual federal cost would be over sixty-seven billion 1983 dollars. If cancer were eliminated as a cause of death, more than eighteen billion 1983 dollars would have to be spent annually on those whose lives would be extended. Even if these figures are off by a factor of two, resolving the two leading causes of death in the United States would cost us from about ten (cardiovascular disease) to over fifty (cancer) times the present annual cost of our efforts to cure the diseases! Cynics might carry this reasoning to its logical conclusion and argue that if everyone would die suddenly in middle age, we could eliminate our national debt and balance the budget in a few years.

Few researchers now study the normal losses in physiological function that occur as we age and how those losses might be slowed or reversed, but these normal losses may eventually become the leading causes of death. If at some future time all deaths in old age result from natural causes, most will occur within a diminishing span of ages. If you live a healthy life until, say, the age of 110 but succumb to ultimately lethal age changes by age 112, you will have approached the maximum human life span. Assuming many others do the same, average life expectation will almost catch up with maximum life span.

I do not believe that we will soon have the ability to manipulate what appears to be the fixed human life span of 115 years. Even if we concede that, on an evolutionary time scale, the human life span will increase naturally, the increase will be imperceptible even over several millennia. If the past is any guide, it might be ten thousand years or more before the maximum human life span reaches even 120 years. I am quite pessimistic that, in the next century, we will learn enough about human evolution to be able to accelerate the processes that drive our increasing life span.

Successful tampering with the processes of biological fitness and adaptation is probably beyond our ability to master, although some of our present actions are certainly having a negative influence on the fitness and adaptation of humans. For example, biomedical sciences and our culture have conspired to preserve and increase the presence of many unfavorable traits in the human gene pool that, without our intervention, would remain at a low level, or disappear entirely. These traits include many genetically determined pathologies that are treatable to the extent that their victims are able to survive long enough to pass on those traits to their progeny. In this way the undesirable traits survive and spread in the human gene pool. The usual processes of fitness and selection, which would have eliminated the biologically unfit before they had a chance to reproduce, are frequently thwarted by human intervention, allowing many of the biologically unfit to survive and reproduce. Our culture demands that we do everything we can to permit all people who suffer from illness to survive as long as possible. Although our intentions obviously are benign, the effect of our actions is to undermine the fundamental process of evolution in which only the fittest survive. . . .

Tampering with the Aging Process

Our increasing ability to control many aspects of our biological destiny has persuaded many people that a technique for slowing the aging process or extending the human life span cannot be more than a few years away. The optimists see the conquering of the major killers—viral and bacterial scourges like poliomyelitis, measles, rubella, tuberculosis, scarlet fever, and diphtheria—during the first half of this century as evidence for their position. Resolution of these diseases depended upon the implementation of better hygienic conditions, the discovery of effective vaccines, and the development of antibiotics. The transplantation of hearts and other organs, enormous advances in diagnostic techniques, and the promise of anticancer therapy are examples of more recent successes by the biomedical research community. All of these accomplishments are thought to herald a second revolution in which recombinant DNA technology and the production of monoclonal antibodies will eliminate the remaining chronic diseases. Because of these monumental achievements, gerontological optimists reason that reversing the aging process, or increasing longevity, are attainable goals.

The Hayflick Limit

Leonard Hayflick overturned the entrenched dogma in cell biology that normal cells can grow indefinitely outside the organism when supplied with necessary nutrients. This cell "immortality" concept was advanced by Alexis Carrel in 1912 and subsequently became a paradigm for the field. It fostered the belief that aging must be an extracellular process. In a classic 1961 paper, Hayflick and Paul Moorhead discovered the opposite—that cultured human cells die after undergoing about fifty divisions. Not only are cells mere mortals, but also aging is indeed an intracellular process. It is perhaps ironic that the individual who debunked cellular immortality has achieved professional immortality via the eponymous route—human cell death at about fifty divisions is now commonly known as the Hayflick Limit.

Eugene Garfield, *The Scientist*, May 15, 1995.

I am not one of the optimists, and I do not believe that we have a sufficient understanding of either the aging process or the determinants of life span to expect to significantly manipulate either during our lifetime. A more important issue, however, is whether it would be desirable to manipulate either process. The capacity to halt or slow the aging process, or to extend longevity, would have consequences unlike most other biomedical breakthroughs. Virtually all other biomedical goals have an indisputably positive value. It is not at all clear whether or not the ability to tamper with the processes that age us or determine our life span would be an unmixed blessing. Resolution of all disease and other causes of death would result in a life expectation of about one hundred years. I am apprehensive about extending average life expectation beyond age one hundred once the leading killers are resolved because the result would be disease-free but nonetheless functionally weaker, still inexorably aging people. We would suffer the fate of Tithonus as memorialized by Alfred, Lord Tennyson: "And after many a summer dies the swan. Me only cruel immortality consumes." Old people will simply become older, condemned to the vicissitudes of a continuing aging process. And that outcome, I believe, is undesirable for most people. . . .

Objective: Eliminate Deadly Diseases

Because immortality and the complete elimination of aging are probably both undesirable, some believe that just slowing the aging process might be the best compromise. This view has many advocates, and the objective may well be useful. We still do not know how to slow the aging process in humans, but we do know how to increase our life expectation by eliminating or reducing causes of death. This approach has, in fact, been remarkably successful throughout most of this century. Nevertheless, the "success" has come at a great cost. Increased life expectation and birth rates have resulted in an explosive increase in the world's population, bringing us dangerously close to destroying what is left of the pristine surface of the planet. Unless the number of humans populating this planet is soon reduced, there will be little purpose in considering the question of slowing the aging process or increasing the human life span. The planet will not be a place on which it is worth spending more time.

After years of thinking about these kinds of issues, I've decided that there is only one objective that is both practical and desirable and that is to strive for maximum human life expectation by eliminating the present leading causes of death. I see no value to society or to the individual in seeking to slow or stop the aging process or to achieve immortality.

The scenario that provokes the least concern is the one in which all humans reach the maximum life span, still in possession of full mental and physical abilities, with death occurring quickly as we approach, say, our 115th birthday. This is the goal that we are tacitly pursuing at this time. Virtually all biomedical research has the implicit goal of eliminating disease in all of its forms. It is logical to ask what will happen if we are successful. The answer seems to be that if we are successful, our life expectation will be increased but we will eventually die from the basic aging processes that lead to failure in some vital system.

"*It appears that many of the warnings of* The Limits to Growth *are as valid as ever.*"

A Forecast of Ecological Collapse Is Accurate

Ian A. Nalder

In 1972, the results of a Massachusetts Institute of Technology computer model that forecast a global ecological catastrophe were published in the book *The Limits to Growth*. In the following viewpoint, Ian A. Nalder argues that recent data show that although it represents "a grossly simplified view of world processes," the model's overall forecast is accurate. Nalder contends that patterns of population growth, resource consumption, and food and industrial production have largely been following the "Limits to Growth" prediction and suggest that changes necessary to avoid a catastrophe have not yet occurred. Nalder is a doctoral student at the University of Alberta's Department of Renewable Resources in Edmonton, Alberta, Canada.

As you read, consider the following questions:

1. What was the intent of the authors of *The Limits to Growth*, according to Nalder?
2. According to Nalder, when was the concept of sustainable development popularized?
3. What three main obstacles have undermined sustainability since the early 1980s, according to *Caring for the Earth*, as cited by the author?

Excerpted from "Ignoring Limits to Growth" by Ian A. Nalder, *IEEE Technology and Society*, vol. 12, no. 3, Summer 1993; ©1993 by the Institute of Electrical and Electronics Engineers, 345 E. 47th St., New York, NY 10017-2394.

In 1968, 30 scientists, educators, economists, industrialists, and government officials from 10 countries met at the *Accademia dei Lincei* in Rome to discuss the present and future predicament of mankind. The first project of the "Club of Rome" examined the consequences of unchecked growth. A computer model developed at Massachusetts Institute of Technology seemed to confirm what many futurologists had been saying: existing growth patterns could not be sustained. There were absolute physical limits which, if ignored, would lead to sudden collapse and to global catastrophe within a hundred years. These results were published as the book *The Limits to Growth* in 1972.

Two decades later, reexamination of the report shows that the world has generally been following the patterns of growth forecast. Yet the implicit warning about continued growth has largely been ignored in the quest for sustainable development.

The World Model

In *The Limits to Growth*, a simulation, termed the World Model, examined five main parameters: population, industrial capital, food, nonrenewable resources, and pollution. Interrelationships were defined and then quantified using global data. As an indication of its complexity, the program had nearly 300 variables and over 100 feedback loops. Nevertheless, it was a grossly simplified view of world processes. No attempt was made to model individual nations or the flows of materials between nations. The contributions of the oceans and aquaculture to food supply were ignored. Nonrenewable resources were treated as one "average" resource and there was only one class of pollution. Also, many assumptions had to be made about [human and other] processes.

The World Model was run for the period 1900 to 2100. Its outputs were adjusted to agree with historical values up to 1970. The model was run many times for varying growth rates and resource levels and showed surprisingly consistent behavior—one of growth and collapse.

The Standard Run

The "standard run," shown in Figure 1, assumed no major changes in the physical, economic, or social relationships that had operated for the previous century. In this scenario, population and industrial output continue to increase exponentially. Industry grows to a level that requires enormous input of material. The resource base is rapidly depleted and prices rise sharply. More and more capital is devoted to extracting the dwindling resources and eventually depreciation outstrips investment leading to a collapse of the industrial base. The agricultural and service sectors, which are dependent on industry, collapse soon after. Food production drops. The increasing population and dwindling food supply soon lead to mass starvation. Combined with the lack of medical services, this causes the population to plummet in what can only be described as a global catastrophe.

Figure 1. World Model Standard Run Output

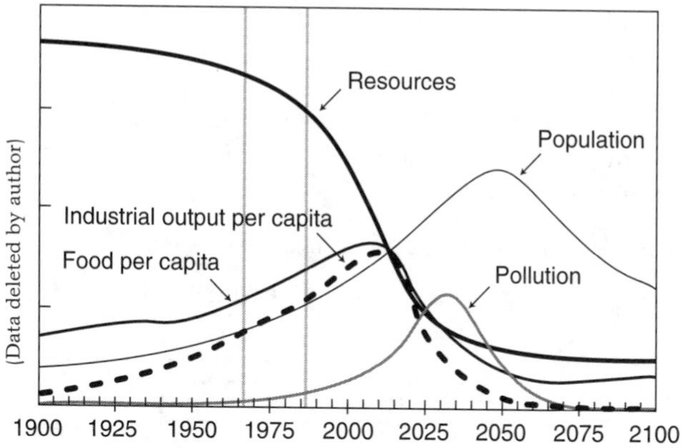

Source: *The Limits to Growth*, 1972.

It must be emphasized that the standard run was never intended to be an accurate prediction. The authors knew as well as anyone that that type of forecasting was impossible. Their interest lay more in the overshoot and collapse mechanism than in the precise year of occurrence—their intent was to propose policy changes that would avoid the catastrophic collapse of the standard run.

Some Criticisms

Nevertheless, the book was widely received as a doomsday forecast and provoked considerable criticism. Much probably arose from the model's challenges to conventional economic assumptions. The most detailed critique, from a group of specialists at the University of Sussex, was inconclusive. In retrospect, one is struck by how many of the arguments either relied on technology to overcome problems or revealed a basic distrust of computer models. Neither the criticisms nor the replies shed much light on the validity of the model.

An acknowledged weakness of the model, however, was that the world was treated as a homogeneous system. A more complex, regionalized model was subsequently developed by Mihajlo Mesarovic and Eduard Pestel. Although providing a better insight

231

into the effects of policies, its limited 50-year forecast neither confirmed nor denied the conclusions of *The Limits to Growth*.

Five Comparisons

Since the validity of any model is best tested by its predictive powers, the question arises whether the standard run has provided a reasonable forecast of the growth patterns of the last 20 years. Some interesting comparisons can be made for each of the five main parameters.

Population. Figure 2 compares the population projections of the World Model standard run for the period 1960 to 2030 with recent U.N. estimates. Over the past 20 years, the world has experienced an even greater increase in population than that predicted by the standard run.

Figure 2. World Population

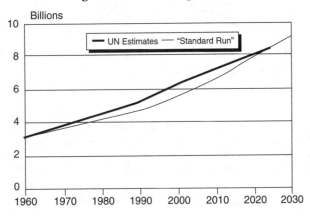

Source: *The Limits to Growth*, 1972.

Nonrenewable Resources. The standard run assumed 250 years' reserve of all nonrenewable resources at 1970 consumption rates. (Reserves are expressed as years of supply at current consumption rates and include only reserves that are economically extractable.) Some reserves such as nickel and iron have decreased as would be expected, but some such as copper and aluminum have actually increased. It should be noted, however, that this apparent imprecision in assessing reserves is not too significant. The important parameter is the growth rate in consumption—at today's level of consumption, there are 41 years' reserve of copper, but even twice current reserves would be exhausted in 42 years given current growth rates of 3.2%. . . .

There has been some variation between what was expected and recent experience, but overall the picture is one of substantially unchanged growth in the consumption of nonrenewable resources.

Food. The standard run predicted a steady increase in food per capita in the medium term. Against these predictions, Figure 3 shows the per capita world cereal production—cereals, which supply about half of people's calorie requirements, provide a convenient indicator of world food production. As can be seen, actual food production per capita has not achieved the rates predicted, mainly due to downturn since 1985.

Industrial Production. A comparison here is more difficult given the ambiguity of data on world industrial production. However, on the assumption that industrial production is closely correlated with energy consumption, Figure 4 compares world energy consumption per capita between 1970 and 1990 with the standard run rate-of-increase of industrial output per capita. The actual per capita output, as measured by energy consumption, continues to increase, but at a significantly slower rate than projected by the standard run.

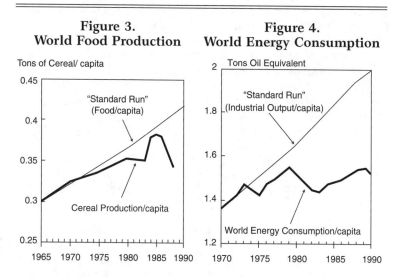

Figure 3.
World Food Production

Figure 4.
World Energy Consumption

Source: *The Limits to Growth*, 1972, and Ian A. Nalder.

Pollution. Since the pollution parameter in the World Model was a gross simplification, it is difficult to make any meaningful comparison against the outputs. It is possible, however, to examine the input data that shaped the model. One very significant, globally-distributed pollutant considered was carbon dioxide. The data then available showed atmospheric carbon dioxide levels were 318 ppm [parts per million] by volume and were predicted to be 353 ppm by 1990. This prediction has been surprisingly accurate—the figure for 1990 is 355 ppm.

It would be a mistake to read too much into the above indicators—they are, after all, only a sampling of today's data against a model that was not intended to provide quantitative outputs. The interesting point, however, is that the world is more or less following the growth patterns forecast by the standard run. This not only lends support to the validity of the model but also suggests that the changes necessary to avoid the catastrophic overshoot and collapse have not yet been made.

Shifts in Concerns

Have we then been ignoring the central message of *The Limits to Growth*? An answer to this question can be found in three publications: *World Conservation Strategy*, *Our Common Future*, and *Caring for the Earth*. Each represents a consensus among leading world experts and is therefore a good barometer of environmental opinion.

In contrast to the broader view of *The Limits to Growth*, *World Conservation Strategy* focused on humans' total dependence on the ecosystem. It pointed out that while population was rapidly increasing, the ecosystem resource was just as rapidly decreasing due to soil loss or degradation, devastation of forests, destruction of aquatic habitats, pollution, and loss of genetic diversity. In offering a solution, *World Conservation Strategy* introduced the idea of sustainable development. However, despite showing that the problems were real and urgent, it made no attempt to quantify the relative urgency.

By 1983, the United Nations had recognized the criticality of environmental issues and called for "a global agenda for change." A commission, chaired by Gro Harlem Brundtland, was established and in 1987 published *Our Common Future*. It was a wide-ranging view of global problems that, in tying growth and sustainability together, popularized the concept of sustainable development. Although based on the premise that growth was essential if brute poverty in the underdeveloped world were to be overcome, it avoided the question of how much growth was possible.

Caring for the Earth is the successor to *World Conservation Strategy*. Its principal aim is to provide a strategy for sustainability. It builds on the preceding three works and focuses on three main obstacles that have undermined sustainability since the early 1980s: the lack of an ethical commitment to the concept; the inequitable distribution of power, resources, and information; and "the notion that conservation and development can be managed separately." Like its predecessors, it relies on illustrative data and anecdotal evidence.

Unheeded Warnings

Over the past two decades, the environmental focus has shifted from concerns about finite limits of growth to the problems of implementing sustainable development. But we appear to be no closer to defining how much growth can be absorbed, or how much development is sustainable. As noted in 1989 by Alexander King, president of the Club of Rome, "it appears that many of the warnings of *The Limits to Growth* are as valid as ever." If we are to truly achieve sustainable development, policies must be based on hard data which defines how much growth is possible without foreclosing on future generations.

*"[Limits to Growth] is a pretty dangerous model
to rely on for predictions of society's future."*

A Forecast of
Ecological Collapse
Is Inaccurate

Kevin Kelly

In the following viewpoint, excerpted from his book *Out of
Control: The Rise of Neo-Biological Civilization*, Kevin Kelly argues that the "Limits to Growth" simulation model that forecasts
unsustainable global growth and an ecological collapse suffers
from a number of flaws, including narrow and wrong assumptions, which undermine its accuracy. Kelly concludes that the
model needs a complete overhaul because it lacks the requisite
features—such as the ability to learn and to simulate growth—to
make accurate forecasts. Kelly is the executive editor of *Wired*, a
monthly magazine covering computers and telecommunications.

As you read, consider the following questions:

1. What is the web of "stocks" and "flows," according to Kelly?
2. In the author's opinion, why are locality and regionalism
   important features of a global simulation model?
3. According to Kelly, why does the Limits to Growth model
   inevitably indicate a collapse?

In the 1970s, after thousands of years of telling tales about the Earth's past and creation, the inhabitants of planet Earth began to tell their first story of what might happen to the planet in the future. Rapid communications of the day gave them their first comprehensive real-time view of their home. The portrait from space was enchanting—a cloudy blue marble hanging delicately in the black deep. But down on the ground the emerging tale wasn't so pretty. Reports from every quadrant of the globe said the Earth was unraveling.

Tiny cameras in space brought back photographs of the whole Earth that were awesome in the old-fashioned sense of the word: at once inspiring and frightening. The cameras, together with reams of ground data pouring in from every country, formed a distributed mirror reflecting a picture of the whole system. The entire biosphere was becoming more transparent. The global system began to look ahead—as systems do—wanting to know what might come next, say, in the next 20 years.

A Global Spreadsheet

The first impression arising from the data-collecting membrane around the world was that the planet was wounded. No static world map could verify (or refute) this picture. No globe could chart the ups and downs of pollution and population over time, or decipher the interconnecting influence of one factor upon another. No movie from space could play out the question, what if this continues? What was needed was a planetary prediction machine, a global what-if spreadsheet.

In the computer labs of MIT [Massachusetts Institute of Technology], an unpretentious engineer cobbled together the first global spreadsheet. Jay Forrester had been dabbling in feedback loops since 1939, perfecting machinery-steering servomechanisms. . . .

Sitting on an airplane on the way home from a conference on "The Predicament of Mankind" held in Switzerland in 1970, Forrester began to sketch out the first equations that would form a model he called "World Dynamics."

It was rough. A thumbnail sketch. Forrester's crude model mirrored the obvious loops and forces he intuitively felt governed large economies. For data, he grabbed whatever was handy as a quick estimate. The Club of Rome, the group that had sponsored the conference, came to MIT to evaluate the prototype Forrester had tinkered up. They were encouraged by what they saw. They secured funding from the Volkswagen Foundation to hire Forrester's associate, Dennis Meadows, to develop the model to the next stage. For the rest of 1970, Forrester and Meadows improved the World Dynamics model, designing more sophisticated process loops and scouring the world for current data.

Dennis Meadows, together with his wife Dana and two other coauthors, published the souped-up model, now filled with real data, as the "Limits to Growth." The simulation was wildly successful as the first global spreadsheet. For the first time, the planetary system of life, earthly resources, and human culture were abstracted, embodied into a simulation, and set free to roam into the future. The Limits to Growth also succeeded as a global air raid siren, alerting the world to the conclusions of the authors: that almost every extension of humankind's current path led to civilization's collapse.

Learning Must Be Accounted For

In real life, the populations of India, Africa, China, and South America don't change their actions based upon the hypothetical projections of the Limits to Growth model. They adapt because of their own immediate learning cycle. For instance, the Limits to Growth model was caught off-guard (like most other forecasts) by global birth rates that dropped faster than anyone predicted. Was this due to the influence of doomsday projections like Limits to Growth? The more plausible mechanism is that educated women have less children and are more prosperous, and that prosperous people are imitated. They don't know about, or care about, global limits to growth. Government incentives assist local dynamics already present. People anywhere act (and learn) out of immediate self-interest. This holds true for other functions such as crop productivity, arable land, transportation, and so on. The assumptions for these fluctuating values are fixed in the Limits to Growth model, but in reality the assumptions themselves have coevolutionary mechanisms that flux over time. The point is that the learning must be modeled as an internal loop residing within the model. In addition to the values, the very structure of the assumptions in the simulation—or in any simulation that hopes to anticipate a vivisystem—must be adaptable.

Kevin Kelly, *Out of Control: The Rise of Neo-Biological Civilization*, 1994.

The result of the Limits to Growth model ignited thousands of editorials, policy debates, and newspaper articles around the world for many years following its release. "A Computer Looks Ahead and Shudders" screamed one headline. The gist of the model's discovery was this: "If the present growth trends in world population, industrialization, pollution, food production, and resource depletion continue unchanged, the limits to growth on this planet will be reached sometime within the next 100 years." The modelers ran the simulation hundreds of times in hundreds of slightly different scenarios. But no matter how they made tradeoffs, almost all the simulations predicted population and living standards either withering away or bubbling up quickly to burst shortly thereafter.

Primarily because the policy implications were stark, clear, and unwelcome, the model was highly controversial and heavily scrutinized. But it forever raised the discussion of resources and human activity to the necessary planetary scale. . . . The authors reissued it on its 20th anniversary, with only slight changes.

How the Model Works

As currently implemented, the Limits to Growth model runs on a software program called Stella. Stella takes the dynamic systems approach worked out by Jay Forrester on mainframe computers and ports it over to the visual interface of a Macintosh. The Limits to Growth model is woven out of an impressive web of "stocks" and "flows." Stocks (money, oil, food, capital, etc.) flow into certain nodes (representing general processes such as farming), where they trigger outflows of other stocks. For instance money, land, fertilizer, and labor flow into farms to trigger an outflow of raw food. Food, oil, and other stocks flow into factories to produce fertilizer, to complete one feedback loop. A spaghetti maze of loops, subloops, and cross-loops constitute the entire world. The leverage each loop has upon the others is adjustable and determined by ratios found in real-world data: how much food is produced per hectare per kilo of fertilizer and water, generating how much pollution and waste. As is true in all complex systems, the impact of a single adjustment cannot be calculated beforehand; it must be played out in the whole system to be measured. . . .

Weaknesses in the Model

The Limits to Growth model has many things going for it. Among them: It is not overly complex; it is pumped by feedback loops; it runs scenarios. But among the weaknesses I see in the model are the following:

Narrow overall scenarios. Rather than explore possible futures of any real diversity, Limits to Growth plays out a multitude of minor variations upon one fairly narrow set of assumptions. Mostly the "possible futures" it explores are those that seem plausible to the authors. They ignored scenarios not based on what they felt were reasonable assumptions of expiring finite resources. But resources (such as rare metals, oil, and fertilizer) didn't diminish. Any genuinely predictive model must be equipped with the capability to generate "unthinkable" scenarios. It is important that a system have sufficient elbowroom in the space of possibilities to wander in places we don't expect. There is an art to this, because a model with too many degrees of freedom becomes unmanageable, while one too constrained becomes unreliable.

Wrong assumptions. Even the best model can be sidetracked by false premises. The original key assumption of the model was that the world contains only a 250-year supply of nonrenewable resources, and that the demands on that supply are exponential. We now know both those assumptions are wrong. Reserves of oil and minerals have grown; their prices have not increased; and demand for materials like copper are not exponential. In the 1992 reissue of the model, these assumptions were adjusted. Now the foundational assumption is that pollution *must* rise with growth. I can imagine that premise needing to be adjusted in the next 20 years, if the last 20 are a guide. "Adjustments" of this basic nature have to be made because the Limits to Growth model has . . .

No room for learning. A group of early critics of the model once joked that they ran the Limits to Growth simulation from the year 1800 and by 1900 found a "20-foot level of horse manure on the streets." At the rate horse transportation was increasing then, this would have been a logical extrapolation. The half-jesting critics felt that the model made no provisions for learning technologies, increasing efficiencies, or the ability of people to alter their behavior or invent solutions. . . .

Geography and the Past

World averages. The Limits to Growth model treats the world as uniformly polluted, uniformly populated, and uniformly endowed with resources. This homogenization simplifies and uncomplicates the world enough to model it sanely. But in the end it undermines the purpose of the model because the locality and regionalism of the planet are some of its most striking and important features. Furthermore, the hierarchy of dynamics that arises out of differing local dynamics provides some of the key phenomena of Earth. The Limits to Growth modelers recognize the power of subloops—which is, in fact, the chief virtue of Forrester's system dynamics underpinning the software. But the model entirely ignores the paramount subloop of a world: geography. A planetary model without geography is . . . not the world. Not only must learning be distributed throughout a simulation; *all* functions must be. It is the failure to mirror the distributed nature—the swarm nature—of life on Earth that is this model's greatest failure.

The inability to model open-ended growth of any kind. When I asked Dana Meadows what happened when they ran the model from 1600, or even 1800, she replied that they never tried it. I found that astonishing since backcasting is a standard reality test for forecasting models. In this case, the modelers suspected that the simulation would not cohere. That should be a warning. Since 1600 the world has experienced long-term growth. If a world model is reliable, it should be able to simulate four centuries of growth—at least as history. Ultimately, if we are to believe Limits to Growth has anything to say about future growth, the simulation must, in principle, be capable of generating long-term growth through several periods of transitions. As it is, all that Limits to Growth can prove is that it can simulate one century of collapse.

"Our model is astonishingly 'robust,'" Meadows told me. "You have to do all kinds of things to keep it from collapsing. . . . Always the same behavior and basic dynamic emerges: overshoot and collapse." This is a pretty dangerous model to rely on for predictions of society's future. All the initial parameters of the system quickly converge upon termination, when history tells us human society is a system that displays marvelous continuing expansion. . . .

The scenarios in Limits to Growth collapse because that's what the Limits to Growth simulation is good at. Nearly every initial condition in the model leads to either apocalypse or (very rarely) to stability—but never to a new structure—because the model is inherently incapable of generating open-ended growth. The Limits to Growth cannot mimic the emergence of the industrial evolution from the agrarian age. . . .

Building a Better Model

The Limits to Growth simulation needs not a mere update, but a total redo. The best use for it is to stand as a challenge and a departure point to make a better model. A real predictive model of a planetary society would:

    1) spin significantly varied scenarios,
    2) start with more flexible and informed assumptions,
    3) incorporate distributed learning,
    4) contain local and regional variation, and
    5) if possible, demonstrate increasing complexification. . . .

In bravely attempting to simulate an extremely complex adapting system (the human infrastructure of living on Earth), in order to feed-forward a scenario of this system into the future, the Forrester/Meadows model highlights not the limits to growth but the limits of certain simulations.

The dream of Meadows is . . . to create a system (a machine) that sufficiently mirrors the real evolving world so that this miniature can run faster than real life and thus project its results into the future. We'd like prediction machinery not for a sense of predestiny but for guidance. . . .

The key insight uncovered by the study of complex systems in recent years is this: the only way for a system to evolve into something new is to have a flexible structure. A tiny tadpole can change into a frog, but a 747 Jumbo Jet can't add six inches to its length without crippling itself. . . . A decentralized, redundant organization can flex without distorting its function, and thus it can adapt. It can manage change. We call that growth.

Living Systems

Direct feedback models such as Limits to Growth can achieve stabilization—one attribute of living systems—but they can't learn, grow, or diversify—three essential complexities for a model of changing culture or life. Without these abilities, a world model will fall far behind the moving reality. A learning-less model can be used to anticipate the near-future where evolutionary change is minimal; but to predict an evolutionary system—if it can ever be predicted in pockets—will require the requisite complexity of a simulated, artificial evolutionary model.

But we cannot import evolution and learning without exporting control. . . . [This is] the greatest fault of the Limits to Growth model: its linear, mechanical, and unworkable notion of control.

There is no control outside of self-making system. Vivisystems, such as economies, ecologies, and human culture, can hardly be controlled form any position. They can be prodded, perturbed, cajoled, herded, and at best, coordinated from within. On Earth, there is no outside platform from which to send an intelligent hand into the vivisystem, and no point inside where a control dial waits to be turned. The direction of large swarmlike systems such as human society is controlled by a messy multitude of interconnecting, self-contradictory agents who have only the dimmest awareness of where the whole is at any one moment.

"The great adventure on which modern
neuroscience has embarked will end up
challenging our most cherished concepts
of who we are."

Neuroscience Will Transform Humanity

J. Madeleine Nash

J. Madeleine Nash, the author of the following viewpoint,
writes that scientific study of the human brain will yield unprecedented breakthroughs in such areas as computer technology and the treatment of mental illness, and will lead to an
increased understanding of human consciousness. Nash is a
senior correspondent for *Time* magazine.

As you read, consider the following questions:

1. According to Nash, what have neural networks
   accomplished?
2. What choices will would-be parents face in the future,
   according to Nash?
3. How will brain scanners help children, in the author's
   opinion?

J. Madeleine Nash, "The Frontier Within," *Time* (special issue), Fall 1992; ©1992 Time, Inc.
Reprinted by permission.

Contemplate for a moment a tangle of seaweed tossed up on the shore. This is what a neuron looks like, surrounded by a thicket of tiny tendrils that serve as communications channels. Now multiply that neuron 100 billion times. Crammed into the skull of every human individual are as many neurons as there are stars in the Milky Way. Each one of these receives input from about 10,000 other neurons in the brain and sends messages to a thousand more. The combinatorial possibilities are staggering. The cerebral cortex alone boasts 1 million billion connections, a number so large, marvels neuroscientist Gerald Edelman in his recent book about the brain, *Bright Air, Brilliant Fire*, that "if you were to count them, one connection per second, you would finish counting some 32 million years after you began."

Assembled by nature and honed by evolution, the convoluted 3-lb. organ positioned between our ears represents a triumph of bioengineering, one that continues to elude comprehension and defy imitation. "The brain," declares molecular biologist James Watson, co-discoverer of the physical structure of DNA, "is the most complex thing we have yet discovered in our universe." The quest to understand the biology of intelligence is likely to occupy the minds of the world's best scientists for centuries to come. The task may prove more challenging than those alive today suppose, requiring perhaps new breakthroughs in physics and chemistry. Meanwhile, the knowledge spawned by this search promises to transform society. Here is what lies ahead:

Computers Will Emulate the Brain but Not Replace It

From the wheeled cart to the printing press, from the telephone to the airplane, inventions have enormously expanded the repertoire of human capabilities, and this trend will continue, even accelerate. In this century computers have provided instant access to awesome number-crunching power and a vast storehouse of information. In coming centuries they will augment and amplify human skills in far more astounding ways. Thus, while the brain will not undergo much in the way of biological evolution, humans, assisted by ever more powerful computers, will become capable of far greater intellectual feats. "We won't recognize any difference in brains themselves," emphasizes Maxwell Cowan, chief scientific officer of the Howard Hughes Medical Institute in Bethesda, Maryland. "But we will recognize enormous differences in what brains know and understand."

Intriguingly, the brain's expanding knowledge of itself has begun to suggest radical new approaches to computer design. Like the brain, the computers of the future will not execute tasks in serial lockstep but will be capable of doing a million things in parallel. The chips of which they are composed may well be silicon, but they will mimic biological systems in almost every other way. A tantalizing hint of what the future holds comes from a type of computer known as a neural network. Employing the time-tested tactic of trial and error, these assemblages of artificial neurons have already "learned" to recognize scribbled handwriting, deduce principles of grammar and even mimic the acoustic sensitivity of the barn owl. By cobbling several of these sensory systems together, scientists will certainly be able to create, say, a robot that combines a barn owl's hearing with the ability to track moving objects and issue an ear-piercing hoot. Home gardeners may well employ an artificial owl to chase away rabbits and deer, but they will hardly consider it an intellectual equal. "Let me put it this way," laughs Caltech physicist Carver Mead, a legendary designer of computer chips. "Two hundred years from now, I will not be having this conversation with a piece of silicon."

The Deaf Will Hear, the Blind See, the Lame Walk

By the end of the next century, if not before, scientific insight into the perceptual centers of the human brain should vanquish these ancient afflictions. Already scientists have developed a cochlear implant that bypasses nonfunctioning hair cells in the ear and stimulates the nerve leading to the auditory cortex of the brain. Says Michael Merzenich, a neurophysiologist at the University of California, San Francisco: "We know that these inputs to the brain are distorted, yet the patients who have worn them for a while insist that what they hear sounds perfectly normal." What appears to occur, says Merzenich, is that the brain somehow manages to adjust its connections to make sense of the distortions it receives. This clear demonstration of the plasticity inherent in the adult brain lends hope that scientists of the future will succeed in performing other similar feats. One of these might well be the ability to equip artificial limbs with electronic "neurons" that can respond to signals relayed by the brain. These circuits might even include the equivalents of the axons and dendrites that link one neuron to another.

Almost certainly, scientists will master techniques for stimulating injured neurons to regenerate themselves. The brains and spinal columns of adult mammals do not possess this ability, at least not yet. A clue that this should be possible comes from frogs and salamanders, whose central nervous systems miraculously regrow following injury. Scientists have discovered several proteins that may eventually be deployed to rejuvenate broken spinal cords and damaged optic nerves. "I don't hold out too much hope for bionic man," says Michael Stryker, a colleague of Merzenich's who specializes in vision. "I think we will get there faster using biological techniques."

Scientists are currently absorbed in tracking down genes believed to be responsible for such mental illnesses as manic depression and schizophrenia. Eventually, they can be expected to broaden their goals and seek out the genetic tool kit for building such intellectual traits as musical talent, mathematical genius and, above all, personality. Shyness, for instance, appears to have a genetic basis; assertiveness and hair-trigger anger probably do as well. Like it or not, predicts Dr. Lewis Judd, chairman of the psychiatry department at the University of California at San Diego, "We are going to find that the attitudes we take, the choices we make, are far more influenced by heredity than we ever thought."

The New Frontier

The new frontier of the nineties and the twenty-first century is not the space between planets and solar systems—it is the space between your ears.

Pushing the outer limits of that frontier are neuroscientists that will lead us further than ever before into the mysterious reaches of the human brain.

"The new frontier is about man defining himself, about understanding our nature at the deepest level and understanding some of the curses of mankind that rob us of our humanity, such as Alzheimer's disease," says Dr. Ira Black, the president-elect of the twenty-thousand-member Society for Neuroscience. "The brain and its functions stand at the center of what we are as humans."

Tim Friend, *USA Today*, October 26, 1992.

For the next century or two, if not beyond, schemes for improving the brain through genetic tinkering are likely to be confounded by a combination of social taboos, legal restrictions and sheer biological ignorance. But when the genes that underlie personality and behavior are isolated and understood, society will reach a critical ethical divide. A Pandora's box of options that were not available in centuries past will suddenly pop wide open. Should would-be parents who learn a fetus has inherited a strong likelihood of developing a serious but treatable mental illness opt for an abortion? Should they choose gene therapy to replace the defective DNA in their newborn child's brain cells? And while they're contemplating all this, might they not also consider conferring on their offspring desirable traits like intelligence?

The machines that make images of the brain today are large, expensive contraptions that only major medical centers can afford. But just as computers have become ever smaller, cheaper and more powerful, so will the ultrafast successors to present-day positron-emission tomography and magnetic-resonance imaging scanners. Washington University neurologist Marcus Raichle predicts, in fact, that the "brain scopes" of the future will make a big splash at Disneyland and other theme parks. One can imagine lines of vacationers waiting to have their thoughts and emotions imaged in garish hues.

But these machines will also be put to serious purpose. Consider, for example, the tantalizing evidence that certain patterns of brain activity correlate with higher achievement levels. Competing educational strategies might someday be judged by whether they stimulate specific areas of the brain and how strongly. "Is phonics really the best way to teach reading?" muses Dr. Raichle. "Or is it just another silly idea? By looking at the brain, I think we'll discover the answer to that question." And to others as well. Many mothers-to-be have wondered whether playing music and reciting poetry can influence embryonic brain development in desirable ways. Someday they may be able to judge for themselves.

More important, tomorrow's brain scanners will be able to assess intellectual strengths and weaknesses in preschool children. A wide spectrum of mental weaknesses will become targets for early intervention. Dyslexia could be diagnosed in infancy, the time when brain plasticity is highest. Therapies could then be monitored by charting changes in neuronal firing patterns.

Brains Will Be Healthier, Happier

Prominent mainstays of the pharmacopoeia of the future will be compounds that prevent nerve cells from dying. Much of the devastation caused by stroke is believed to occur because the directly injured neurons release massive quantities of the neurotransmitter glutamate. Normally, tiny bursts of glutamate act as signals between one neuron and another, triggering the brief opening of minuscule channels that allow calcium to pass through the cell's protective membrane. Too much glutamate, however, causes the channels to remain open too long, permitting an abnormal, and lethal, influx of calcium. Soon drugs that mop up excess glutamate or block its action may make this sort of stroke-related brain damage as preventable as tissue damage from gangrene. Similar strategies should likewise succeed in protecting neurons from the ravages of Alzheimer's disease.

Needless to say, expanding knowledge of the brain's complex biochemistry and how it goes awry will bring about more effective treatments for depression and schizophrenia, panic attacks and obsessive compulsions, alcoholism and drug addiction. Along the way, scientists will gain profound insights into the biochemical signals that create the astounding range of human emotions. "Which peptides make you sad, which ones make you happy, and which ones make you feel just grand?" wonders Columbia University neuroscientist Eric Kandel. That knowledge could conceivably translate into an ability to fine-tune those states at will—through either pharmacology or sophisticated biofeedback techniques.

Certainly nothing in the past 100,000 years of cultural evolution can prepare future generations for the moment when science lays bare, as it most certainly will, the secrets of the human mind. "We will be rendered naked," predicts Tufts University philosophy professor Daniel Dennett, "in a way that we've never been naked before. The mind boggles at the varieties of voyeurism, eavesdropping and intrusion that will become possible." Concepts like good and evil, free will and individual responsibility will presumably survive the upheaval, but not before being shaken to their deepest foundations. Imagine, for a moment, that a psychiatrist could peer into the psyche of a serial killer. Could the doctor see what was wrong? If he could, would he know how to fix it?

The great adventure on which modern neuroscience has embarked will end up challenging our most cherished concepts of who we are. "In the end, we will even figure out how this tissue in our skulls produces the states of self-awareness we refer to as consciousness," ventures John Searle, a philosopher of science at the University of California, Berkeley. But just as understanding the Big Bang has not permitted humans to create new universes at will, understanding consciousness will probably not allow us to construct an artificial brain. Besides, says University of Iowa neurologist Dr. Antonio Damasio, "a brain is not likely to work without a body." At the very least, a disembodied brain would be extremely disoriented and terribly unhappy.

In the coming centuries, one imagines, the desire to create monstrous caricatures of ourselves will dissipate. At long last, we will reclaim the awe and wonder our predecessors reserved for machines and turn them back toward our biological selves. Like Narcissus, we will behold the image of our minds and lose ourselves in endless admiration.

*"The fourth robot generation and its successors
. . . could replace human beings in every
essential task."*

Robots Will
Become Humanlike

Hans Moravec

For decades, inventors and science fiction writers have contemplated robots with humanlike characteristics. In the following viewpoint, robotics researcher Hans Moravec argues that such robots will evolve by the middle of the twenty-first century. Moravec describes progressive stages of robot evolution, from robots operated by simple programs to those performing almost every essential human task. He concludes with a scenario describing the transfer of a human mind to a robot. Moravec is the director of the Mobile Robotics Laboratory at Carnegie Mellon University's Robotics Institute in Pittsburgh, Pennsylvania.

As you read, consider the following questions:

1. How are cybernetics and Artificial Intelligence different, according to Moravec?
2. What two forms of heredity do human beings have, according to Moravec?
3. In the author's brain surgery scenario, what are the effects of faster brain speed?

Excerpted from "Robots and Artificial Intelligence" by Hans Moravec, in *The World of 2044*, edited by Charles Sheffield, Marcelo Alonso, and Morton A. Kaplan (New York: Paragon House, 1994). Reprinted with permission.

Instincts regarding the nature and quantity of work we enjoy probably evolved during the one hundred thousand years our ancestors lived as hunter-gatherers. Less than ten thousand years ago the agricultural revolution made life more stable, and richer in goods and information. But, paradoxically, it requires more human labor to support an agricultural society than to live in a primitive one, and the work is of a different, "unnatural," kind, out of step with old instincts. The effort to avoid it has resulted in domestication of animals, slavery, and the industrial revolution. Many jobs must still be done by hand, engendering for hundreds of years the fantasy of an intelligent but soulless being that can tirelessly dispatch the drudgery.

Thinking Machines

But only in this century have electronic sensors and computers given machines the ability to sense their world and to think about it, and so offered a way to fulfill the wish. As in the fables, the side effects are likely to dominate the resulting story. Most significantly, these perfect slaves will continue to develop, and will not long remain soulless. As they increase in competence they will have occasion to make more and more autonomous decisions, and so will slowly develop a volition and purpose of their own. At the same time they will become indispensable. Our minds evolved to store the skills and memories of a Stone Age life, not the enormous complexity that has developed in the last ten thousand years. We've kept up, after a fashion, through a series of social inventions—social stratification and a division of labor, memory aids like poetry and schooling, written records stored outside the body, and recently machines that can do some of our thinking entirely without us. The portion of absolutely essential human activity that takes place outside of human bodies and minds has been steadily increasing. Hard-working intelligent machines may complete the trend.

Serious attempts to build thinking machines began after World War II. One line of research, called cybernetics, used simple electronic circuitry to mimic small nervous systems, and produced machines that could learn to recognize simple patterns, and turtle-like robots that found their way to lighted recharging hutches. An entirely different approach, named Artificial Intelligence (AI), attempted to duplicate rational human thought in the large computers that appeared after the war, and by 1965 had demonstrated programs that proved theorems in logic and geometry, solved calculus problems, and played good games of checkers. In the early 1970s, AI research groups at the Massachusetts Institute of Technology (MIT) and Stanford University attached television cameras and robot arms to their computers, so their "thinking" programs could begin to collect their information directly from the real world.

What a shock! While the pure reasoning programs did their jobs about as well and about as fast as college freshmen, the best robot control programs took hours to find and pick up a few blocks on a table, and often failed completely—a performance much worse than a six-month-old child. This disparity between programs that reason and programs that perceive and act in a real world holds to this day. . . .

Emulating the Human Nervous System

By comparing the edge- and motion-detecting circuitry in the four layers of nerve cells in the retina, the best understood major circuit in the human nervous system, with similar processes developed for "computer vision" systems that allow robots in research and industry to see, I've estimated that it would take a billion computations per second (the power of a world leading Cray 2 supercomputer) to produce the same results at the same speed as a human retina. By extrapolation, to emulate a whole brain might take ten trillion arithmetic operations per second, or ten thousand Crays worth. This is for operations our nervous systems do extremely efficiently and well. . . .

In *arithmetic* today's average computers are one million times more powerful than human beings. In very narrow areas of *rational thought* (like playing chess or proving theorems) they are about the same. And in *perception* and *control of movement* in the complex real world, and related areas of common sense knowledge and intuitive and visual problem solving, today's average computers are a million times less capable. . . .

Robotics Research and Evolution

I feel that the fastest progress on the hardest problems will come from the field of robotics, the construction of systems that must see and move in the physical world. Robotics research is imitating the *evolution* of animal minds, adding capabilities to machines a few at a time, so that the resulting sequence of machine behaviors resembles the capabilities of animals with increasingly complex nervous systems. This effort to build intelligence from the bottom up is helped by biological peeks at the "back of the book"—at the neuronal, structural, and behavioral features of animals and humans.

The best robots today are controlled by computers just powerful enough to simulate the nervous system of an insect, cost as much as houses, and so find only a few profitable niches in society (among them, spray painting and spot welding cars and assembling circuit boards). But those few applications are encouraging research that is slowly providing a base for a huge future growth. Robot evolution in the direction of full intelligence will greatly accelerate, I believe, in about a decade, when the mass-produced general purpose, *universal*, robot (which I will also refer to as the "Volks-Robot," from the German "people") becomes possible.

The Volks-Robot (ca. 2000–2010)

The first generation of universal robot will need to navigate reliably and safely over stairs and rough and flat ground. It must be able to manipulate most objects, and to find them in the world in front of it. . . .

The slow operation of [experimental robots] suggests one other element needed for the Volks-Robot, namely a computer about one thousand times as powerful as those found on desks and in robots today. Such machines, able to do one billion computations per second, would provide approximately the brain power of a mouse (with different abilities).

Fear of Falling

Third-generation robots—advanced robots, say, forty years from now—will simulate the world. So if one runs into a situation where it almost falls down some stairs, it won't just stop with conditioning itself not to do whatever led up to that. It will simulate everything, what would've happened if it had fallen. And its simulation will produce an internal picture of itself crumpled in a heap down at the bottom of the stairs. And that will look really awful. If the robot's internal problem detectors have any sense at all, there will be one for saying, "Crumpled in a mass at the bottom of the stairs is really, really bad. So whatever it was you did—*really, don't do that!*" If the robot has the ability to run through scenarios of the previous day, looking for improvements, then it's going to be running through this scenario, with this terrible possible consequence, a lot. And it's going to be looking for all sorts of ways to avoid it. So now this *fear*, you might say, has gotten a lot richer. It's starting to resemble human fear. If you were to ask the robot what it felt, it might say, "Yes, I think I was afraid, because all my analogies to physiological states mimicked what I know happens in humans in similar circumstances."

Hans Moravec, *Discover*, November 1992.

Universal robots will find their first uses in factories, where they will be cheaper and more versatile than the older generation of robots they replace. Eventually they will become cheap enough for some households, extending the reach of personal computers from a few tasks in the data world to many in the physical world. . . .

Learning (2010–2020)

Useful though they will be, the first generation of universal robots will be rigid slaves to simple programs. If the machine bangs its elbow while chopping beef in your kitchen making stroganoff, you will have to find another place for the robot to do its work, or beg the software manufacturer for a fix. Second generation robots with more powerful computers will be able to host a more flexible kind of program able to adjust itself by a kind of conditioned learning. In other words, they will be adaptive robots. First generation programs will consist primarily of sequences of the type "Do step A, then B, then C. . . ." The programs for the second generation will read "Do step A1 or A2 or A3 . . . then B1 or B2 or B3 . . . then C1 or C2 or C3. . . ." In the beef stroganoff example, A1 might be to chop with the right hand of the robot, while A2 is to use the left hand. Each alternative in the program has a "weight," a number that indicates the desirability of using it rather than one of the alternate tasks. The machine also contains a "pain" system, a series of programs that look out for problems, such as collisions, and respond by reducing the weights of recently invoked branches, and a "pleasure" system that increases the relevant weights when good conditions, such as well-charged batteries or a task efficiently completed, are detected. As the robot bangs its elbow repeatedly on a microwave in your kitchen, it gradually learns to use its other hand (as well as adapting to its surroundings in a thousand other ways). A program with many alternatives at each step, whose pain and pleasure systems are arranged to produce a pleasure signal on hearing the word "good" and a pain message on hearing "bad" could be slowly trained to do new tasks, like a dog or a cat.

Imagery (2020–2030)

Adaptive robots will find jobs everywhere, and the hardware and software that supports them could become the largest on earth. But teaching them new tasks, whether by writing programs or through punishment and reward, will be very tedious. This deficiency will lead to a prodigious innovation, a software *world-modeler* (requiring another big increase in computer power), that allows the robot to simulate its immediate surroundings and its own actions within them, and thus to think about its tasks before acting. Before making beef stroganoff in your kitchen, the new robot would simulate the task many times. Each time its simulated elbow bangs the simulated cabinet, the software would update the learning weights just as if the collision had physically happened. After many mental runthroughs the robot would be well trained, so that when it finally cooks for real, it does it correctly.

The simulation can be used in many other ways. After a job, the robot can run through its previous actions and try variations on them to improve future performance. A robot might even be configured to invent some of its own programs by means of a simpler program that can detect how nearly a sequence of robot actions achieves a desired task. This training program would, in repeated simulations, provide the "good" and "bad" indications needed to condition a general learning program like the "dog or cat" program of the previous decade.

It will take a large community of patient researchers to build good simulators. A robot entering a new room must include vast amounts of prior knowledge in its simulation, such as the expected shapes and probable contents of kitchen cabinets and the effect of (and force needed for) turning faucet knobs. It needs instinctive motor-perceptual knowledge about the world that took millions of years of evolution to install in us, that tells us instinctively when a height is dangerous, how hard to throw a stone, or if the animal facing us is a threat. Robots that incorporate it may be as smart as monkeys.

Reasoning (2030–2040)

In the decades while the "bottom-up" evolution of robots is transferring the perceptual and motor faculties of human beings into machinery, the conventional Artificial Intelligence industry will be perfecting the mechanization of reasoning. Since today's programs already match human beings in some areas, those of forty years from now, running on computers a million times as fast as today's, should be quite superhuman. Today's reasoning programs work from small amounts of clear and correct information prepared by human beings. Data from robot sensors such as cameras is much too voluminous and too noisy for them to use. But a good robot simulator will contain nearly organized data about the robot and its world—for instance, if a knife is on the countertop, or if the robot is holding a cup. A robot with simulator can be married to a reasoning program to produce a machine with most of the abilities of a human being. The combination will create a being that in some ways resembles us, but in others is like nothing the world has seen before.

First Generation Technicalities

Both industrial robot manipulators and the research effort to build "smart" robots are twenty-five years old. Universal robots will require at least another decade of development, but some of their elements can be guessed from the experience so far. One consideration is weight. Mobile robots built to work in human sized spaces today weigh too many hundreds of pounds. This dangerously large mass has three major components: batteries, motors, and structure. Lead-acid batteries able to drive a mobile robot for a day contribute about one-third of the weight. But nickel-cadmium aircraft batteries weigh half as much, and newer lithium batteries can be half again as light. Electric motors are efficient and precisely controllable, but standard motors are heavy and require equally heavy reducing gears. Ultrastrong permanent magnets can halve the weight and generate high torque without gears. Robot structure has been primarily aluminum. Its weight contribution can be cut by a factor of four by substituting composite materials containing superstrength fibers of graphic, aramid, or the new material Spectra. These innovations could be combined to make a robot with roughly the size, weight, strength, and endurance of a human.

The first generation robot will probably move on wheels. Legged robots have advantages on complicated terrain, but they consume too much power. A simple wheeled robot would be confined to areas of flat ground, but if each wheel has a controlled suspension with about a meter of travel, the robot could slowly lift its wheels as needed to negotiate rough ground and stairs. . . .

The robot's travels would be greatly aided if it could continuously pinpoint its location, perhaps by detecting the signals from a handful of small synchronized transmitters distributed in its environment. . . .

Mind Children (2050 +)

The fourth robot generation and its successors, with human perceptual and motor abilities and superior reasoning powers, could replace human beings in every essential task. In principle, our society could continue to operate increasingly well without us, with machines running the companies and doing the research as well as performing the productive work. Since machines can be designed to work well in outer space, production could move to the greater resources of the solar system, leaving behind a nature preserve subsidized from space. Meek humans would inherit the earth, but rapidly evolving machines would expand into the rest of the universe.

This development can be viewed as a very natural one. Human beings have two forms of heredity, one the traditional biological kind, passed on strands of DNA, the other cultural, passed from mind to mind by example, language, books, and recently machines. At present the two are inextricably linked, but the cultural part is evolving very rapidly and gradually assuming functions once the province of our biology. In terms of information content, our cultural side is already by far the larger part of us. The fully intelligent robot marks the point where our cultural side can exist on its own, free of biological limits. Intelligent machines, which are evolving among us, learning our skills, sharing our goals, and being shaped by our values, can be viewed as our children, the children of our minds. With them our biological heritage is not lost, it will be safely stored in libraries at least, but its importance will be greatly diminished.

What about life back on the preserve? For some of us the thought of being grandly upstaged by our artificial progeny will be disappointing, and life may seem pointless if we are fated to spend it staring stupidly at our ultra-intelligent progeny as they try to describe their ever more spectacular discoveries in baby-talk that we can understand. Is there any way individual humans might join the adventure?

More Machine than Human

You've just been wheeled into the operating room. A robot brain surgeon is in attendance, and a computer waits nearby. Your skull, but not your brain, is anesthetized. You are fully conscious. The robot surgeon opens your brain case and places a hand on the brain's surface. This unusual hand bristles with microscopic machinery, and a cable connects it to the computer at your side. Instruments in the hand scan the first few millimeters of brain surface. These measurements, and a comprehensive understanding of human neural architecture, allow the surgeon to write a program that models the behavior of the uppermost layer of the scanned brain tissue. This program is installed in a small portion of the waiting computer and activated. Electrodes in the hand supply the simulation with the appropriate inputs from your brain, and can inject signals from the simulation. You and the surgeon compare the signals it produces with the original ones. They flash by very fast, but any discrepancies are highlighted on a display screen. The surgeon fine-tunes the simulation until the correspondence is nearly perfect. As soon as you are satisfied, the simulation output is activated. The brain layer is now impotent—it receives inputs and reacts as before, but its output is ignored. Microscopic manipulators on the hand's surface excise this superfluous tissue and pass it to an aspirator, where it is drawn away.

The surgeon's hand sinks a fraction of a millimeter deeper into your brain, instantly compensating its measurements and signals for the changed position. The process is repeated for the next layer, and soon a second simulation resides in the computer, communicating with the first and with the remaining brain tissue. Layer after layer the brain is simulated, then excavated. Eventually your skull is empty, and the surgeon's hand rests deep in your brain stem. Though you have not lost consciousness, or even your train of thought, your mind has been removed from the brain and transferred to a machine. In a final, disorienting step the surgeon lifts its hand. Your suddenly abandoned body dies. For a moment you experience only quiet and dark.

Then, once again, you can open your eyes. Your perspective has shifted. The computer simulation has been disconnected from the cable leading to the surgeon's hand and reconnected to a shiny new body of the style, color, and material of your choice. Your metamorphosis is complete.

Mind Speed

Your new mind has a control labeled "speed." It had been set at 1, to keep the simulations synchronized with the old brain, but now you change it to 10,000, allowing you to communicate, react, and think ten thousand times faster. You now seem to have hours to respond to situations that previously seemed instantaneous. You have time, during the fall of a dropped object, to research the advantages and disadvantages of trying to catch it, perhaps to solve its differential equations of motion. When your old biological friends speak with you, their sentences take hours—you have plenty of time to think about the conversations, but they try your patience. Boredom is a mental alarm that keeps you from wasting your time in profitless activity, but if it acts too soon or too aggressively it limits your attention span, and thus your intelligence. With help from the machines, you change your mind-program to retard the onset of boredom. Having done that, you will find yourself comfortably working on long problems with sidetracks upon sidetracks. In fact, your thoughts routinely become so involved that you need an increase in your memory. These are but the first of many changes. Soon your friends complain that you have become more like the machines than the biological human you once were. That's life.

"The main reason for going into space in future will be the pursuit of cash."

Space Exploration Will Become Commercialized

Vincent Kiernan

According to Vincent Kiernan, the author of the following viewpoint, the age of space exploration is ending and will be followed by an age of commercial exploitation of space. Kiernan contends that once the cost of rocket launches is reduced, there will be numerous commercial ventures in outer space. Kiernan is a science writer for *New Scientist*, a biweekly British science magazine.

As you read, consider the following questions:

1. According to Kiernan, what are the space exploration goals of various nations?
2. On what concept would a lunar rover entertainment system be based, according to the author?
3. How could the isotope helium-3 be used as an energy source, in Kiernan's opinion?

Vincent Kiernan, "Plundering the Final Frontier," *New Scientist*, vol. 143, no. 1935, July 23, 1994; ©IPC Magazines Ltd. Reprinted with permission.

"Hello and welcome to the final of the Space Rugby World Cup, broadcast to you live from Japan's Olympus Sports Complex, orbiting hundreds of kilometres above the Earth." A vision of the future for space? Perhaps. After the 25th anniversary of the 1969 Apollo 11 moon landing, it may seem mundane to suggest that space will be used for activities such as sport. But some space analysts would go further. They say the era of noble feats of exploration is over. The main reason for going into space in future will be the pursuit of cash, and a new generation of astro-entrepreneurs could make their fortunes trading materials manufactured only in space, taking tourists into orbit or even selling sponsorship of space sports.

Why the change? In the past, civilian space programmes have acted as showcases for state-of-the-art technology and engineering in the propaganda battle between East and West during the Cold War. Before the collapse of the Soviet Union, NASA and the Russian Space Agency had the clearly defined task of beating each other. No longer. "The Cold War is over and with it many of the reasons for justifying a civil space programme," says Peggy Finarelli, who helps plan future projects at NASA. Now governments refuse to spend the large quantities of taxpayers' money needed to support the massive programmes of the past, she says.

The Promises of Space

So space agencies have been casting around for another *raison d'etre* [reason for being]. Dan Goldin, the head of NASA, says the space agency needs a simple goal that will be easy to understand and will generate public support. One possibility, he says, could be to put a major effort behind the search for a habitable planet orbiting a nearby star. He believes such a goal, and the possibility of finding extraterrestrial life, would grab the public's imagination and give people a reason to support the programme.

Others think the Earth should be the focus of attention, with satellites used mainly to monitor the Earth's changing environment to bring about a better understanding of its climate. The Russian space agency says it is concentrating on environmental space missions. The European Space Agency is developing a new generation of weather satellites known as Metop which will be launched at the end of the decade. And NASA has ambitious plans to launch 17 satellites between 1998 and 2012, at a total cost of $8 billion, to monitor the environment. Goldin says that such research could form part of his programme by helping space scientists understand how to examine environments on other planets.

The Japanese have not been involved in this show of strength in space. Instead, they are being more pragmatic. Earlier this year, the National Space Development Agency launched its own

H-2 rocket designed and built by Japanese industry and widely regarded as the world's most advanced expendable rocket. Looking to the future, Japan is hoping to make money in space by manufacturing materials in the near weightless conditions, mining raw materials from the surface of the Moon and pampering rich tourists in orbiting hotels.

Just as the hunger for gold and raw materials drove the exploration of the New World 500 years ago, the commercial promise of space could entice entrepreneurs to take on ventures that NASA would never envision. "The commercial potential of space is ultimately the reason why we will go back in large numbers," says Lori Garver, executive director of the National Space Society, a group of space enthusiasts based in Washington, DC. William Braselton, a vice-president of Harris Government Aerospace Systems, a NASA and Pentagon contractor based in Melbourne, Florida, calls space business "the world's largest industry of the early 21st century."

Space Satellites

Virtually all that business will be generated indirectly on Earth. Constellations of telecommunications satellites could provide instant links between any two points on the globe with portable phones, making businesses in far-flung corners of the world easier to run. The Teledesic Corporation based in Kirkland, Washington, for example, has a plan to place 840 satellites in orbits 700 kilometres above the surface by 2001.

One system is in place—the Global Positioning System, a network of 24 military navigational satellites which can pinpoint the position of a hand-held receiver on Earth to within 100 metres. The GPS has created a new business in the manufacture of receivers and is already being used by fishermen to navigate more easily at sea and by surveyors to make maps more quickly. In future, the GPS could be used for other terrestrial applications such as relaying the position of driverless cars to the computer which controls them. Such a system would allow closely packed queues of traffic to travel safely at speed.

Another idea is to use satellites to transmit power from one part of the globe to another. Electricity generated at one spot would be converted into microwaves and beamed towards an orbiting microwave mirror which would reflect it to a receiving station. The idea was embraced by a committee at the Institute of Electrical and Electronics Engineers (IEEE) based in New York. The same panel suggested dumping nuclear waste in orbit around Earth, an idea also being toyed with by Russian scientists.

The waste would be launched from isolated areas such as Antarctica or Greenland to reduce the risk to humans should a rocket explode and release its payload into the atmosphere. In theory, the waste would stay in orbit until it ceased to be radioactive. The committee decided that the basic difficulty was not technological but the public apprehension regarding all things nuclear.

Of course, such a proposal is hugely controversial. Steve Aftergood of the Federation of American Scientists, a pressure group based in Washington, DC, believes it will never happen because of the cost and the public outcry. In 1989, antinuclear activists, worried about the possibility of an accident, took legal action against NASA to block the launch of the nuclear-powered space probe Galileo. The action failed but NASA has not proposed any further missions involving nuclear power.

In any case, disposing of waste in this way would be very expensive, says Aftergood. To minimise the risk of nuclear contamination in the event of an accident, the waste would have to be packed in strong protective containers that add weight to the payload and push up the cost of each launch. The National Academy of Sciences, an advisory group to the US government, says that the containers required for 50 tonnes of plutonium would weigh more than 1000 tonnes and cost more than $10 billion to put in orbit. What is more, adds Aftergood, space is becoming crowded: "Earth orbit—even a very high orbit—is valuable real estate." He says that better use could be found for such orbits than for the waste disposal industry.

Marketing Outer Space

One of the most lucrative space industries could be entertainment. Luna Corp, an entertainment company based in Virginia, plans to build a robotic rover and land it on the Moon by 1997 at a cost of between $90 and $120 million. The vehicle would be controlled remotely from Earth using a virtual reality system. Luna Corp hopes to sell opportunities to take the machine's controls and hopes to organise a worldwide competition to find the first driver.

But the real impact of space industry will be in new businesses away from the Earth's surface requiring workers with the skills to build space stations, orbiting hotels and sports centres while working in weightless conditions. Patrick Collins, an economist at Imperial College in London and at the Institute of Space and Aeronautical Science in Tokyo, says that building and launching such a stadium in space might cost $800 million and a hotel as little as $250 million. In contrast, the international space station Alpha will cost the US alone $17.8 billion through 2002.

Collins says his complex will be cheap to build because it will be a simple modular structure requiring little new technology; in fact, most of the technology needed is no more advanced than that used for the Skylab orbiting research station launched in the 1970s. He also expects the advent of reusable rockets to reduce the cost of launching materials from current levels of up to $40,000 per kilogram to around $200. And money could be recouped by selling the rights to televise such events and by charging fans as much as $2,000 a week to stay.

In fact, space tourism has already begun. In 1990, the Tokyo Broadcasting Service paid the Russians $12 million to send a journalist to the orbiting space station Mir. Surveys in America and Britain show that up to 45 per cent of adults would like to travel in space. The IEEE estimates such a figure translates into 250 million adults worldwide.

Low-Earth Orbit

Rocket liftoffs as common as airplane takeoffs. Spaceports sprinkled throughout the world. Making dinner reservations at a low-Earth orbit hotel.

It's a healthy serving of the future, courtesy of William Gaubatz, director-program manager of Delta Clipper programs for McDonnell Douglas Aerospace's Space Systems Unit in Huntington Beach, California. What's even better, Gaubatz is far from being a viewgraph visionary. When the smoke clears following every flight of the firm's Delta Clipper-Experimental (DC-X) rocket, an early surge of the future becomes ever more visible.

Low-Earth orbit could well become a high-speed off ramp for manufacturing, be it a new biomedicine made in microgravity, advanced metals or exotic optical glass. It's the "Who knows?" factor that will likely transform space into a site for large-scale manufacturing, Gaubatz says. "Somebody will make a ton of money just selling jewelry made in space, or something," he adds.

Leonard David, *Final Frontier*, July/August 1995.

Garver believes that space tourism will be a viable proposition within 25 years. The key, she says, is finding a cheaper way to launch passengers into orbit. The next generation of rockets that will do the trick are already being developed. In 1993, the aerospace company McDonnell Douglas demonstrated an experimental reusable rocket called the Delta Clipper. By the end of the decade, a full-sized version could be taking passengers into space at a cost of only $500 per kilogram.

Others have more ambitious visions of business in space. Harrison Schmitt, a geologist who walked on the Moon in 1972 as a member of the Apollo 17 mission, points out that the isotope helium-3, which does not exist in large quantities on Earth, is found in large quantities on the Moon. Helium-3 can be used in fusion processes to generate large amounts of energy more efficiently than the current favourite, tritium-deuterium fusion. One tonne of helium-3 could provide enough energy to supply electricity to a city of 10 million people for a year. Twenty-five tonnes—an amount the space shuttle could carry—could power the whole of the US for a year. Schmitt argues that helium-3 could also be used to power rockets launched from the Moon to explore the Solar System and, eventually, nearby stars.

But crewed visits to other planets in our Solar System are a long way in the future. "I don't think a crewed mission to Mars will be possible within the next decade," says Goldin. He believes such a mission would not receive political backing unless a spacecraft could be designed and launched within ten years and cost only tens of billions of dollars—current estimates suggest the programme would take decades to complete and cost hundreds of billions of dollars. And scientists would have to find ways to help astronauts prevent the muscle and bone loss that prolonged weightlessness can cause and also ways of protecting them against cosmic radiation. Goldin says that if we send humans to Mars and back we must ensure we can do it safely.

Flight into Danger

Not everyone agrees, however. Noel Hinners, a space scientist at the aerospace company Martin Marietta, suggests that some scientists would leap at the chance to go to Mars, even if there were no way of bringing them back to Earth. He says there is an inconsistency in our attitudes towards scientists and safety, citing the unsung deaths of 55 scientists since 1946 while working on Antarctic projects funded by the American government. But the death of even one astronaut can bring the entire US space programme to a standstill, as happened in the wake of the Challenger space shuttle disaster in 1986. "We go to incredible lengths to protect life at all costs," says Hinners, but those costs make exploration too expensive. He says we have to be more realistic about the risks of exploring space.

And of all the forecasts about space exploration, the easiest to make is that astronauts will die, joining the ten Americans and four Soviets who have died carrying out their duties. Recent budget cuts are fuelling worries that NASA may no longer be able to fly the space shuttle safely. Since the Challenger disaster the ageing shuttles have flown 38 times. "Sooner or later, one of those things is going to blow up again," says John Pike, a space policy analyst at the Federation of American Scientists. Such an event would ground the shuttle fleet and might even lead to the cancellation of the shuttle programme, says Pike. But Goldin insists that NASA will spend whatever it takes to prevent another disaster: "We will have the shuttle flying safely or we will ground it."

Flying the shuttle is crucial for the construction of the space station Alpha, which will be the focus of international space efforts over the next 30 years. "It may not be the world's most perfect vehicle. But it is the only machine capable of putting 40 tonnes into orbit and bringing 40 tonnes back," says Goldin. Grounding the fleet would seriously hamper construction.

By the end of the decade, Goldin says NASA will decide whether to replace the shuttle altogether. The most likely candidates for the next generation of rockets are reusable models that can reach orbit with a single stage, unlike the shuttle which throws its huge external fuel tank every time it flies. The Delta Clipper is an example of these so-called single stage to orbit rockets. They will be easily serviced, have short turnaround times and could make space travel as routine as commercial flight is today. And because they fly more than once, the cost of building the craft can be recouped over many flights.

Launch costs have also hampered scientists' efforts to send probes into space. The main reason for this is that probes are now so big and complex that they are too expensive to build and launch. Future craft will be simpler, smaller and cheaper.

Early satellites were small because early rockets couldn't lift much into space. Sputnik 1, the first satellite, launched in 1959, weighed 86 kilograms while the first US satellite, Explorer 1, weighed only 4.8 kg. Since then satellites have grown bigger and heavier. For example, the Cassini space probe due to be launched in 1997 to study Saturn and its moons will weigh a whopping 5,634 kg.

The great expense of modern spacecraft means fewer missions eat up all available funds. And with fewer missions there is greater pressure to ensure success. This forces scientists to build in backup systems and to test the device extensively before launch, driving up costs still further. The result has been a vicious circle of fewer spacecraft that cost more and take longer to build. The Cassini mission is expected to cost $3.7 billion. In 1958, Explorer 1 cost $5.9 million.

Cutting Costs

But now NASA is trying to break this cycle with a spacecraft built under a programme known as Discovery. These spacecraft will be simple and built with lightweight components. They will be cheap and there will be plenty of them—if one fails it will not be such a big blow to the entire space effort. The first mission, which will visit a near-Earth asteroid, will be launched in 1998 at a cost of only $150 million. Future missions could be designed to collect sample materials from throughout the Solar System and bring them back to Earth. The advantage is that such a spacecraft will be light and simple because it will not need to carry any analytical equipment. Also, the spacecraft's scientific bounty can be examined by scientists from many disciplines under ideal laboratory conditions.

Costs are the key issue. The cheaper it is to get into space, the easier it will be for businessmen and scientists to operate there. As the space industry matures it will require more launch pads and more companies dedicated to building satellites, as well as better rockets. In future, historians may say that the development of such a space infrastructure had the same boost on the world's economy in the early 21st century as did the construction of major road networks this century and the building of rail networks in the last.

"It's possible that out there may be thousands of species more intelligent than we are."

The Wild Card
of Alien Contact

Arlan Andrews, Yoji Kondo, and Charles Sheffield, interviewed by *Science Fiction Age*

In the following viewpoint, *Science Fiction Age* magazine interviews scientists and science fiction writers Arlan Andrews, Yoji Kondo, and Charles Sheffield about the possibility of humans encountering aliens from outer space. Andrews is the manager of the Advanced Manufacturing Initiatives Department at Sandia National Laboratories in Albuquerque, New Mexico. Kondo is a director at NASA's Goddard Space Center in Greenbelt, Maryland. Sheffield is a consultant for Earth Satellite Corporation in Rockville, Maryland.

As you read, consider the following questions:

1. According to Sheffield, how many worlds are there in the universe?
2. What do humans assume about aliens' cultural views, in Kondo's opinion?
3. According to Andrews, how do many in the UFO community believe aliens were attracted to Earth?

Excerpted from an interview with Arlan Andrews, Yoji Kondo, and Charles Sheffield by *Science Fiction Age*, vol. 3, no. 2, 1994. Reprinted by permission of Sovereign Media Co., Herndon, VA.

SF Age: Before we discuss what it might be like to come face to face with an alien, perhaps we should see if we have any consensus on whether or not the universe holds anything alien out there for us to find in the first place.

Sheffield: I consider it is not only unknown, but it is unknowable. The only way you'll know there's an alien life form is when you encounter one, if you encounter one. Until that happens, it's rather like a discussion of angels, except that you can imagine encountering an alien; it's rather difficult for me to imagine encountering an angel.

Andrews: I see your presumption here is that if and when we do encounter aliens, we would recognize them as life. They don't have to be only anthropoid or humanoid, and maybe they're not even anything recognizable. They would not have to even be corporeal, as we recognize it. They might be energy forms, miasmas, plasmas, or colonies.

Alien Intelligence

Sheffield: One of the problems is that in science fiction, when one talks of alien life forms, it is usually assumed to be some sort of *intelligence*. In other words, if we were to discover a slime mold on one of the satellites of Jupiter, that would in fact be an alien life form (assuming we hadn't taken it there with us). However, it would not be a very satisfactory alien in the terms usually used by science fiction. You need smart *aliens* in science fiction. Otherwise, you might as well write about slime molds here on Earth, and that would have limited audience appeal.

Kondo: Still, an alien would not necessarily interact with human beings, even when they come to us. It is not to be assumed a priority. Consider the alien in *The Black Cloud* by Fred Hoyle. They manage to communicate with the black cloud, but one might have passed by us without really having ever established communication with human beings. That is also possible. Let me answer your first question by saying that I am inclined to be agnostic about aliens. And I guess to this extent I agree with Charles, except I think we should include the possibility of encountering aliens that may not be intelligent. As long as they are not really creatures from this planet, I think we could include them as aliens.

Sheffield: Then the first question is, do we believe there is any form of life outside of the Earth, and to that, I say that I believe there is. There has to be. We're looking at ten to the eleventh stars in the galaxy, and ten to the eleventh galaxies, so you've probably got on the order of ten to the twentieth worlds. Now yes, I believe that life does exist on one of them. The question is, if it's in a galaxy that's three billion parsecs [one parsec equals 3.26 light-years] from us, is that very interesting to us, since we would never realistically be able to communicate with that life form? The answer is, it's interesting, but it's not of *practical* interest.

Andrews: If we knew that life was there, under any circumstances, there would be a great deal more than academic interest. It would impact philosophy and everything else. Let me weigh in on the side that I *do* think that there will be intelligent life elsewhere, because we've explored one solar system, albeit not thoroughly. But in that one solar system we've explored, there is at least one intelligent race and the probability of life in that one solar system—namely ours—is a hundred percent. So if you wanted to extrapolate our limited knowledge, you could say that the odds would be that *all* solar systems would support intelligent life.

Kondo: For the probability of detecting planets around any given star, it is not necessary to think only in terms of a solar type star. Solar type stars are unique in the sense that they tend to provide a stable environment for about ten or fifteen billion years. Therefore, there is a chance for life to evolve and develop into an intelligent being. So to that extent I agree with you. But planets may be found around stars other than solar types.

Sheffield: One of the troubles is, we are dealing with, as Arlan said, a set with one member at the moment, which is ourselves, and extrapolation to the rest of the universe becomes tricky. . . .

Alien and Human Aspects

Kondo: As I said earlier, I am agnostic about the existence of aliens to begin with. But assuming that aliens exist, about which I have no proof or disproof, I tend to disagree with Charles in the sense that any indication of their existence is sufficient to cause interest in more intense search. I would agree with Arlan, if we had any indication that they existed. Having said that, I think I should point out that we tend to assume that aliens have similar cultural views. Even the most bizarre aliens in SF [science fiction] stories still tend to share some of our cultural values. This may not be the case at all; aliens may have their own cultural values, especially if their survival depends on very much different circumstances.

SF Age: In SF, however, it seems that you can't make an alien truly alien, because then no one would understand it. If we met something that was truly alien, would any sort of communication be possible?

Kondo: You're probably right. But Fred Hoyle at least partially succeeded in his *Black Cloud*. I think it's possible. You can come up with very alien concepts.

Sheffield: In writing about aliens, I think about what Konrad Lorenz wrote in his book on aggression, "If a lion could speak, we would not understand it." And I have a suspicion that if we met a real live alien, we would be totally unable to communicate with it for a long period, maybe a few hundred years, except perhaps on the most basic level of mathematical theorems. We wouldn't understand its motivations. In fact, I suspect that we don't even understand the motivations of other people on Earth.

You don't even have to go very far abroad. Go down to the poorer parts of Southeast Washington [D.C.] and try to understand what life is like. I think that we have a big problem in adapting our own world view to theirs. Most of our troubles come because of that. So I think we might meet aliens, but I don't think we'll be able to talk to each other, even if they are smart.

'Could you please give the door a kick? It sticks a bit.'

Reprinted by permission of *The Spectator*.

SF Age: Would we even recognize them as smart?

Andrews: If they arrived in spaceships, we might think that they had a technological society, but they might do this out of instinct. They might build spaceships and interstellar craft out of instinct, and they might land and practice what they're doing without being interested in what we're about. . . .

Kondo: Let me comment on this. Actually, I think we can speculate about the probability of intelligent alien beings developing technical culture. If you have a large enough number of alien cultures, if we're talking about billions of such cultures, surely some of those would be sufficiently advanced to come across the distance of interstellar or even intergalactic space. In some cases, then, we might assume that their technology is so advanced that, the way *we* might communicate with some lower forms of animal life they would figure out a way to communicate with us, not because *we* are smart enough to understand them, but because *they* are intelligent enough to figure out a way.

So I think there is a possibility of communication. I do agree with Charles that, if our development levels are comparable, communication may be fairly difficult.

Sheffield: If, in fact, the other society is very much more advanced than ours, then you get back to the old problem—why haven't they done something? Why haven't they given us any evidence of their activities?

One plausible argument is that there are many, many planets bearing life, and that we happen to have come along first. And if that were the case, then we're the ones who are going to have to go out and explain to the developing intelligences how one communicates. We're a long way away from being able to do that, but then we're only three and a half billion years old. If we've got ten to the ten to the twenty-six years or thereabouts still to go, we should be a lot better at it in a few billion years.

So the real question is, do we believe that there is at least one other intelligent organism in the universe? We have no evidence, but we like to think the answer is yes. Nobody likes to be on their own. The very idea that we're in the universe as the only intelligent species is unnerving. To me, even more disturbing is the concept of the universe with *no* intelligent species, because at that point, the universe itself seems to have no reason to exist. Certainly, this is almost a theological argument. The universe doesn't need a reason to exist. . . .

When Aliens Arrive

SF Age: So what are we likeliest to do should the spaceship show up? Are we going to blow it out of the sky, or are we going to let it crash into the side of the White House? What is the likeliest scenario when the contact comes?

Sheffield: Let's set the groundwork. This is a situation in which the alien spaceship arrives in Earth orbit, a classical theme that has been used many many times. I think that most people will first disbelieve it; they will have a healthy dose of cynicism and skepticism. A few cities will have to be obliterated or something before most people will believe. Remember, a large fraction of the American population does not believe that humans went to the Moon. . . .

Andrews: I think there are millions of people on Earth today who do believe that Earth is being visited and has been visited by aliens, and they're already perfectly willing to accept it. In the last twenty years, I have given many talks about UFOs; I used to be a consultant for a UFO organization hoping someday to get a piece of one, hoping that if one crashed or landed, we'd be called in to look at it.

People have asked why would they be here, if they are here. I always responded that I would have no idea. I don't even understand how Iraq works, so I certainly wouldn't understand how an alien culture would work.

But I wouldn't be surprised if they do exist here already, that they are already interacting with those people and doing those things that they wish to do. They may not be at all interested in human civilization and human society. We might not be a very interesting species to interact with. I've said in the past, if aliens came, they might be interested in our oil, who knows? Or they might be interested in harvesting human beings for meat. There are millions of people who disappear every year. Damon Knight's "To Serve Man" could be real. Maybe, like Charles Fort said, we're cattle.

So you could have aliens here, doing what they want to do, and we wouldn't know about it. And the way people are treated who report any of these things . . . we all ridicule it.

Sheffield: I certainly do!

Andrews: I've been meaning to talk to you about that.

Sheffield: I would be honestly amazed if there were any form of aliens creeping around on Earth with unadvertised presence. That's because I'm a cynic and a skeptic.

Government Secrets

Kondo: Let me say that they could be here, but they could be sufficiently advanced that they do not recognize us as being very intelligent. There are a large number of people who believe that NASA is hiding dead aliens somewhere. They are serious. But if you understand anything at all about how tight the NASA budget is, if NASA had any brains at all in its hierarchy, they would not hide dead alien bodies. Because dead alien bodies would increase the NASA budget by a hundredfold.

Sheffield: People have been saying since 1948 that the Air Force has aliens who crashed in New Mexico. Can you imagine the U.S. Government keeping a secret for forty-six years at that level of interest? They can't even keep a secret that is of no interest to anyone. . . .

Kondo: Getting back to your original question of what we would do if aliens showed up in orbit, I think there's a good chance today that we could communicate with them. Especially if they are smart enough to come all the way across the gulf. If they can figure that out, they can figure out how to communicate with us, assuming that that is what they wish. We have no idea what they'd want. If they want to wipe us out, they'd probably have the ability to do so. Assuming that they are here for anthropological purposes other than eliminating us, I think at least a significant number of us would see the possibility of communicating with them. I don't know whether or not we'll succeed, but I think we'll make attempts.

Sheffield: The CIA would try to keep their existence secret, the Defense Department would seek to destroy them, the State Department would bore them to the point where they'd go away. We seem to be somewhat skeptical about intelligent aliens showing up any time soon. We may detect that life exists on other planets around other stars, and we may make our own intelligences. But as for somebody showing up on our doorstep within fifty to one hundred years—the timing would be incredible. After all, we have just become a technological society, and life has been on Earth for three and a half billion years. If you say that humans have been intelligent for even as long as three million years, it's very unlikely that somebody shows up just at this time.

Andrews: One of the arguments in the UFO community is that the first major sighting in this country occurred about two years after the nuclear blasts in 1945. So some people suggested that somebody could have been cruising the neighborhood, the local galactic cops could have been zoning by a light-year away, and saw the flash. They could have said, "Wait, these people are violating the firearms ordinance," and just popped in to see what was happening.

Aliens and DNA

Sheffield: One of my favorite theories is that aliens did come a long time ago, and they decided they didn't want to talk to us until we were smart. So they put a coded message into our DNA, and when we are smart enough to read our own genetic code, we'll find a coded message in there that tells us what to do to get in touch with them. They don't have to keep coming back. All they have to do is let us reproduce from one generation to the next until the organism is smart enough to read and has the technology to read the message. We're just about at that point now. We're reading the genome. Once we sort out the introns from the exons, we'll find, lo and behold, the specifications for the starship are there, in a certain code.

And that's a very economical way of doing it. You don't have to hang around, you don't have to keep watch. You wait for people to develop, and if they never come to see you, then they never got smart. If you do that to all the life-bearing planets in your galaxy, you solve the problem. The aliens have done their job. They've made sure that anybody who does come to see them has passed the screening test.

Kondo: There are variations to your story, actually. You may speculate how we made the jump to *Homo sapiens*. It may be that alien interference caused *Homo sapiens* to be created, in which case the entire DNA may be thanks to the alien technology.

SF Age: Which would make us the aliens. Any final words?

Andrews: Given an infinitely large universe, and at least ten billion years, I'm sure nature has cooked up surprising life forms. I only hope they don't believe in using pesticides on troublesome immature species like humans.

Sheffield: There is a quote from the late, lamented [comic strip] *Pogo* that is relevant to this, in which they are sitting looking up at the stars, and one of them says, "You know, it's possible that out there may be thousands of species more intelligent than we are. On the other hand, we may be the most intelligent species in the universe. Either way, it's a mighty sobering thought."

Periodical Bibliography

The following articles have been selected to supplement the diverse views presented in this chapter.

Edward Edelson — "Robo Surgeons," *Popular Science*, April 1995.

James Gleick — "The Doctor's Plot" (book review of John E. Mack's *Abduction: Human Encounters with Aliens*), *New Republic*, May 30, 1994.

Edward Golub — "The Constant Presence of Death," *Bio/Technology*, February 1995. Available from Reprints Dept., 65 Bleecker St., New York, NY 10012-2467.

Douglas Groothuis — "To Heaven and Back?" *Christianity Today*, April 3, 1995.

Michael D. Lemonick — "Glimpses of the Mind," *Time*, July 17, 1995.

Gene Levinson — "Artificial Life: Biotechnology of the Twenty-first Century?" *Bio/Technology*, February 1995.

Margaret McKelway — "Time Travel," *National Geographic World*, March 1995.

Marvin Lee Minsky — "Will Robots Inherit the Earth?" *Scientific American*, October 1994.

New Scientist — "Trends That Are Transforming the World," October 15, 1994. Available from 1350 Connecticut Ave. NW, Suite 403, Washington, DC 20036.

Omni — "*Omni*'s Project Open Book," March 1995.

Thomas T. Perls — "The Oldest Old," *Scientific American*, January 1995.

A.J.S. Rayl — "Anatomy of an Abduction," *Omni*, February 1995.

John D. Rockfellow — "Wild Cards: Preparing for the 'Big One,'" *Futurist*, January/February 1994.

Jonathan Rosen — "Rewriting the End: Elisabeth Kübler-Ross," *New York Times Magazine*, January 22, 1995.

Carl Sagan — "The Search for Extraterrestrial Life," *Scientific American*, October 1994.

Kanji Yonemoto — "Lending a Hand," *Look Japan*, April 1994. Available from 24 Raffles Pl., 25-02 Clifford Centre, Singapore 0104.

For Further Discussion

Chapter 1

1. Al Gore and Paul Kennedy assert that overpopulation is leading to environmental harm, impoverishment, and instability within and among some nations. What else contributes to instability, according to Kennedy? How do you think Thomas Lambert would respond to Gore's and Kennedy's arguments?

2. Peter Schwartz argues that the impact of the global baby boom and the "global teenager" will dwarf other demographic factors for the next two generations. Wolfgang Lutz argues that an unprecedented increase in elderly populations will jolt the world's demographic makeup. Based on your reading of these two viewpoints, which trend do you believe will have the greater impact on societies? Why? Evaluate both authors' use of statistics. Which author uses statistics to sketch future social conditions?

Chapter 2

1. Herbert Kaufman contends that superintelligent machines in the future will evolve and work without the aid of humans, most likely coexisting with and benefiting humanity. Warwick Collins envisions that such machines could turn against humans and cause the downfall of the human species. Which viewpoint is more convincing? Explain your answer. Does the prospect of superintelligent machines comfort or frighten you? Why? What measures do you think could be taken to prevent such machines from harming humans?

2. Edmund Storms suggests that cold fusion and its production of excess heat could develop into a future energy source. David Goodstein argues that cold fusion is impossible to achieve with current scientific knowledge. Which author most effectively cites researchers' experiments to support his position? Explain your answer.

Chapter 3

1. Alan Thein Durning asserts that people should eat less meat because of the ecological and health benefits of doing so. Kathleen Meister disagrees and argues that beef should be part of one's diet because of its nutritional advantages. Which viewpoint do you find more convincing? Why? If meat is a part of your diet, would you consider eating less of it? Explain your answer.

2. Martin W. Holdgate calls the environment "real national wealth" and argues that governments should define how to manage natural resources. Thomas J. DiLorenzo argues that government control of such resources would cause environmental ruin. Do you believe that government has a responsibility to protect the environment? If so, how far should government go in pursuing environmental protection? Support your answer with examples from the viewpoints.

Chapter 4

1. Riccardo Petrella argues that increased economic competition worldwide—including evolving corporate-national alliances—is affecting the vast majority of the world's population in many ways. Based on your reading of the viewpoint, what do you believe to be the most important priorities for the world's inhabitants? Rank these in order of importance.

2. Joseph F. Coates describes an increasingly conflict-ridden world and the forms of collective violence that he predicts will occur in the twenty-first century. Bruce Russett contends that the spread of democracy among nations could increase peace and stability around the world. Taking into account both new democratic regimes and new regional conflicts that have emerged during the 1990s, which author's view do you believe will prove to be more accurate? Explain your answer.

Chapter 5

1. J. Madeleine Nash describes a "critical ethical divide" facing parents who, through genetic engineering, could improve their newborn child's health or traits. Imagine yourself in their position. Would you choose to alter your child's genes or would you "let nature take its course"? Explain your reasoning.

2. Speculating on alien beings, Charles Sheffield maintains that humans like to think that "there is at least one other intelligent organism in the universe." Do you agree with Sheffield? Why or why not? Do you believe that intelligent aliens exist? On what do you base your answer?

Organizations to Contact

The editors have compiled the following list of organizations concerned with the issues debated in this book. The descriptions are derived from materials provided by the organizations. All have publications or information available for interested readers. The list was compiled on the date of publication of the present volume; names, addresses, and phone numbers may change. Be aware that many organizations take several weeks or longer to respond to inquiries, so allow as much time as possible.

Australia's Commission for the Future (ACF)
PO Box 115, Carlton
Melbourne 3053
AUSTRALIA
(011) 61 3 663 3620

ACF is an independent, multidisciplinary futures-planning organization that provides futures analysis for corporations and government. It works to identify emerging issues, including social and technological trends, and performs strategic policy analysis. ACF's publications include the periodicals *21-C* and *Apocalypse? No!* and the book *Energy Futures: Efficient Energy Scenarios to 2020* (1991).

Chinese Society for Futures Studies (CSFS)
86 Xueyuannan Rd.
Beijing 100081
CHINA
(011) 86 10 831 8877, ext. 462

The society serves as a futures-research clearinghouse for professionals and the interested public of China. It encourages members to study the future development of Chinese economics, society, and technology and to establish methods and theories in futures research. Its publications include the periodicals *Future and Development* and *A Guide to Soft Sciences* and the multivolume book *China and the World in the Twenty-first Century*.

Club of Rome
34 Ave. D'Eylau
Paris 75116
FRANCE
(011) 33 1 4704 4525
fax: (011) 33 1 4704 4525

Members from fifty-seven nations and thirty national associations make up the Club of Rome, which studies and attempts to resolve global problems. The club's programs and projects include continuing analysis of long-term world problems, study of the interactions among these problems, long-term forecasting and policy formulation, and evaluation of international cooperation for development. Books and reports published by the club include *The Limits to Certainty* (1990) and *The First Global Revolution* (1991).

Institute for Alternative Futures (IAF)
100 N. Pitt St., Suite 235
Alexandria, VA 22314
(703) 684-5880
fax: (703) 684-0640

The institute consults with and provides speakers to various organizations concerned with health futures, information futures, and business and community futures. Books published by IAF include *Mending the Earth: A World for Our Grandchildren* (1990), *Regulating Change: The Regulation of Foods, Drugs, Medical Devices, and Cosmetics in the 1990s* (1990), and *20-20 Visions: Health Care Information, Standards, and Technologies* (1993).

Institute for Futures Research
Studies of the Future Program
2700 Bay Area Blvd.
Houston, TX 77058-1090
(713) 283-3320

This academic program offered by the University of Houston at Clear Lake is currently the only one in America to offer a master's degree in futures studies. The curriculum covers a detailed review of the techniques used to understand and plan the long-term future. The program also sponsors workshops with industry and government regarding futures-related activity. Its research reports have been published in the periodicals *Futurist* and *Futures*. Books it has published include *Information and the Future* (1988) and *Changing Images of Man* (1988).

Institute for Futures Studies and Research (IFSR)
University of Akron, Gallucci Hall
Akron, OH 44325-7906
(216) 972-7616
fax: (216) 972-5101

The institute's objectives are to initiate and provide comprehensive programs in salient and vital policy research, including a structural network that encompasses strategic planning, environmental scanning, trends analysis, and other innovative research methods. IFSR publishes the bimonthly *Ohio Foresight* and the books *Cities in Global Society* (1989) and *The Future of Urban Environments* (1993).

Open University Futures Research Center
Novo-Cheremushki 54-4
Moscow 117418
RUSSIA
(011) 7 095 120 13 47
fax: (011) 7 095 120 13 97

The center's objectives include applied forecasting methodologies in such areas as business, environment, technology, trade, and urbanization. Its publications include the book *Russia 1904–2004: From Colossus to Collapse and Back* (1993).

Policy Studies Institute (PSI)
100 Park Village E.
London NW1 3SR
UNITED KINGDOM
(011) 44 171 387 2171
fax: (011) 44 171 388 0914

PSI's objectives include undertaking empirical research of use to policymakers. In addition to futures studies, its research areas include arts, culture, education, employment, environment, health, industry, new technologies, race relations, social security, and welfare. The institute's publications include the book *Britain in Europe: 2010* (1994).

Resources for the Future (RFF)
1616 P St. NW
Washington, DC 20036
(202) 328-5000
fax: (202) 939-3460

RFF is a nonprofit research organization concerned with the conservation, management, and development of natural resources. Its research areas include forestry economics, land use and planning, surface and groundwater resources, energy, and environmental quality. Among RFF's publications are the quarterly newsletter/magazine *Resources*, a biannual Center for Risk Management newsletter, and the books *Public Policies for Environmental Protection* (1990) and *Mineral Wealth and Economic Development* (1992).

United Nations Development Programme (UNDP)
1 United Nations Plaza
New York, NY 10017
(212) 906-5315
fax: (212) 906-5364

UNDP funds six thousand projects in more than 150 developing countries and territories. It works with governments, UN agencies, and non-governmental organizations to enhance self-reliance and promote sustainable human development. Its priorities include improving living standards, protecting the environment, and applying technology to meet human needs. UNDP's publications include the weekly newsletter *UNDP Flash* and the annual *UNDP Human Development Report*.

World Future Society
7910 Woodmont Ave., Suite 450
Bethesda, MD 20814
(301) 656-8274
fax: (301) 951-0394

The society serves as a national clearinghouse for ideas and information about the future, including forecasts, recommendations, and alternative scenarios. These ideas help people to anticipate what may happen in coming years and to distinguish between possible, probable, and desired futures. The society publishes the bimonthly *Futurist* magazine, *Futures Research Quarterly*, the annual *Futures Research Directory: Organizations and Periodicals*, and the book *The 1990s and Beyond* (1990).

World Future Studies Federation (WFSF)
c/o Turku School of Economics
Rehtorinpellonkatu 3
Turku sf-20500
FINLAND
(011) 358 21 2330 835
fax: (011) 358 21 2330 755

The federation promotes and encourages the opening of futures studies to all scientific initiatives in different disciplines, provides a forum for generating ideas concerning the future, and assists with national and global futures research activities. Its publications include the *WFSF Newsletter*.

World Resources Institute (WRI)
1709 New York Ave. NW
Washington, DC 20006
(202) 638-6300
fax: (202) 638-0036

WRI is a nonprofit research foundation. Its policy research is concerned with global resources, environmental conditions, emerging issues, and the public's understanding of these issues. WRI publishes books, reports, and papers; holds briefings, seminars, and conferences; and provides the print and broadcast media with new perspectives and background materials on environmental issues. The institute publishes the quarterly newsletter *NGO Networker* and research reports covering such topics as climate and energy, land development, and sustainable forestry and agriculture.

Worldwatch Institute
1776 Massachusetts Ave. NW
Washington, DC 20036-1904
(202) 452-1999
fax: (202) 296-7365

Worldwatch is a research organization that analyzes and focuses attention on global problems, including environmental concerns such as nuclear waste and the relationship between trade and the environment. It compiles the annual *State of the World* book and publishes the bimonthly magazine *World Watch* and the Worldwatch Paper Series of booklets.

Bibliography of Books

John A. Baden, ed. — *Environmental Gore: A Constructive Response to "Earth in the Balance."* San Francisco: Pacific Research Institute for Public Policy, 1994.

Gerald O. Barney — *Global 2000 Revisited: What Shall We Do?* Arlington, VA: Millennium Institute, 1993.

Lester R. Brown — *Saving the Planet: How to Shape an Environmentally Sustainable Global Economy.* New York: Norton, 1991.

Lester R. Brown et al. — *State of the World 1995: A Worldwatch Institute Report on Progress Toward a Sustainable Society.* New York: Norton, 1994.

Richard Carlson and Bruce Goldman — *Fast Forward: Where Technology, Demographics, and History Will Take America and the World in the Next Thirty Years.* New York: HarperBusiness, 1994.

Daniel Crevier — *AI: The Tumultuous History of the Search for Artificial Intelligence.* New York: BasicBooks, 1993.

Trevor N. Dupuy — *Future Wars: The World's Most Dangerous Flashpoints.* New York: Warner Books, 1993.

Environmental Technology Strategy Staff — *Technology for a Sustainable Future: A Framework for Action.* Washington, DC: Office of Science and Technology Policy, 1994.

Jeffrey A. Fisher — *Our Medical Future: Breakthroughs in Health and Longevity by the Year 2000 and Beyond.* New York: Pocket Books, 1993.

Al Gore — *Earth in the Balance: Ecology and the Human Spirit.* Boston: Houghton Mifflin, 1992.

John Harris — *Wonderwoman and Superman: The Ethics of Human Biotechnology.* Oxford: Oxford University Press, 1992.

Robert Heilbroner — *Visions of the Future: The Distant Past, Yesterday, Today, and Tomorrow.* New York: Oxford University Press, 1995.

Michael Heim — *The Metaphysics of Virtual Reality.* New York: Oxford University Press, 1993.

Walter J. Karplus — *The Heavens Are Falling: The Scientific Prediction of Catastrophes in Our Time.* New York: Plenum Press, 1992.

281

Paul Kennedy	*Preparing for the Twenty-first Century.* New York: Random House, 1993.
Ervin Laszlo	*The Choice: Evolution or Extinction? A Thinking Person's Guide to Global Issues.* New York: Jeremy P. Tarcher/Putnam, 1994.
Harold A. Linstone	*The Challenge of the Twenty-first Century: Managing Technology and Ourselves in a Shrinking World.* Albany: State University of New York Press, 1994.
Bruce Mazlish	*The Fourth Discontinuity: The Co-Evolution of Humans and Machines.* New Haven: Yale University Press, 1993.
Laurie Ann Mazur, ed.	*Beyond the Numbers: A Reader on Population, Consumption, and the Environment.* Washington, DC: Island Press, 1994.
Hamish McRae	*The World in 2020: Power, Culture, and Prosperity.* Boston: Harvard Business School Press, 1995.
Donella H. Meadows, Dennis L. Meadows, and Jorgen Randers	*Beyond the Limits: Confronting Global Collapse, Envisioning a Sustainable Future.* Post Mills, VT: Chelsea Green, 1992.
George D. Moffett	*Critical Masses: The Global Population Challenge.* New York: Viking, 1994.
National Research Council	*Atomic, Molecular, and Optical Science: An Investment in the Future.* Washington, DC: National Academy Press, 1994.
Donald A. Norma	*Things That Make Us Smart: Defending Human Attributes in the Age of the Machine.* Reading, MA: Addison-Wesley, 1993.
John L. Peterson	*The Road to 2015: Profiles of the Future.* Corte Madera, CA: Waite Group Press, 1994.
Clive Ponting	*A Green History of the World: The Environment and the Collapse of Great Civilizations.* New York: St. Martin's Press, 1992.
David B. Roe and Jay G. Wilpon, eds.	*Voice Communication Between Humans and Machines.* Washington, DC: National Academy Press, 1994.
John Roper et al.	*Keeping the Peace in the Post–Cold War Era: Strengthening Multilateral Peacekeeping.* New York: Trilateral Commission, 1993.
Bruce M. Russett	*Grasping the Democratic Peace: Principles for a Post–Cold War World.* Princeton, NJ: Princeton University Press, 1993.

Marshall T. Savage   *The Millennial Project: Colonizing the Galaxy in Eight Easy Steps.* Boston: Little, Brown, 1994.

Max Singer and   *The Real World Order: Zones of Peace/Zones of Turmoil.* Chatham, NJ: Chatham House, 1993.
Aaron Wildavsky

Gregory Stock   *Metaman: The Merging of Humans and Machines into a Global Superorganism.* New York: Simon & Schuster, 1993.

Charles W. Taylor   *A World 2010: A New Order of Nations.* Carlisle Barracks, PA: U.S. Army War College Strategic Studies Institute, 1993.

Michael Tobias   *World War II: Population and the Biosphere at the End of the Millennium.* Santa Fe, NM: Bear, 1994.

Alvin Toffler   *Powershift: Knowledge, Wealth, and Violence at the Edge of the Twenty-first Century.* New York: Bantam Books, 1990.

Alvin Toffler and   *War and Anti-War: Survival at the Dawn of the Twenty-first Century.* Boston: Little, Brown, 1993.
Heidi Toffler

World Bank Group   *Learning from the Past, Embracing the Future.* Washington, DC: World Bank Group, 1994.

Robin Wright and   *Flashpoints: Promise and Peril in a New World.* New York: Knopf, 1991.
Doyle McManus

Michael G. Zey   *Seizing the Future.* New York: Simon & Schuster, 1994.

Index